Development in an Era of Capital Control

Palgrave Socio-Legal Studies

Development in an Era of Capital Control

Corporate Social Responsibility within a Transnational Regulatory Framework

Ciara Hackett
Queen's University Belfast, UK

macmillan education palgrave

First published 2017 by
PALGRAVE

Palgrave in the UK is an imprint of Macmillan Publishers Limited, registered in England, company number 785998, of 4 Crinan Street, London, N1 9XW.

Palgrave® and Macmillan® are registered trademarks in the United States, the United Kingdom, Europe and other countries.

ISBN: 978–1–137–48527–4 hardback

This book is printed on paper suitable for recycling and made from fully managed and sustained forest sources. Logging, pulping and manufacturing processes are expected to conform to the environmental regulations of the country of origin.

A catalogue record for this book is available from the British Library.

A catalog record for this book is available from the Library of Congress.

Printed and bound by CPI Group (UK) Ltd, Croydon, CR0 4YY

Contents

Acknowledgments

When I took this project on, I don't think I had any idea of what lay ahead. Thankfully, it turns out I have a fantastic network of colleagues, friends and family who supported me every step of the way. Not only that, but they endured my vacant expression as I retreated into my head – thinking of something I had not included in a particular chapter, among other things – and my general lack of craic for a few months. I will make up for it. Although I am not able to thank everyone, there are some people whom I would like to particularly acknowledge.

I work with amazing people at Queen's University Belfast, and their support has been tremendous. In particular, I would like to thank Professor Sally Wheeler and Dr Ciarán O'Kelly, who inspired me to research in this area. They read and reread material from the earliest inceptions. and their endless patience with me will not be forgotten. I thank Dr Bruce Wardhaugh, who, along with Professor Dave Cowan, guided me through the book proposal process, assuring me that this was something that people would be interested in reading. Finally, I would like to mention Dr Anne-Marie McAlinden and Dr Luke Moffett, who between them reviewed endless material, answered my numerous stupid questions and provided great support. I hope I will be in the position to return the favour.

To my friends who kept in contact even when I abandoned all technology and social media in the dying days of the project, thank you for continuing to text and call, feeding me and generally making me turn up to things. I am very lucky! In particular, I am grateful to Clare, Michelle, Donal, Sarah, Aisling, Charles, Anne E, Russell and Faith – also to Rory and Ann, who provided food and checked in almost daily to see how things were progressing.

I have a small but fantastic family. My wonderful aunt and uncle – Margaret and Owen – who have done so much for me over the years – I am so lucky to have you. I have fabulous siblings, who have supported me in their own strange ways: in particular, Niall (20), who suggested that I finish the book on a cliff-hanger so that we could spend some time together; and Kyla (17) who reminded me of the importance of 'YOLO' and to eat plenty of chocolate. I did! And finally more than thanks go to my mammy: without you, none of this would have been possible. You are the best mammy in the world – thank you so much for everything you have done and sacrificed for me.

Finally, to my other half, Brian, we did it! It has been a long few months, and every step of the way you were there, providing tea (caff or de-caff depending on the time of day), making dinner, cracking jokes and generally, in your support, reminding me how lucky I am to have you. I can't wait to spend the rest of my life with you.

I write this book in loving memory of Nellie – who did not live to see the finished product but always had faith that I had it in me.

If I have left anyone out, my apologies! You have all touched me so much with your kindness.

Preface

On 23 June 2016 the United Kingdom, through an advisory referendum, voted by 52% to 48% to leave the European Union. In the immediate aftermath, market instability, seismic political upheaval and media reports of racist hatred dressed up as 'Britishness' has ensued. For the first time in centuries, the United Kingdom is depicted as small and relatively insignificant. As the home of the British Empire, and then a core element of the European Union, the United Kingdom had a reach and power beyond its small size. The pound was seen as a currency of worth and the City of London (home of the FTSE) had a solid reputation. Now, the pound is not as safe as it once was, and threats of departures by MNCs from London are being documented in the media. The future for a United Kingdom outside the European Union remains uncertain. Indeed, because the results demonstrate that Scotland and Northern Ireland (as well as City of London and Gibraltar) strongly wish to remain within the EU (all with similar majority 'Remain' votes), the future of the 'United' Kingdom itself is unclear.

The narrative of this book is that nation states are less significant than they once were. Instead, in a global capitalist system, it is the relationships with key actors that identify the regions perceived as being more developed than others. To demonstrate this, this book takes a theory that was used to explain the process of decolonialisation and applies it in a modified format to the capitalist system. If all nation states are dependent on capital (to varying degrees) to develop a region, then 'independence' is unrealisable. Instead what emerges are a series of relationships between nation states and capital, which can lead to a dependent development within the nation state's borders. At this point, corporate initiatives such as Corporate Social Responsibility could be used to shape 'development' within a region, but ultimately, for nation states in a dependent relationship with capital, investment is of more importance than a commitment to social and environmental initiatives. However, there is the potential for nation states to direct CSR initiatives through legislation, principles and codes. Help for the strength of these initiatives can come from bodies such as the EU. With their collective bargaining power and population size, the EU is in a better position to bargain with capital to ensure that the symptoms of dependent development are alleviated.

Throughout this book, the United Kingdom is regarded as something of a success story. Typically, small nations struggle to carve an identity on the global market. However, with its history as a driver of the British Empire and the infrastructure that this resulted in, the United Kingdom became a world leader in areas of trade and indeed CSR. With the United Kingdom's decision to leave the European Union, it is now in a position where it must bargain with capital and other states to gain access to markets and to ensure that the import/export requirements of the country are maintained. It remains to be seen whether the historical reputation of the UK with capital and CSR advances can be preserved, or whether it now must suffer the fate of small open economies as discussed throughout this book. Regardless, it will prove to be an interesting test case for modified dependence as this story unfolds.

Ciara Hackett
8 July 2016

Tables

Table of Cases

Table of Cases (UK)

Hutton v West Cork Railway Company, (1883) 23 Ch.D.654.

Table of Cases (US)

AP Smith Management Company v Barlow 13 N.J. 145 (1953) 98 A.2d 581.

Brown v Board of Education of Topeka, 347. U.S. 483, (1954).

Citizens United v Federal Election Commission, No. 08–205, 558 U.S. 310 (2010).

Dodge v Ford Motor Company, 170 NW 668 (Mich 1919).

Paramount Communications Inc v Time Inc., 571 A. 2d 1140, (Del. 1990).

Unocal v Mesa Petroleum (493 A.2d. 946, (Del. 1985)).

Table of Legislation

Table of Directives (EU)

Directive 2014/95/EU on disclosure of non-financial and diversity information by certain large undertakings and groups. Available at http://eur-lex.europa.eu/legal-content/EN/TXT/?uri=CELEX:32014L0095 (Accessed 29 September 2015).

Directive 2013/34/EU of the European Parliament and of the Council of 26 June 2013 on the annual financial statements, consolidated financial statements and related reports of certain types of undertakings. Available at http://eur-lex.europa.eu/legal-content/EN/TXT/?uri=celex:32013L0034 (Accessed 29 September 2015).

Directive 2004/25/EC of the European Parliament and of the Council of 21 April 2004 on takeover bids. Available at http://eur-lex.europa.eu/LexUriServ/LexUriServ.do?uri=OJ:L:2004:142:0012:0023:EN:PDF (Accessed 29 September 2015).

Table of Statutes and Regulations (Germany)

Mitbestimmungsgesetz 1976 (Codetermination Act 1976).

Table of Statutes and Regulations (India)

Companies Act (India) 2013. Available at www.mca.gov.in/Ministry/pdf/CompaniesAct2013.pdf (Accessed 11 October 2016).

Table of Statutes and Regulations (Ireland)

Companies Act 2014. Available at www.irishstatutebook.ie/2014/en/act/pub/0038/print.html (Accessed 29 September 2015).

Companies (Auditing and Accounting) Act 2003. Available at www.irishstatutebook.ie/eli/2003/act/44/enacted/en/html (Accessed 29 September 2015).

Companies Consolidation Bill 2012. Available at www.oireachtas.ie/documents/bills28/bills/2012/11612/b11612d-Memo.pdf (Accessed 10 October 2016).

Directors' Compliance Statement – proposed section 45 of the Companies (Auditing and Accounting) Act 2 003. Act No. 44 of 2003. Tithe an Oireachtais. Available at www.irishstatutebook.ie/eli/2003/act/44/section/45/enacted/en/html (Accessed 10 October 2016).

Table of Statutes and Regulations (UK)

Climate Change Levy www.gov.uk/green-taxes-and-reliefs/climate-change-levy (Accessed 1 September 2015).

Community Investment Tax Credit Scheme. Available at www.gov.uk/government/publications/community-investment-tax-relief-citr (Accessed 27 September 2015).

Companies Act 2006 (Strategic Report and Director's Report) Regulations 2013). Available at www.legislation.gov.uk/ukdsi/2013/9780111540169/introduction (Accessed 29 September 2015).

Companies Act 2006. Available www.legislation.gov.uk/ukpga/2006/46 (Accessed 29 September 2015).

Criminal Justice Act 1993, Available at www.legislation.gov.uk/ukpga/1993/36/contents (Accessed 29 September 2015).

Draft Order: The Greenhouse Gas Emissions (Directors' Reports) Regulations 2013. Available at www.gov.uk/government/uploads/system/uploads/attachment_data/file/82573/consult-ghg-regulations-20131.pdf (Accessed 13 September 2015).

Enterprise Act 2002. Available at www.legislation.gov.uk/ukpga/2002/40/contents (Accessed 29 September 2015).

Enterprise and Regulatory Reform Act 2013. Available at www.legislation.gov.uk/ukpga/2013/24/contents/enacted (Accessed 29 September 2015).

Financial Services Act 2012. Available at www.legislation.gov.uk/ukpga/2012/21/pdfs/ukpga_20120021_en.pdf (Accessed 29 September 2015).

Financial Services Act 2010. Available at www.legislation.gov.uk/ukpga/2010/28/pdfs/ukpga_20100028_en.pdf (Accessed 29 September 2015).

Financial Services and Markets Act, 2002. Available at www.legislation.gov.uk/ukpga/2000/8/contents (Accessed 29 September 2015).

Financial Services and Markets Act 2000, (Consolidated). Available at www.gov.uk/government/uploads/system/uploads/attachment_data/file/81410/consolidated_fsma050911.pdf (Accessed 29 September 2015).

Landfill Tax. Available at www.gov.uk/green-taxes-and-reliefs/landfill-tax (Accessed 10 July 2015).

Public Services (Social Value Act) 2012. Available at www.legislation.gov.uk/ukpga/2012/3/section/3/enacted (Accessed 29 September 2015).

Table of Statutes and Regulations (US)

Banking Act 1935. Available at www.federalreservehistory.org/Media/Material/Event/26-284 (Accessed 10 October 2016).

Dodd–Frank Wall Street Reform and Consumer Protection Act (Pub. L. 111–203, H.R. 4173) 2010. Available at www.gpo.gov/fdsys/pkg/PLAW-111publ203/html/PLAW-111publ203.htm (Accessed 29 September 2015).

Glass–Stegall Act 1933. Available at www.legisworks.org/congress/73/publaw-66.pdf (Accessed 29 September 2015).

Investment Advisers Act 1940. Available at www.sec.gov/about/laws/iaa40.pdf (Accessed 29 September 2015).

Investment Company Act 1940. Available at www.sec.gov/about/laws/ica40.pdf (Accessed 29 September 2015).

Public Company Accounting Reform and Investor Protection Act (2002, (SOX)) Sarbanes Oxley, Pub. L. 107–204 116 Stat. 745. Enacted July 30, 2002. Available at www.gpo.gov/fdsys/pkg/PLAW-107publ204/html/PLAW-107publ204.htm (Accessed 29 September 2015).

Securities Exchange Act 1934. Available at www.sec.gov/about/laws/sea34.pdf (Accessed 29 September 2015).

Trust Indenture Act 1939. Available at www.sec.gov/about/laws/tia39.pdf (Accessed 29 September 2015).

Constituency Statutes (State-Level Legislation US)

Ariz. Rev. Stat. Ann. § 10–1202 (1990 & Supp. 1993)
Conn. Gen. Stat. Ann. § 33–313(e) (West Supp. 1993)
Fla. Stat. Ann. § 607.0830(3) (West 1993)
Ga. Code Ann. § 14–2-202(b)(5) (1989)
Haw. Rev. Stat. § 415–35(B) (Supp. 1992)
Idaho Code § 30- 1702 (Supp. 1993)
Ill. Ann. Stat. Ch. 805, Para. 8.85 (Smith-Hurd 1993)
Ind. Code Ann. § 23–1-35–1(D) (West 1989)
Iowa Code Ann. § 491.101(B) (West 1991)
Ky. Rev. Stat. Ann. § 271b.12–210(4) (1989 & Supp. 1992)
La. Rev. Stat. Ann. § 12:92(G) (West Supp. 1994)
Me. Rev. Stat. Ann. Tit. 13-A, § 716 (West Supp. 1993)
Mass. Gen. Laws Ann. Ch. 156b, § 65 (Supp. 1993)
Minn. Stat. Ann. § 302a.251(5) (Supp. 1994)
Miss. Code Ann. § 794–8.30(D) (Supp. 1993)
Mo. Ann. Stat. § 351.347 (Vernon 1991)
Neb. Rev. Stat. § 21–2035(1) (1991)
Nj. Stat. Ann. § 14a:6–1 -14 (West Supp. 1993)
N.M. Stat. Ann. § 53–11–35(D) (Michie Supp. 1993)
N.Y. Bus. Corp. Law § 717(B) (Mckinney Supp. 1994)
Ohio Rev. Code Ann. § 1701.59(E) (Anderson 1992)
Or. Rev. Stat. § 60.357(5) (Supp. 1992)
15 Pa. Con. Stat. Ann. § 1715, 1716 (Supp. 1993)
R.I. Gen. Laws § 7–5.2- 8 (1992)
S.D. Codified Laws Ann. § 47–33–4 (1991)
Tenn. Code Ann. § 48–35–204 (1988)
Wis. Stat. Ann. § 180.0827 (West 1992)
Wyo. Stat. § 17–16–830(E) (Supp. 1993)

Table of Statutory Instruments

(United Kingdom)

Occupational Pension Schemes (Disclosure of Information) Regulations (1996) SI No. 1655. Available at www.legislation.gov.uk/uksi/1996/1655/contents/made (Accessed 29 September 2015).

Occupational Pension Schemes (Investment) Regulations 2005 SI, No. 3378. Available at www.legislation.gov.uk/uksi/2005/3378/regulation/2/made (Accessed 10 October 2016).

(Ireland)

European Union (Cross Border Mergers) (Interconnection of Business Registers) Regulations 2014, SI no. 309 of 2014. Available at www.irish statutebook.ie/eli/2014/si/309/made/en/pdf (Accessed 29 September 2015).

Codes and Principles

2012 Revised Guidelines on Audit Committees. Available at www.frc.org.uk/Our-Work/Publications/Corporate-Governance/Guidance-on-Audit-Committees-September-2012.aspx (Accessed 29 September 2015).

2014 UK Corporate Governance Code. Available at www.frc.org.uk/Our-Work/Publications/Corporate-Governance/UK-Corporate-Governance-Code-2014.pdf (Accessed 29 September 2015).

2011 Update on the OECD Guidelines for Multinational Enterprises. Available at www.oecd.org/corporate/mne/oecdguidelinesformultinational enterprises.htm (Accessed 29 September 2015).

Caux Principles for Business. Available at www.cauxroundtable.org/index.cfm?menuid=8 (Accessed 29 September 2015).

Disclosure and Transparency Rules regarding corporate governance statements and audit committees (DTR 7). Available at www.iasplus.com/en-gb/resources/other-regulatory/market-rules/disclosure-and-trans parency-rules (Accessed 29 September 2015).

Global Reporting Initiative. Available at www.globalreporting.org/Pages/default.aspx (Accessed 29 September 2015).

Global Sullivan Principles of Social Responsibility. Available at www.marshall.edu/revleonsullivan/principles.htm (Accessed 10 October 2016).

Guidance on Risk Management, Internal Control and Related Financial and Business Reporting. Available at www.frc.org.uk/Our-Work/Publications/Corporate-Governance/Guidance-on-Risk-Management,-Internal-Control-and.pdf (Accessed 29 September 2015).

ILO Tripartite Declaration of Principles concerning Multinational Enterprises on Social Policy. Available at www.ilo.org/empent/Publications/WCMS_094386/lang--en/index.htm (Accessed 29 September 2015).

ISO 26000 Guidance Standard on Social Responsibility. Available at www.iso.org/iso/home/standards/iso26000.htm (Accessed 29 September 2015).

Listing Rules. Available at www.handbook.fca.org.uk/handbook/LR/ (Accessed 29 September 2015).

Norms on the responsibilities of transnational corporations and other business enterprises with regard to human rights. Available at www1.umn.edu/humanrts/business/norms-Aug2003.html (Accessed 29 September 2015).

Principles for Global Corporate Responsibility Benchmark. Available at www.bench-marks.org (Accessed 29 September 2015).

Social Accountability 8000 (SA8000). Available at www.sa-intl.org/index.cfm?fuseaction=Page.ViewPage&PageID=937 (Accessed 29 September 2015).

The City Code on Takeovers and Mergers. Available at www.the takeover-panel.org.uk/wp-content/uploads/2008/11/code.pdf (Accessed 10 October 2016).

The OECD Guidelines for Multinational Enterprises. Available at www.oecd.org/corporate/mne/ (Accessed 29 September 2015).

UKLA's Disclosure and Transparency Rules. Available at www.handbook.fca.org.uk/handbook/DTR/ (Accessed 29 September 2015).

United Nations Global Compact. Available at www.unglobal compact.org (Accessed 29 September 2015).

United Nations Guiding Principles on Business and Human Rights. Available at www.ohchr.org/Documents/Publications/GuidingPrinciplesBusinessHR_EN.pdf (Accessed 29 September 2015).

List of Abbreviations

AIB	Allied Irish Bank
BitC	Business in the Community
CCI	Corporate Community Involvement
CIME	Committee on International Investment and Multinational Enterprises
CLRG	Company Law Review Group
CSR	Corporate Social Responsibility
DCS	Director's Compliance Statement
DRC	Democratic Republic of Congo
EC	European Commission
ECLA	United Nations Economic Commission for Latin America
EEOC	Equal Employment Opportunity Commission (US)
ERT	European Round Table of Industrialists
EU	European Union
EUI	European University Institute
FDI	Foreign Direct Investment
FSA	Financial Services Authority
GDP	Gross Domestic Product
ILO	International Labour Organisation
IMF	International Monetary Fund
MNC	Multinational Corporations
NAFTA	North American Free Trade Agreement
NCP	National Contact Point
NGO	Non-governmental Organisation
OECD	Organisation for Economic Cooperation and Development
OPEC	Organisation of the Petroleum Exporting Countries
OSHA	Occupational Safety and Health Administration (US)
PPP	Public–Private Partnerships
PRA	Prudential Regulatory Authority
SEC	Securities and Exchange Council
SOX	Sarbanes Oxley Act
SRI	Socially Responsible Investment
TCC	transnational capitalist class
TNP	Transnational Practices
UK	United Kingdom
UN	United Nations
US	United States
WWII	World War

Introduction

I Who is in charge?

When something does not go according to plan, or disaster strikes, the 'go to' position is to find out who is to blame for any detrimental effects that may have befallen those questioning. Apportionment of blame is not a new concept and indeed underscores some of the key premises of society, and our legal infrastructure, as it exists today. Financial crises are no different. With the most recent global financial crisis, many sought to apportion blame, with numerous groups being targeted: bankers, regulators, politicians, market participants, credit rating agencies, and so on. Much has been written on who is at fault for the recent crisis and why it was allowed to occur. Whereas these texts give much insight into the *fault* element of this crisis and others before it, perhaps of more interest are discussions around who is *in charge* of the global economic market. By focusing in on the key actors in the global system, the cause of crisis becomes clearer.

This book operates on the premise that our scale of measurement is incorrect. The way in which we have been thinking about the global system and analysing 'crisis' has been so grounded in the nation state and the effect that financial crisis is having *on* a nation state or nation states that we forget to look at the global scale. Capitalism has transitioned beyond the nation state, and therefore our conceptions of crisis need to also move beyond this inward-focused state analysis. This may seem somewhat cold, and in no way do I wish to undermine the impact of financial crisis, but there is a need to recognise the systemic inevitability of liquidity issues. It is within the global arena that more and more business transactions are taking place. With this global focus, we must also take into account the very nature of capitalism: winners and losers. In order to ensure continued market efficiency and profit, there is a constant need to re-evaluate the system and make necessary adjustments. With the premise of capitalism being a survival of the fittest and a race to the bottom in terms of production costs, the human cost of the withdrawal of capital from an area, or indeed of a 'crisis', as the market reimagines its position is not considered. Capitalism, with an economic focus, is so embedded in economic efficiency that crisis is regarded in a different manner. Far from the rise in homelessness, numbers of people taking their own lives, job losses and savings losses, the capitalist articulates crisis in a more emotionally detached manner – specifically, diminished production, limited profit accumulation and corporate scandal. Much of this has to do with shifts in power. Governments, with a mandate to consider the 'human' element to capitalism, are now lesser actors in the capitalist system, with those in charge of corporations and banks increasingly the ones whose decisions have an impact on society.

Those, then, that are in charge, in this most recent manifestation of capitalism, are corporations. It is they that are in control of the processes of globalisation, of the business transactions that shape national economies and imagine our understanding of crisis. What we perceive as a crisis may not be viewed as such by corporations. Again, as products of the capitalist system, they are conditioned to accept winners and losers in the markets; and when they are on the losing side, corporations resolve to reimagine their business plan to ensure that they can once again be perceived as 'winners'. When viewed through this lens, financial crisis becomes less 'emotional' and more a systemic reaction within the markets: not a disaster as such but a type of flashing error code to corporations of the need to reboot and rethink their business practice.

As governments have become less powerful within the market system, the reach of corporations has become greater. Governments are increasingly turning to corporations to fill the interstices in society, and perhaps this is why the most recent liquidity crisis was so keenly felt. This partnership between business and government has produced many successes, but in times of crisis, the difference in the outlook and approach of these entities becomes particularly noticeable. Governments have a 'human element': they have a mandate to a large section of the population. They also have a loyalty to their state, their culture and their people, which underpins how they do business. This is not the case for corporations. Whereas increasingly corporations are engaging in the 'social' or 'human' element of business, when times are tough, and this need for a reboot occurs, the corporation needs to revert back to its primary objective, namely profit maximisation, in order to stabilise its niche in the market. So, in times of crisis, national governments react by implementing social protections because the corporate reaction has been to shore up the economic side of capitalism. Thus, problems occur. The corporate social responsibility (CSR) approach of corporations is insufficient on its own as, when it is most needed, it is the time when corporations are less willing to engage more proactively and innovatively with the policies in place. Governments however need to engage with corporations to ensure that social policy developments are maintained. Crisis leaves something of a vacuum, and it is within this scenario that this book is situated.

II Structure of this book

This book is focused on government–business interactions in the global market. Focused specifically on the role of business in supplementing (or even replacing) social-development initiatives within some regions, this book is concerned with whether a corporation's corporate social responsibility (CSR) policy can create 'true' development for the region in which it is operating or if the 'development' which occurs is an attempt by the corporation to legitimise its operation within the region. The capacity of corporations to facilitate true development is conditioned by the fact that they owe no loyalty to a culture or state. Simply, the corporation's key objective is capital accumulation. With the shifts in governance, however, the value of these organisations to the governance discourse is increasing, and their contribution to development is becoming more precious. Although the power of national governments has diminished considerably as the global market has become more globalised, their role as external stakeholders cannot be undervalued. As vehicles for influencing corporate policy, there is scope for CSR to be further developed by introducing a regulatory framework to ensure effective CSR. However, the strength of government as an external stakeholder can be constrained by a number of other factors, including its dependence on the corporation for development within a particular region. This book concludes by trying to find a middle ground – one that recognises the constraints on government while pursuing the potential of effective CSR.

Chapter 1 traces the evolution of the CSR concept. From its inception in the charitable donations of influential businessmen, the model has been developed, refined and mass produced – to the extent that CSR has become, in theory, as much a part of a business as profit making. To emphasise the evolution in CSR writings and practice, Chapter 1 looks specifically at the character of CSR in the US and the UK. The rationale behind focusing on these two countries is that CSR developed within the wider Anglo-American corporate governance sphere. Whereas this has experienced a divorce of ideology, the key principles in each system remain comparable and offer an interesting insight into how different governments can shape CSR meaning, practice and policy, in different ways. This chapter finishes with the recognition that CSR can contribute to the development of a region, especially when working in tandem with the national government to ensure that CSR policy best meets the needs of the particular nation state.

Chapter 2 is concerned with the challenge of developing an effective CSR policy (which will lead to development), where the two parties in partnership are not equal. In order to demonstrate the challenge that this presents, this chapter focuses on a development theory from the 1960s and

1970s known as dependency theory. This theory originally emerged to describe the unequal relationship between newly nationalised states and their colonisers. Focused primarily on issues of inequality, this theory fell into disuse with the demise of the Bretton Woods system of market regulation. This chapter proposes the existence of dependency but that this dependency is slightly different from the dependency described in the early literature. Modified dependency suggests a ubiquitous dependence on capital generated by MNCs. This dependency manifests in a similar fashion to traditional dependence. Development becomes dependent and the underdevelopment of development becomes the norm. This chapter also introduces the idea that whereas all states are dependent, some are more dependent than others. The history of a state and whether it was considered dependent under traditional understandings of the theory all contribute to the status of the state under a modified dependence, which has implications on the power of the state to hold corporations to account, enforce accountability mechanisms and drive CSR policy. Other elements such as population size become relevant also – to the point that it can be said that small open economies tend to be more dependent than others. This theme is teased out throughout this book with many examples used.

Chapter 3 builds on Chapter 2 by looking at the now dominant actor in the global system: the corporation. Looking at the class that can be said to oversee the corporation, the transnational capitalist class (TCC), this chapter focuses on the challenge of relying on corporations and the TCC to drive an effective CSR agenda in dependent regions. The reason for this perceived challenge lies in the function of the corporation. Profit maximisation must be a primary function. Whereas a more societal element is increasingly on the corporate agenda, this can only be second to profit maximisation. This chapter explores the shifts in the power structures within the global system and notes that the TCC has no loyalty to a people, culture or class. With the rise in dominance of the corporation, the role of national governments has changed. Less powerful now, the national government is reimagined within the governance infrastructure.

Chapter 4 then looks at the role of government in this problem. CSR can assist with development. The challenge is in ensuring that this development is 'true' development and not dependent development. Dependence on corporate investment has led to dependent development and indeed questions the effectiveness of any CSR mechanisms that have been introduced at state level. CSR has the power to develop a region, but is the wherewithal there to ensure that this development is effective? Chapter 4 therefore addresses the role of the government within this new governance system. Although national governments are lesser players in the governance infrastructure, they still have a role to play. This piece is something of a mesh between the language of corporate governance (specifically CSR) and international relations (through the narrative on dependence, globalisation, etc.). In so doing, the position of the government needs to be translated into this language. In assuming the rise of the transnational capitalist class (TCC), international relations are becoming increasingly more 'corporate'. In following this through to the role of national governments within this new world order, then, they are external stakeholders of the corporation. Corporates are increasingly in control of capitalism. This is not to say that national governments have no role to play. In theory, they can influence the direction of the corporation, particularly on shaping the social and environmental contributions of the corporate form (a form that was not envisaged as being anything more than a vehicle for profit accumulation). However, the dependence discussed in Chapters 2 and 3 may mean that, rather than *influencing* the corporation, the government is *influenced* by the corporation. Such is the inequality in the relationship between state and corporation: the government of more dependent states may be resigned to the whim of the corporation and, as such, can be described as being as a hostage to capital.

Chapter 5 expands on this point. CSR could develop a region. However, in order to offset the condition of dependence, CSR needs to be effectively directed or shaped by government. Government, particularly government in a dependent state, may be unable to effectively do this. Legislation or regulation is needed that can introduce a comprehensive CSR regulatory regime which can develop a region and, in so doing, alleviate the symptoms of dependency. Some initiatives already exist: from state level to federal level, to international codes and principles. The voluntary nature of these initiatives (especially those at federal or international level) re-emphasise the challenge for smaller, more open and traditionally more dependent economies. For these states to have effective CSR, which may in turn inspire development, CSR regulation must be mandatory, implemented and enforced at a federal or international level. With the increasing competitiveness of the global market, however, dependence has become the norm, and it is unlikely that innovation in CSR direction and influence will ever override the desire to retain competitiveness. Dependence is here to stay and, as it becomes more ingrained, financial crises become increasingly prevalent with the impact on regions becoming more and more detrimental. Capitalism revolves around winners and losers. For now, society appears to be losing out.

1
The Evolution of the CSR Concept: From Sharing to Caring

1.1 Introduction and overview

Corporate social responsibility (CSR) has been heralded as the manner in which corporations position themselves in society. In recent times the scope of CSR has evolved beyond management school and business rhetoric to become a term recognised by most in society. Whereas the term CSR may be part of general parlance, the nuances of the concept evade many people. This may be attributed to the fluid development of the ideology and, in accordance its evolution has been in a constant state of flux. Discussions on CSR have developed considerably in recent years, to the extent that CSR can now be considered a strategic tool in the relationship between business, government and stakeholders alike. This book is concerned with capital generated by MNCs and the relationship between MNCs and the state. The government's role within CSR, then, is primarily as an external stakeholder of MNCs. This, and stakeholder management more generally, is explored in more detail in Chapter 4, but the idea behind this chapter is to introduce CSR and to consider the character of CSR today. These two tasks provide a useful lens to analyse the evolution of CSR in both academic literature and practical application – from 'indirect' methods such as disclosure legislation and other regulatory practices to the more direct methods of CSR-influenced legislation which is becoming more commonplace today.

1.2 Overview of CSR

Corporate social responsibility (CSR) has spent the last 50 years developing, evolving and reimagining its purpose and value within the company and in broader society. And that is the beauty of it. It is designed to ebb and flow with business trends, to align with market patterns and to gauge societal interpretations of the concept. As such, it has undergone significant rebranding from early inceptions of philanthropy and gift giving. Today, the idea of CSR is tied in with a self-regulatory function (as it relates to tax, compliance, etc.). It can be viewed as an inclusion of public interest into corporate decision making (Elkington, 1997) and as a means of recognising and protecting stakeholders by taking their needs and concerns into consideration while making corporate decisions. More recent developments have centred on the role of business within the sphere of human rights, and the 'corporate responsibility' to protect human rights has further embedded the language of CSR into a business, legal and governance space (for example, the UN Guiding Principles on Business and Human Rights).

Carroll (1999) provides a useful review of the themes and concepts of CSR from Bowen's Social Responsibilities (1953) to Corporate Social Performance initiatives (Wood, 1991). More recent discussions have centred on the impact of global financial crises and what crises tell us about the effectiveness of CSR theory and practice (Kemper and Martin, 2010; Carroll, 2015). It is in piecing these puzzle pieces that the fluidity of the concept can be best understood. It can be attributed in part to the failure of academics, practitioners and governments to agree on a particular definition: for example, Godfrey, Hatch and Hansen (2010) describe CSR as a 'tortured concept' (2010, p. 316). The proliferation of definitions through the years has contributed to the success of the concept but also the criticisms of CSR as a model. There is constantly a reimagining of the definition of CSR within the literature (see Schwartz and Carroll, 2003 (which is particularly critical of Carroll, 1991); Carroll 2015) and with bodies like the European Commission reimagining CSR as 'the responsibility of enterprises for their impact on society' (Corporate Social Responsibility: Accountable, transparent and responsible business behaviour and sustainable growth, 2013b).

The 'modern' definition of CSR is perhaps attributable to Bowen (1953) but refined by Carroll in 1979. Carroll's definition, describes CSR as 'the social responsibility of business [that] encompasses the economic, legal, ethical and discretionary expectations that society has of organizations *in any given point in time*' (Carroll, 1979, p. 500, emphasis added). Note the fluidity of the definition, where 'any given point in time' suggests that the characterisation of CSR adapts as business trends change. In later years, though, McWilliams and Siegel's definition of CSR as an action that *appears* to further some social good extends beyond the explicit interests of the firm but is not required by the law (2001, p.117, emphasis added) has garnered considerable popularity (Godfrey et al., 2010: Lawler and Conger, 2015). Indeed, this idea of going *beyond* the law is something that has gained traction in more recent years (McBarnet, 2007) and does still lend itself to the 'appearance' of social good. Windsor is critical of the concept and the emphasis on the appearance of social good, especially with the 'anti-responsibility' trends in the literature, noting in particular that 'the leitmotif of wealth creation has a veneer of respectability' as it 'progressively dominates the managerial conception of responsibility' (2001, p.226). This suggests that CSR is not so much a conscious desire to *do* good, but rather a conscious desire to *look* good, which challenges the potential of CSR especially in the context of this book.

More recently, Carroll has again reconceptualised CSR, but this time as 'the benchmark and centre-piece of the socially conscious business movement' (2015, pp. 87–88). Here, he notes that every generation expects more from business and life generally – something that can be traced particularly from the social consciousness movements of the 1960s. With these shifts, social responsibility has had to adapt to globalisation and can be used as a tool for legitimacy as globalisation proliferates. Interestingly, Carroll is now less persuaded by the altruism of companies, suggesting that CSR in the 21st century now takes the form of alternative concepts, rationales and frameworks (2015, p. 89). This does reflect Godfrey et al., who note that the construct is more defined by the confusion surrounding it than by the clarity that a good definition would bring to scientific inquiry and practical application (2010, p. 317).

The failure to define the concept does, in part, contribute to the struggles of academics (and indeed business leaders and governments) to develop a concrete identity for CSR. Nonetheless, some constants can be identified. One such constant, and one which can be traced throughout this book generally and particularly in this chapter, is the contribution of Carroll to the academic understanding and identification of trends in the CSR literature. From his definition of CSR (1979), to his pyramid construct (1991) (where he looked at the different types of CSR and placed these on a pyramid to demonstrate types of CSR contributions and their relationships to each other), to his general overviews of the masses of literature (1999; 2015), Carroll has provided a pathway for understanding the evolution of CSR.

CSR was 'invented' as a modern concept in the 1950s (Bowen, 1953) with definitions emerging in the 1960s (e.g. McGuire, 1963 – although a bit fuzzy in terminology, this can be seen as a precursor to Carroll's 1979 definition and indeed his 1991 pyramid). These definitions continued into the 1970s and, to a point, fragmented the ideology (See, Sethi, 1975; Manne and Wallich, 1972; Frederick, 1994). By the end of the 1970s and more definitively in the 1980s, CSR had evolved from definitive to pragmatic, with streams of CSR-influenced research adopting a more empirical flavour in areas such as corporate social performance, business ethics, corporate citizenship and stakeholder management. Context is everything. After the definitional stage of the literature, the late 1970s–1980s are where CSR tries to make the transition from the literature to policy. At this stage too, the nature of business is experiencing a drastic evolution from the Fordist model of business to the MNC. Although this transition had been in place since WWII, it was at this stage picking up speed. On a politico-ideological level, the prime minister of the UK was Margaret Thatcher and the president of the US was Ronald Reagan. Their political ideologies were very much in line with the writings of Friedman and the Chicago School of Economics as broadly conceived – that is, the importance of tying CSR policies to the bottom line. Perhaps this in part explains the nature of CSR trends at this time specifically the linking of CSR to corporate financial performance. Corporate social performance was, at this point, the more popular choice, a trend that continued into the 1990s with Wood (1991) and Carroll's pyramid construct of CSR (1991). If the 1950s and 1960s were defined by definitions, and the 1970s and 1980s were more pragmatic (and grounded in the context of that time), then the 1990s and 21st century became more thematic. By this stage, corporate governance is encroaching more emphatically into the CSR space, as are issues around financial crisis and CSR and notions of sustainable development.

Even as this evolution has produced marked differences from early understandings of CSR to interpretations today, some key themes have prevailed: Carroll notes that 'whereas sometimes nomenclature to CSR is used – the themes remain the same' (2015, p. 94). The following are the main focuses of this book: first, definitional dissatisfaction which may have prompted fragmentations of thinking around CSR; second, the relationship between CSR and financial performance; and third, the voluntary nature of the concept.

Throughout this book, and particularly in Chapters 4 and 5, I explore solutions to the CSR impasse, especially the voluntary nature of the concept and the underlying economic focus of CSR specifically as this relates to governance and dependency. The future of CSR has been the focus of academic discussion in recent years, with Filatotchev and Stahl (2015) arguing for transnational CSR. They argue that transnational CSR demands that 'companies develop a global template for their CSR activities to guide managerial decision making and ensure consistency across the organization but allows executives of local subsidiaries to adapt that template according to their specific needs and circumstances' (Filatotchev and Stahl, 2015, p. 123). In so doing, they are promoting a hybrid between global CSR centred on hyper-norms (which in itself may lead to criticism of 'cultural arrogance' and 'ethical imperialism' (2015, p. 122)) and a local approach to CSR. The transnational approach is not without criticism in that the cost is not explored, nor is the scenario of the weaker government that may be unable to direct local policy. The sheer number of resources needed for local information and knowledge would require a body of expertise in each subsidiary. Aside from this being at odds with the underlying economic focus of CSR, there are wider issues, particularly regarding whether this approach would limit fluidity within a company if expertise is limited to a particular region. In exploring the future of CSR, Carroll (2015) argues that the continuation of the norm is the most probable scenario due to 1) business acceptance of the concept, 2) the global growth of the concept and 3) academic proliferation around the subject. Carroll's approach is the one most closely aligned with the views outlined in this book. CSR is now an accepted 'add-on' of business practice, be it through an integrated engagement with stakeholders or independent philanthropic activities (Lawler and Conger, 2015). With the acceptance of CSR as an aspect of business practice, there is also the increasing globalisation of business and society's expectation of business practice (Filatotchev and Stahl, 2015; Carroll, 2015). In short, business today is about more than shareholder profits. CSR *could* be used in an innovative manner, *could* inspire development and *could* alleviate the symptoms of a dependence on capital as explored in Chapters 2 and 3. For this to happen, CSR may need to occur at a transnational level as proposed by Filatotchev and Stahl (2015) and enforced. However, academic proliferation on CSR has so closely linked CSR with an underlying economic focus and has characterised CSR as 'voluntary', that the capacity for CSR to 'develop' may be limited. This is not to say that CSR has not inspired development. The next section of this chapter addresses the character of CSR in the US and the UK before considering how the evolution of CSR in academia and practice has contributed to a more robust CSR environment today.

1.3 Characterising CSR

1.3.1 'Layers' of CSR

As a paradigm, CSR has been constantly evolving as academic literature, social concerns and government interventions have each made their own contributions to the theory's development (Vurro, 2006; Carroll, 1999). As the aims and approaches of governments' policies differ with the social requirements and obligations of their citizens, national variations can be found within CSR. What has been created then are 'layers' – these layers within CSR are in part characterised by particular contributions in government policy. With nuances at state-level, federal interventions and international obligations, what emerges is a global melting pot of CSR policy, shifts and persuasions. This chapter refers to developments in the UK and the US primarily given the origins of CSR within the Anglo-American construct. However, reference to other jurisdictions is also made. Despite both the UK and the US originally being advocates of the Anglo-American mode of governance, factors such as structural differences, reactions to scandal, and so on have helped to redefine each country's governance structure, each of which has, in turn, had an impact on the direction of CSR within both nations. By considering these two case studies – and the particular nuances that have emerged – I am able to situate the case of small open economies within a CSR spectrum. However, as the information on dependency and development informs, it may be that context is key. Innovation on how that capital operates in a region may be only the utopic ideal as opposed to the potential reality for many of states.

Traditional divisions in corporate governance suggest two main modes of governance: the Anglo-American (outsider) mode and the European/Japanese (insider) mode. However, as this chapter illustrates in Sections 1.3.1.2 and 1.3.3 especially, advances in the UK governance structure in particular suggest an ideological divorce between British and American modes of governance. Approaches to CSR, in both jurisdictions, have arguably been a major factor in the division of the corporate structures. This evolution, in the UK especially, towards an expanded social and environmental disclosure mandate (e.g. the business review, s. 417 Companies Act 2006; Directive 2014/95/EU; DEFRA, 2011; Draft Greenhouse Gas Emissions (Directors' Reports) Regulations 2013) is evidence that the UK's 'enlightened share value' is beginning to occupy a unique position between the American shareholder wealth-maximising model and the continental stakeholder model (Williams and Corely, 2005; Andreasson, 2011).

Although this shift has not been complete – as can be noted in the UK and EU's sometimes parallel approaches to takeovers, for example (for the UK, see The City Code on Takeovers and Mergers (which goes beyond Art. 3 general principles in the Directive); Companies Act 2006 (Part 28); Financial Services and Markets Act, 2002; Financial Services Act 2012, Criminal Justice Act 1993; Enterprise Act 2002; Enterprise and Regulatory Reform Act 2013: For the EU – see primarily the Takeovers Directive (2004/25/EC); EU Merger Regulations 2014 (for takeovers which are concentrations within a community direction)) – the compromise of the Third Way with regard to CSR in the UK has meant that there is now a significant division in the 'historically, unified Anglo-American front' (Williams and Corely, 2005, p. 495). As such, they now represent two alternative approaches to CSR and are both included in this chapter to demonstrate the capacity for divergence in approaches to CSR, even when similarities exist in broader governance structures.

By addressing the status of CSR today in the UK and the US, this chapter highlights how specific societal requirements and modes of governance, together with the strength of the government's ability to influence, affect the national approach to CSR. This will facilitate discussion later in this book on the relationship of CSR to development and in particular to capital investment in a region from MNCs. It may be that profit maximisation remains the key goal of governments in, for example, small and open economies, as dependence on capital from MNCs limits the government's role as an influential stakeholder. In these countries, capital may not need to legitimise its existence via robust CSR activities. In a global system emerging from financial crisis, the role of CSR within nation states in contributing to development is very much open to debate.

1.3.1.1 CSR in the US today

Despite being traditionally a firm advocate of shareholder primacy, the effect of scandals such as Enron, WorldCom, Refco (and perhaps more recently, inter alia, Lehman Bros and AIG) on the public's perception of the MNC and wider regulatory controls has had an impact on the US governance structures. Added to this, the US itself has been keen to depict an accurate and secure market for investors, despite such scandals - arguably calling for advances *beyond* the traditional principles-based approach to governance. In part, this has been achieved by the implementation of federal legislation such as the Public Company Accounting Reform and Investor Protection Act (2002, (SOX)) and, more recently, the Wall Street Reform and Consumer Protection Act (2010 (Dodd–Frank)).

In aiming to promote a 'culture of integrity' through a rules-based approach to governance, the Sarbanes Oxley Act (SOX) has aimed to increase transparency and accountability of corporate actions (Oxley, 2007; Merino, Mayper and Tolleson, 2010). Although not evincing CSR policy, it is a marked change in attitude with regard to governance, and it perhaps reflects how the character of American governance is changing, with the view to CSR expectations at a federal level in the future. Moving on from SOX, the Dodd–Frank Act follows a similar rhetoric and perhaps goes further with CSR-influenced approaches embedded in legislation. Whereas the Act itself has come under heavy criticism from a number of areas (and for a number of reasons) (Wilmarth Jr, 2010; Rapp, 2012), the underpinning aims around Title VII (Wall Street Transparency and Accountability) and Title IX (Investment Protections and Improvements to the Regulation of Securities) do enhance regulatory requirements and both transparency and accountability. Title VII (Wall Street Transparency and Accountability) is concerned with the regulation of swap markets. These are customised contracts that are traded in the over-the-counter market between private parties. This market has been challenged for its role in the 2008 financial crisis. Title IX (Investment Protections and Improvements to the Regulation of Securities) focuses on the issues that commonly appear in any discussion of corporate governance issues: accountability, executive compensation, regulation of credit rating agencies, increasing regulatory enforcement and so on. These two Titles, therefore – in enhancing reporting requirement, transparency and accountability – provide, along with creating investor security through minimising risk, a secondary function that creates a more responsible environment for business to operate.

Also of relevance are the provisions in Title X (Bureau of Consumer Financial Protection) in protecting and representing the consumer. Again, the provisions contained within are somewhat reactionary in how they look at the fairness, transparency and the competitiveness of financial products on the market, albeit they do add to a culture of responsibility that is emerging as an aside to the more risk-averse market for investors. However, in noting the more CSR-influenced elements of Dodd–Frank, the miscellaneous provisions of Title XV are most relevant, focusing specifically on the disclosure requirements on conflict materials in or near the DRC; Mine Safety Reports; and the reporting on payments by oil, gas and mineral industries for the acquisition of licences (Woody, 2012; for criticism of this approach, see Narine, 2012). By requiring the Comptroller General of the US and the Federal Deposit Insurance Corporation to conduct studies and issue reports to Congress on these issues – CSR regulation 'by the back door' is being created, in part. However, the fact that these reports have to be completed within one year of the enactment of the Title does delimit the potential of this type of legislation in fostering CSR – their value may instead lie in creating the environment for CSR to develop.

Regardless of the limitations of these pieces of legislation, when combined with advances at state level, in the form of constituency statutes,[1] it is clear that there is some departure from the traditional shareholder-oriented American governance system in how the US thinks about the MNC and its role within society. Although this remains somewhat tentative and

---

1 Constituency Statutes are state-level pieces of legislation that encourage boards of directors to take into consideration the impact of their business decisions on their constituency – or stakeholder group. For examples of current constituency statutes, see Ariz. Rev. Stat. Ann. § 10–1202 (1990 & Supp. 1993); Conn. Gen. Stat. Ann. § 33–313(e) (West Supp. 1993); Fla. Stat. Ann. § 607.0830(3) (West 1993); Ga. Code Ann. § 14–2-202(b)(5) (1989); Haw. Rev. Stat. § 415–35(B) (Supp. 1992); Idaho Code § 30- 1702 (Supp. 1993); Ill. Ann. Stat. Ch. 805, Para. 8.85 (Smith-Hurd 1993); Ind. Code Ann. § 23-1-35–1(D) (West 1989); Iowa Code Ann. § 491.101(B) (West 1991); Ky. Rev. Stat. Ann.

§ 271b.12–210(4) (1989 & Supp. 1992); La. Rev. Stat. Ann. § 12:92(G) (West Supp. 1994); Me. Rev. Stat. Ann. Tit. 13-A, § 716 (West Supp. 1993); Mass. Gen. Laws Ann. Ch. 156b, § 65 (Supp. 1993); Minn. Stat. Ann. § 302a.251(5) (Supp. 1994); Miss. Code Ann. § 794–8.30(D) (Supp. 1993); Mo. Ann. Stat. § 351.347 (Vernon 1991); Neb. Rev. Stat. § 21–2035(1) (1991); Nj. Stat. Ann. § 14a:6–1, -14 (West Supp. 1993); N.M. Stat. Ann. § 53–11–35(D) (Michie Supp. 1993); N.Y. Bus. Corp. Law § 717(B) (Mckinney Supp. 1994); Ohio Rev. Code Ann. § 1701.59(E) (Anderson 1992);

Or. Rev. Stat. § 60.357(5) (Supp. 1992); 15 Pa. Con. Stat. Ann. § 1715, 1716 (Supp. 1993); R.I. Gen. Laws § 7–5.2- 8 (1992); S.D. Codified Laws Ann. § 47–33–4 (1991); Tenn. Code Ann. § 48–35–204 (1988); Wis. Stat. Ann. § 180.0827 (West 1992); Wyo. Stat. § 17–16–830(E) (Supp. 1993).

flawed, in requesting that directors take into consideration the impact of their actions on stakeholders, for example, a more *stakeholder-friendly* form of governance is beginning to emerge: a form of governance that may even be shaped by government intervention and regulation.

1.3.1.2 CSR in the UK today

The UK has divorced from traditional 'Anglo-American' modes of governance. In advancing the 'Third Way', the accession of the New Labour government considerably altered the face of CSR and government–business interaction in the UK to the point where the UK today is recognised as being a global leader in CSR. Within the UK government there had been a minister for CSR up until 2010. This in itself had provided a focal point for CSR within government regarding the encouragement of research and the development of CSR issues and planning. An annual CSR report was released: this, together with the increasingly global focus on CSR, contributed to amendments within the regulatory framework (as it related to CSR). Today, CSR is subsumed primarily under the Department of Business, Innovation and Skills; Department of Work and Pensions; Department of the Environment, Food and Rural Affairs; and the All Party Parliamentary Group for Corporate Responsibility (www.apcrg.org.uk/home), and rhetoric around CSR in government has been superseded by talk of the 'Big Society' (Westwood, 2011; Bowles, 2010; Parkes, Scully and Anson, 2010) – which would appear to be the Lib-Dem/Conservative and now, albeit to a much lesser extent, Conservative manifestation of business and societal governance (see, for example, 'Responsible Business Champions Scheme' (www.apcrg.org.uk)).

Despite the change in rhetoric, and the shift to more vague all-encompassing statements on CSR-influenced activities, social issues *are* being considered – not just by welfare state services but those investing in the UK (increasingly so with the changes in governance structure in the UK). CSR activities have become normalised behaviours – a mark of legitimisation (as Carroll, 2015 predicted) – a standard rather than a badge of exception. Public–private partnerships (PPP) and increased disclosure legislation (for example, Listing Rules, 2014; UK Corporate Governance Code, 2012; Revised Guidelines on Audit Committees; Disclosure and Transparency Rules regarding corporate governance statements and audit committees (DTR 7); and Guidance on Risk Management, Internal Control and Related Financial and Business Reporting), which attempt to regulate MNCs operating in the UK (Moon, 2004), have served to enhance the profile of the 'Third Way' and illustrate the success of this approach in identifying and considering stakeholding interests in MNC policy. Moon (2004) speculates that this interest in corporate governance and CSR is due to the fact that the government is no longer willing to accept blame for perceived failures through non-reaction. This has been emphasised by subsequent advancements, such as the Companies Act 2006 as detailed below. The limitations of the PPPs especially in relation to the private finance initiative have been well documented elsewhere, but again, they illustrate the role of business in society in the UK and the recognition of other interests.

This has culminated in the introduction of s. 172 of the Companies Act 2006. Whether or not it represents a strategic or a committed desire to foster stakeholding relationships has been discussed elsewhere (Copp, 2009), but for the purposes of this book, its importance cannot be disputed. By legislating on the advantages of strategic philanthropy and recognising the need to consider the impact of the company's operations on the community and the environment (s. 172 (1) (d)), section 172 has arguably provided a platform for CSR in the UK, where this type of model can be accepted as a business strategy. What this suggests is that, far from being of economic detriment to the MNC, an effective, strategic CSR strategy could, in fact, lead to profit maximisation in the long run, fulfilling the rhetoric of Freeman (1984) discussed below and indeed emphasising the link postulated in academia between CSR and financial performance (e.g. Godfrey et al., 2010; Carroll, 1991). However, these legislative provisions are not developed within a vacuum. It is imperative to recognise the impact of the structure of the UK's economy and the bargaining power which its potential consumer base incites, in any assessment of the success of the UK CSR approach. It may be the case that, rather than fostering a vibrant CSR environment, capital has legitimated its existence in the UK through CSR, which in turn represents a manifestation of brand marketing to appeal to the large population and potential consumer base that the UK contains. Perhaps, therefore, the UK is not a global leader in CSR but simply *more proficient* in shaping CSR through its pre-existing structures, which warrants a deeper integration in the economy for MNCs. What this is referring to is the London Stock Exchange (LSE) and how it is recognised as a formidable entity in the UK economy.

By combining legislative and policy developments with an increasing amount of disclosure legislation, we can see to what extent the UK governance structure has progressed from the charitable donations of businessmen (Climate Change Levy, Landfill Tax, Community Investment Tax Credit Scheme). Although these pieces of legislation may not be very radical in their wording, they have marked a significant shift in the British culture of corporate governance. Disclosure legislation, although not mandatory, has quietly advanced market pressures and therefore encouraged voluntary CSR (McBarnet, 2007). This move, from tell me to show me, has had the effect of shaping CSR practice more and more in the UK (McBarnet, 2007). As McBarnet (2007) argues, the UK government's strategy with regard to

CSR has been to legislatively support and strengthen market pressures on companies to pay attention to CSR issues.

In sum, what we have today is a very complex combination of business, government and societal groups interacting, together with self-regulation and legislated regulation. It is theoretically the most positive stage of CSR thus far in its development, with the idea of government and business being on a more equal standing. Applying Carroll's (1999, p. 268) Venn diagram to a different set of circumstances – as opposed to being separate entities – governments, businesses and NGOs are now interrelated, where the business rules supreme. CSR can be viewed as a journey, and a journey that will, and can, evolve as long as government and business work together, analysing how past success could be made more successful and how perceived failures can be avoided in the future. As noted in Section 1.2 of this chapter, the ability of CSR to reinvent itself, to imagine business responsibilities at 'any given point in time' (Carroll, 1979, p. 500) has aided the rise of the concept in managerial, business, government and academic circles.

But the question remains as to how CSR has evolved to the point where an Anglo-American structure of governance – traditionally founded on share value maximisation – can be considered a 'global leader' (Ward and Smith, 2006, p. 5). How have governmental issues and policies in the last number of decades contributed to the character of CSR in the UK and the US? The next subsection addresses these questions. Looking at the US and the UK, it considers the impacts of various social issues, together with governmental developments, on the character of CSR today. By highlighting a selection of governmental contributions to the CSR paradigm (both direct and indirect), the next subsection aims to illustrate how the government, as an external stakeholder, has evolved with CSR as its own role within the MNC has become more defined.

1.3.2 The US

Although CSR literature attributes the 1950s as the beginning of CSR in the modern era, businesses had long been encountering a sense of social awareness. CSR prior to this stage, however, was in an embryonic state, centred on charitable donations from business leaders and company chairpersons, such as Henry Ford, Andrew Carnegie and John Rockefeller. The characterisation of CSR as philanthropy at this time owed something to the perception of the role of business. Profit maximisation was regarded as the primary (and sole) aim of business and to go beyond that was considered *ultra viries*. For example, in the US, *Dodge v Ford Motor Company* (1919) reflects courts' and society's perception of the role of business at that time: profit maximisation. The success of the Ford Motor Company had meant that by 1916 they had amassed a considerable capital surplus. At the same time, the cost of the car had decreased while employees' wages increased. Henry Ford wished to capitalise on this development and wanted to end special dividends for shareholders in order that new plants could be developed, leading to even cheaper cars and even greater employment. Oft cited with his utilitarian approach to labour, the Michigan Supreme Court thwarted this attempt at socially responsible behaviour noting that a business corporation is organised primarily for the profit of the shareholders – not for the benefit of the community or, in this case, employees. Any philanthropy therefore had to come from the businessmen, as opposed to the business, in order to protect the relationship between profit and shareholder.

The political climate of two world wars, and the reliance on government for welfare provision, did highlight the inadequacies of the existing system. By emphasising the need for social issues to be supplemented by charitable donations from businesses, the sociopolitical climate around both World War I and World War II aided the development of the CSR concept in their illustration of the limitations of national governments, in provision of services. Although the contribution of business was still grounded in philanthropy, the *admission* of the role of business in society and welfare provision proved instrumental in the development of the concept of CSR. It also led to a number of questions being asked with regard to the governance of the 'big business', especially as to their obligations and duties to the law (Hansmann and Kraakman, 2000). Academic literature began to note the influence of business on society with Bowen (1953) and contemporaries (e.g. Selekman, 1959; Eells, 1956) commenting on the pivotal role of business in influencing and being influenced by society: '[social responsibility] refers to the obligations of businessmen to pursue those policies, to make those decisions, or follow those lines of action which are desirable in terms of the objectives and values of our society' (Bowen, 1953, p. 6).

Questions being asked about the role of business in society also led to the recognition of the need to control the MNC via government regulation. At this time in the US, this was marked by banking reforms (e.g. Glass–Stegall Act 1933; Securities Exchange Act 1934; Banking Act 1935; Trust Indenture Act 1939; Investment Company Act 1940, Investment Advisers Act 1940), together with the establishment of the Securities and Exchange Council (SEC) under the New Deal (s. 4 Securities and Exchange Act 1934) (Leuchtenburg, 1963)). Although not concerned with CSR in the conventional sense, the establishment of the SEC in particular, together with other reforms listed above, prompted some limited regulation of the business community in the US. When taken in conjunction with judicial advances in judgments such as *AP Smith Manufacturing Company v Barlow* (1953) – the old idea of profit maximisation of business was beginning to fade – to be tenuously replaced by a new era of philanthropy. In *AP Smith Manufacturing Company v Barlow*, the courts recognised a legal link between corporate philanthropy and goodwill. Also noted in the judgment was the idea that:

> the appellants, as individual stockholders whose private interests rest entirely upon the well-being of the plaintiff corporation, ought not be permitted to close their eyes to present-day realities and thwart the long-visioned corporate action in recognizing and voluntarily discharging its high obligations as a constituent of our modern social structure. (1953, at 161)

In addition, the judgment recognised that socially responsible actions may actually lead to long-term profit maximisation, heralding, if you will, a tentative embrace of the concept of stakeholders and indeed this link between financial performance and CSR which dominates the literature (Cochran and Wood, 1984; Godfrey et al., 2010; for criticism of this link, see Windsor, 2001).

By the 1960s and 1970s, CSR literature expanded and formalised considerably (Davis, 1960; Frederick, 1960; Walton, 1967). Many of the developments at this stage seemed to be gradually recognising the shift in the business context from the Fordist model of business to the increasing role of the MNC. Davis (1960) discussed CSR through his Iron Law of Responsibility. There, he suggests that social responsibilities of businesspeople need to be commensurate with their social power. Initially, Davis held that the social impact of businesses' power on society was an evolving concept, believing that the nucleus of social power was constantly shifting from the economic to the social to the political. Interestingly, he also points to the negative connotations of failing to use the power: 'whoever does not use his social power responsibly will lose it. In the long run those who do not use power in a manner which society considers responsible will tend to lose it because other groups eventually step in to assume those responsibilities' (1960, p. 73). This seems to point to the requirement that business legitimise their position in society by contributing back to society – something which he expands on with talk on the social power principle, namely that the 'social responsibilities of businessmen arise from the amount of social power that they have' (Davis, 1967, p. 48). Here, he also looks at the functional role of business and managers and seems to allude to the importance of external stakeholders, which he describes as constituency groups whose purpose is to 'limi[t] [the] functional power of the business'. This has implications for this chapter and indeed this book by questioning whether or not business has become too powerful for stakeholders to actually limit the functional power of the business. In recent years, corporations have exponentially increased in size, and the consumerism drive, combined with the implications of financial crisis, has impacted on the capacity to be an effective limitation on business power as a 'constituent' or 'stakeholder' (Garriga and Mel, 2004). This will be discussed in greater detail in Chapter 3.

At this stage, too, there existed the first hints at criticism of the concept of CSR. Friedman (1962), for example, stressed the vagueness of the definitional constructs of CSR, along with difficulties in foreseeing the economic effects of responsible behaviour. By the 1970s this criticism had formalised somewhat, and indeed, criticism of CSR is one of the dominant themes in 1970s academic literature (Friedman, 1970). Much of the literature on CSR fails to recognise just how much Friedman contributed to CSR. Much writing on CSR subsequent to Friedman seems to be haunted by the spectre of 'the social responsibility of business is business' and arguably exists only as a response to Friedman. It may be that his writings have contributed to the policy development at government level (in both the US and the UK) and indeed to the embracing of neoliberalism, thereby suggesting that the main naysayer to CSR has actually been the inspiration for how we have characterised CSR for a number of decades.

Aside from Friedman, Davis focuses, in the 1970s, more on the characteristics of CSR, noting that CSR begins where the law ends (1973, p. 313). Noting that simple compliance was not enough, Davis makes the distinction between good citizenship and CSR. Manne and Wallich (1972) set about defining CSR as 'a condition in which the corporation is at least some measure of a free agent. To the extent that any of the foregoing social objectives are imposed on the corporation by law, the corporation exercises no responsibility when it implements them' (p. 40). This approach is described as the economics of responsibility and links wealth with social welfare. This theme has prevailed in the literature with the work of Sternberg (2009, 2011), Jensen (2001, 2002) and McWilliams and Siegel (2001). Indeed, Windsor is quite critical of this approach, describing it as a 'supply and demand' model of CSR. Definitions generally were the prevalent theme of the 1970s, with the decade ending with Carroll's monumental definition of CSR as 'the social responsibility of business encompasses the economic, legal, ethical and discretionary expectations that society has of organisations at a given point in time' (Carroll, 1979, p. 500).

Social pressures in the US focused on mounting unemployment and the ensuing problems in the American economy. The increased momentum of groups such as those who championed civil rights (*Brown v Board of Education of Topeka* 1954; Guinier, 2004) and the environmental (Carson, 1962; Lutts, 1985), combined with the Vietnam War, enabled social movements to be swept together, which in turn impacted on the business community, forcing it to be more defensive (Kline, 1985). All in all, business began to learn in these decades, especially in the United States, that it had to try harder: 'Business's task has been uphill, not just because of the general trend towards interventionism' (Robinson and Pearce, 1983, p. 197).

The US government, in the years between 1965 and 1977, set up regulatory agencies that, according to Jones (www.iaf.gov), shaded most of the internal CSR benchmarks (for example, see the EPA (Environmental Protection Agency), EEOC (Equal Employment Opportunity Commission) and OSHA (Occupational Safety and Health Administration)). These regulatory agencies have created standards for responsible corporate practices, which have become the threshold for minimal CSR behaviours. As Epstein (1998) noted, 'A critical difference throughout much of the 1960s was that federal and state governments were no longer reluctant to enact laws that transformed general public expectations about business responsibilities into specific legal requirements. A new era in the interaction between business and other sectors of society was emerging' (p. 7). Despite the introduction of more regulatory agencies and policies within this layer of CSR, the failure of contemporary literature to define and refine the government's role as an external stakeholder is reflected in the type of CSR advances. By this stage, the government was not integrating with the business community, in order to develop the most effective type of CSR policies for the specific requirements of local communities at that time.

The next layer – the 1980s – marked the emergence of a number of state constituency statutes (for an up-to-date listing of constituency statutes, see Mickels, 2009; see Table of legislation; for an analysis of constituency statutes, see Orts, 1992), which authorise, but do not obligate, corporate boards of directors to consider the interests of constituencies, other than shareholders, in making corporate decisions (Mitchell, 1992; Bisconti, 2008; Bainbridge, 1992). Due to the still predominately shareholder-primacy attitude to corporate governance in the US, it is perhaps not surprising that criticism is rife with regard to the perceived interference of the government in business affairs (von Stange, 1994; Bainbridge, 1992). However, if we are to address even the shift of attitude, regardless of the practicalities of the legislation among other things, the change has been momentous for the development of CSR through government influence: '[t]he increasing recognition of the modern corporations' profound effect on the lives of a variety of groups, not traditionally within the corporate law structure, has the potential to lead corporate law into the next century in a manner more reflective of the role that this type of organisation actually plays in our society' (Mitchell, 1992, p. 579).

Together with legislative advances, the idea of business complementing government practice became more commonplace. As Moon (2005a) suggests, 'CSR can fill interstices of public policy.' This has certainly been the case in the US. In the United States, the corporation has increased interaction with government and governmental policies. This manifests itself in a number of ways. First, charity is considered to be a moral obligation and is therefore no longer voluntary (Schwartz and Carroll, 2003). Given the privatised structure of the country, especially in relation to the healthcare system, donations from MNCs are essential for the operation of society. Second, due to the close relationship between the government and the MNCs, corporations are inclined to follow government political agenda (or vice versa) with regard to their CSR policies (for the relationship between government and business and the implications of this relationship, see *Citizen's United v FEC* (2010)).

In the years from the conception of the modern era of CSR, developments of the paradigm can be traced in the US. Donations towards charitable causes by notable businesspeople developed into a more strategic philanthropy, which engages areas of social policy not covered by the government. Therefore, not only does CSR supplement government policy in the US, but also in areas such as the arts and healthcare, it replaces the government where policy is lacking.

1.3.3 The UK

As with the US, early manifestations of modern CSR comprised primarily charitable donations from the wealthy chairpersons of businesses, such as Lever Bros and Cadbury. In a similar vein to the *Dodge Bros* case discussed above, *Hutton v West Cork Railway Company* (1883) provided a colourful judgment on the role of business in society (Pettet, 1997). It notes that '[t]he law does not say there are to be no cakes and ale, but there are to be no cakes and ale except such as are required for the benefit of the company' (*Hutton v West Cork Railway Company*, 1883, Bowen, LJ). Profit maximisation, therefore, was considered to be the aim of a company. Social concerns were irrelevant. While the effects of the world wars were to affect the role of the government and that of business in society, the welfare state meant that it was more difficult to extend CSR beyond charitable giving. Whereas the US had notable 'gaps' in its social infrastructure, the UK provided for healthcare, education and so on, as a matter of course, through general taxation.

The literature of the 1960s and 1970s was to be reflected in government attitudes of the time also (Davis, 1960; Frederick, 1960; Walton, 1967, Friedman, 1962; Friedman, 1970: Manne and Wallich, 1972; Carroll, 1979). Towards the end of the 1970s, in the UK, there appears to have been recognition that the extent of governmental, social and economic commitments, coupled with the demands of society, may have been overloading the government and therefore diminishing legitimacy (King, 1975). This was due, in part, to the failure of the government to fight controversial issues such as unemployment, inflation, public debt and the lack of economic growth. Added to this was the continued existence of a much centralised government structure. It was not until the 1980s and the Thatcherite years that the UK began to fully acknowledge the role that the government could play in fostering CSR (Marchak, 1993, p. 93).

Freeman's (1984) landmark work on stakeholders in the next layer (1980s) helped to define the government's role in business. In the UK, the government became more prepared to go beyond the 'you cannot do this' towards the 'you *ought* to do this'. This transition is discussed in greater detail in Chapter 4. As a result, in the 1980s and 1990s, CSR entered a transitionary phase. Government and business, in this layer, alter from being dichotomous at the beginning of the 1980s to being more complementary by the end of the 1990s – moving from government incentivising business at the start of the 1980s to partnerships with business at the end of the 1990s (Moon, 2005b). With regard to public policy issues, the UK had attempted to resolve the overloaded state by the introduction of the 'hollowed out state' (Rhodes, 1994; Peters, 1993). Globalisation created and is creating sets of relationships that transcend the nation state (Skelcher, 2000). From a European perspective, the developing supranational and regional institutions of government posed particular challenges to the nation state (Skelcher, 2000).

However, the hollowing out of the state stimulated the widespread use of strategies designed to foster collaborations in this fragmented landscape. The result was, and has increasingly been, the creation of partnerships between business and government: tertiary partnerships (Skelcher, 2000). As mentioned with regard to the overloaded state of the 1970s, public debt and unemployment (among other things) had been major sources of contention. This culminated in the urban riots of the 1980s. For a government concerned with 'the free economy and the strong state' (Gamble, 1988), cooperation with corporations was needed in order to respond effectively to these problems (Moon and Richardson, 1985).

One of the results was the 'urban development corporations' forwarded by Michael Heseltine to combat urban decay (Lean, 1999). Although it provided jobs and rejuvenated inner-city areas, jobs went to those outside the city and the poor remained poor. The levels of cooperation, planning and development at ground level that would be necessary for such schemes to succeed were not present. The role of the government in CSR still needed some refining. However, this first constructive attempt, in encouraging the business community to complement the government in social matters, had paved the way for others.

Hollowing out the state evolved into collaboration or congestion, as termed by Skelcher (2000), which enabled partnerships to be formed between government and business leaders. Strategic philanthropy became more strategic. The benefits of localism, and partnerships were described as, 'not just a joining up of services, but also a joining up of finances and funding, and a joining up of people with key interests in what goes on in the area. It is reconnecting citizens and a whole range of services' (Woolas, 2007). By exploiting the benefits of the hollowed out state, and harnessing the business community, the then-Prime Minister Tony Blair would be able to foster partnerships that would strategically and cooperatively address social issues to a level considered impossible by state services alone.

This has been augmented by the creation of the CSR umbrella group – 'Business in the Community' (BitC) – which still functions today in the stimulation of public–private partnerships in the form of local enterprise. The creation of BitC has contributed to the advances of the UK CSR agenda, through its role in identifying such a wide range of CSR issues for British business and in continuing to work closely with the Department of Work and Pensions ('Generation Talent'); the Cabinet Office (volunteering and supporting the social sector); the Department for Business, Innovation and Skills (responsible business policy, diversity issues, etc.); and the Department for the Environment, Food and Rural Affairs.

The widespread advances of the UK CSR agenda, too, prompted some legislative advances in this 'layer' of CSR development. Although for the most part 'soft' or disclosure regulation, it provided business with the opportunity to highlight their social agenda to a wide range of stakeholders. If one considers the example of the Occupational Pension Schemes (Investment) Regulations (2005) (or indeed the earlier Occupational Pension Schemes (Disclosure of Information) Regulations 1996), and the manner in which this called for reporting on social impacts (s. 2 (3) (b) (vi)), we can see how far the government has advanced since the 'cakes and ale' (*Hutton v West Cork Railway*) of the 19th century towards the idea of 'enlightened shareholder value', which is the underpinning CSR rhetoric in the UK today (s. 172 (1) (d) Companies Act, 2006; Keay, 2007a, 2007b; Clarke, 2014). By requiring pension funds to disclose *how* they take account of social, environmental or ethical considerations in the selection, retention and realisation of investments (2005), a type of responsibility via transparency is created, which requires a more explicit behaviour from business with regard to CSR.

1.4 Conclusion

CSR in both the UK and the US has progressed significantly from the respective cases of *Dodge v Ford Motor Company* (1919) and *Hutton v West Cork Railway Company* (1883). From the traditional profit-maximisation approach, towards a more stakeholder-oriented framework of regulation, CSR has evolved considerably. By using the UK and the US as case studies, a map of CSR emerges from Bowen's seminal work (1953) to the point that today, in the US, it is seen as supplementing and indeed replacing the role of government in some cases and, in the UK, it is seen as complementing and supplementing government practice. Whereas this partnership between business and state in social endeavours promises many rewards for society, the continued prominences of key themes within CSR do cause some concern. The need for CSR to be 'voluntary' is much lauded, but post-financial crisis, the voluntary nature of CSR could actually *limit* the scope of business engagement in development. Whereas the CSR story in the US and the UK has demonstrated only a positive engagement between business and society, other factors may have contributed to this dynamic engagement. The prominent status of the US and the UK in the global system up until this point may mean that businesses are more willing to promote CSR policies to ensure a place in a robust market.

Today, government is significantly weaker than it was in the 1950s. Partly the symptoms of the financial crisis, the processes of globalisation and the rise of the MNC have limited the government's ability to influence, shape and direct CSR activities. And so, we stand at the crossroads – the rhetoric espoused by governments (such as the UK and the US) suggests the *value* of 'voluntary' CSR. However, post-financial crisis, a more robust CSR agenda *could* empower local economies and assist in development. That very much depends on how government can push the CSR agenda to promote development.

As business transactions become more global, and the power of the corporation grows, the potential for CSR is boundless. However, if CSR is accepted as an articulation of the *appearance* of social good while generating or promoting promising financial returns, the strategy behind an effective CSR policy may be inspired or directed by exogenous factors such as the strength of the government in the area where the business is operating, the financial climate at that time or the potential economic returns in furthering a social agenda. It may be that the primitive attempts at CSR in the charitable donations of businesspeople offered a greater chance at 'true' development, as articulated in later chapters of this book, than many of the more robust and comprehensive CSR policies that exist today, reminding us of the reimagining of the concept over the decades and reminding us particularly that responsibilities are conditioned by 'any given point in time' (Carroll, 1979, p. 500).

2 The Problem With CSR for the Sake of CSR: A Study in Development

2.1 Introduction and overview

With the power shifts in the global system between business and government, and the evolution of our relationship with capital, the role that capital generated by MNCs plays in society has developed considerably in the last century or so. The lines between government and business are becoming increasingly blurred, with CSR policies often complementing, supplementing or even replacing state governments' agendas on some societal issues. Through the CSR ideology, and increasingly in the wider implication of human rights, business is generally coming to the fore in societal and environmental issues. As we emerge from financial crisis, the challenge is in maintaining and advancing engagement between government and business in social issues (for the benefit of the communities in which the business operates) and in ensuring that CSR benefits national development as well as the MNC's agenda. The challenge is augmented somewhat by the inequalities in the relationship between government and MNCs.

Although not necessarily focused on CSR, much has been written on the contribution of MNCs to national development and specifically how the rising role of the MNC within a state can influence and shape development within its borders (Blowfield, 2005; Luetkenhorst, 2004; Idemudia, 2008; Bondy, Moon and Matten, 2012). However, less has been written on what we mean by development. Although this may seem like a simple question, our interpretation of 'development' very much determines our analysis of the success of said development. For the most part, assessments of development have been grounded in Western ideologies and, as such, skew both measurements and understandings of development. This book, however, portrays an alternative view on 'development' and is grounded in a Latin American theory, dependency that emerged after World War II. This chapter updates this theory of development somewhat and widens its application to explain the relationship between states and business. It challenges the parameters of the existing theory, specifically the key actors engaged in unequal relationships, the interstate application and the emphasis on the market. Using this modified theory, this book offers an alternative understanding of relationships within the global system and indeed our grasp of development. This has implications for the need, scope and application of CSR and more widely on the exchanges between government and business.

2.2 The context

Dependency is a branch of development theory and is predicated on the idea that there exists a centre/core or metropole of wealthy 'developed' states and a periphery or satellite of poorer 'underdeveloped' states. In order to bolster economic growth in the core, resources are extracted from the periphery and channelled to the core to sustain growth. Of the various branches of development and in particular dependency theories, Frank's (1967a, 1991) work on 'underdevelopment' through dependency theory coupled with Dos Santos's (1970) 'conditions of dependence' approach are most useful as they provide a means to understand dependent relationships that can be adapted to shifts in the global order today (i.e. the rise of the MNC and the diminishing power of national governments). As such, much of the material used in this chapter can be traced to the 1960s and 1970s. Although this might appear quite dated, the value of these contributions to the literature – and specifically to this book – lies in how they can be applied to a different set of relationships (particularly the relationship between nation states and capital) and provide an alternative way to understand the global system as it exists today.

Dependency theory emerged after WWII. Prior to WWII, writings on development appear limited to the work of Marx and Hegel (Tucker, 1978; Hegel, 1953, pp. 14–35, 445–458). Leys (1996) attributes Hegel and Marx as 'true originators of development theory', (p. 4) by the way that they 'recognized that it was the sudden acceleration in the rate of change that the establishment of capitalist production and bourgeois society has generated that made it necessary and possible to ... view world history as a process of development' (Leys, 1996, p. 4). The timing of the theory is noteworthy, and parallels can be drawn between the economic environment in which the theory emerged and the current financial climate. Roxborough (1979, p. 63) notes that the theory needed the push of the change in world order (i.e. the dissolution of the empires after the war), whereas Kay (1975, p. 1) referred to the shift away from pinning division on race and climate. Today, the inherent problems of engaging with a capitalist system have led to financial crisis and a rethinking of how we engage with and control capital.

Transformations in the global system after WWII provided the climate for new theoretical approaches to development to emerge (Frank, 1967a, 1967b). Decolonisation, independence and nationalisation not only provided a means to disengage with former masters and theoretically assert independence but in doing so provided a smokescreen around these states' continued dependence on world economic structures (and indeed their former masters) (Zartman, 1976, p. 325). A need to move away from conventional development theories was apparent, with Kay referring to their failure to acknowledge the work of Marx generally, in particular his 'Law of Value' and their existence as 'a thinly veiled apology for colonialism' (Kay, 1975, p. 2). This 'Law of Value' is a regulative principle of the economic exchange of the products of human work. At its most basic (and a rather crude explanation at that), the value of a product is expressed in terms of a price (money). This price is proportional to the cost of production (in terms of labour). Therefore, the exchange value of products is regulated by their value – with value being a quantity of human labour (Pilling, 1972). This is not to say that 'value' and 'price' are the same – indeed, this is something to which Marx refers when talking about the transformation problem. Here, he (and indeed many others, including Ricardo and Smith) notes that an algorithm is needed which encompasses the magnitude of value added by labour in proportion to its intensity and duration. The said algorithm needs to account for this, after value has been distributed through prices that reflect an equal rate of return on capital advanced. Marx, however, does recognise the importance of 'supply and demand' – he refers to Smith when speaking of the cost production argument, citing it as Smith's 'adding up theory of value'. Where Marx differs then from Smith and Ricardo is in his starting point as "society" not the individual (specifically socially necessary abstract labour time) together with the idea of commodity values (Marx, 1868 (1969), ch. 6; 1891). In thinking about 'society', Marx introduces a social element that makes his theory on labour value distinct from his predecessors and neoclassical economists.

The failure of development theories generally to acknowledge Marx can be attributed to the relative shallowness of such theories. For example, such theories can fail to take into consideration the historical (or social) aspect of developing nations. Of course, this was also part of the wider political context in which this theory emerged. After WWII, the 'Cold War' era tainted discussions on development insofar as they traded on the value of newly independent nations and took the Marx/anti-Marx stance depending on whether they were East/West theorists.

Not only did the post-WWII climate create an environment for theories on development to evolve, it also arguably stifled the potential for these theories. The theories on development that emerged were undeniably tinged with 'conservative bias' (Kay, 1975, Introduction), and many took the form of propaganda-style publications (e.g. Rostow, 1960), which proposed to enlighten readers to 'the processes of economic and social evolution, but also its alleged power to dispose once and for all of the Marxian dragon with which so many others have done battle but failed to slay' (Baran and Hobsbawn, 1973, p. 234). Rostow's *stages of growth* did become a key publication in development theories after World War II. However, it was not without widespread criticism, and this criticism extended beyond the anti-Marxist bias that prevailed throughout the work. Many of the key concepts were both under-explained and underexplored – for example, the idea of 'stages'. Such was the vagueness of this term that Baran noted that the use of 'stages' fails to inform on anything, other than there are 'stages'. Rostow's 'stages' reduce economic growth to a single pattern and assume every, and any, country follows the same growth pattern. Criticism of this theory also came from Rostow's failure to regard growth as a 'homogenous continuum', but instead he viewed it as a discontinuous course involving qualitative changes. Berrill (1960) challenges this with the idea that there is continuity in history, while Cairncross (1961) highlights again the lack of criteria for discerning stages, which leads to an unnecessary exaggeration of discontinuity.

In addition, the existence of Bretton Woods *facilitated* the emergence of early, arguably flawed development theories, due to the manner in which it assisted national economic planning. Although established as a system of money management, a side-effect of Bretton Woods meant that national governments could manage their economies to maximise growth and employment (due to the requirement of government permission for capital to cross domestic borders). National economic planning, therefore, became a way for transition economies (lesser-developed regions) to engage in development which would allow them to 'catch up' with more developed countries (Helleiner, 1994). Leys comments that 'it is not a great oversimplification to say that "development theory" was originally just theory about the best way for colonial and then ex-colonial states to accelerate national economic growth in this international environment' (Leys, 1996, p. 7). He takes this further, noting that 'the goal of development was growth, the agent of development was the state, and the means of development were these macroeconomic policy instruments' (Leys, 1996, p. 7). Therefore, the Keynesian approach, via Bretton Woods, presented an easy solution to early theorists as a means of encouraging growth and development while bolstering the economy – and perhaps, most importantly for early theorists such as Rostow, doing so without adherence to Marxist views on the subject (Eichengreen, 2004; Rostow, 1960; Baran and Hobsbawn, 1973). Such a heavy reliance on one aspect of development (state intervention), meant that any change in the status quo (for example, the collapse of Bretton Woods and its subsequent effect on developing nations), could be potentially catastrophic (Myrdal, 1968; Brohman, 1995; Levy-Yeyati and Sturzenegger, 2001). Marx even acknowledged this, recognising that the state posed merely one aspect of development and one should not become too focused upon it (Marx, 1999, chs 25–33 inclusive, especially pp. 542–547).

Turning again to the economic, social and political climate in which development theories emerged, after WWII, there was a worldwide recession. Closed economies at the time (such as the Soviet Union) served to question the success of 'invisible hand' economics. This in turn precipitated the popularity of Bretton Woods (Helleiner, 1994). This Keynesian approach inevitably had implications for the development of, or the failure to develop of, some states, with early development theories primarily concerned with economic development. Therefore, despite early theorists perpetuating the broad social and democratic ethos of the era, their concerns were primarily economic, and this became one of the main problems with development theories which dependency theory attempted to overcome. Most of the perceived 'underdeveloped' nations were encountering a new age of political, social, cultural and economic development. Arguably, then, in order for any new development theory to survive, it would be imperative to consider all aspects of development: social, cultural, political and economic. This particular stage in development theories is quite interesting when considered alongside theories of the firm at this time. In Chapter 1, Section 1.3, I considered the character of CSR in the US and the UK. After WWII, MNCs were concerned with only the economic function of the firm (profit maximisation for shareholders), and the idea of even considering social issues in particular only tentatively emerged after *AP Smith Manufacturing Company v Barlow* (1953). Indeed, societal issues were considered an 'add-on' – philanthropy and not to be mixed up with the primary function of the firm, which was economic. Thus it is clear to see that the distortion of economic development at the expense of cultural, political and social development was not limited to international relations and political economy but rather was reflective of wider thinking at that time.

After WWII no serious or coherent theory existed that took into consideration the effects of imperialism on social structures and inequalities between developed and 'less-developed' states. Theorists on post-WWII development can be divided into two main schools of thought. The first camp espoused the work of Rostow, albeit with some modifications. This camp became known as the 'modernisation' or 'diffusionist' theorists. The basic maxim of modernisation is that technological advancements and economical changes will serve to 'develop' a society socially as well as economically. With its roots in the work of French philosopher Marquis de Condorcet (1975), it is the extension of his belief in the interrelation of economic and social development that this idea of developing the social aspects of a nation through technological advancement. In diffusing 'modern' ideas via education and technology transfer to the elite in the periphery, theorists in this area believed that the particular region could develop (Bilgin and Morton, 2002; Scully, 1988; Bernstein, 1971; Booth, 1975). Major criticisms of this approach included the political climate that the theory emerged in (ignorance of Marx, Cold War and so on); the manner in which it supposed that historical development was the same in every country (the US approach to a 'non'-US problem); and finally the supposition that if you 'solved' economic underdevelopment, social and political development would stem from this solution (Cardoso, 1972, 1977; Frank, 1966, 1967a, 1977a, 1977b, 1991; Wallerstein, 1974; Chilcote, 1978; Griffin 1973; Chew and Denmark, 1996).

The second camp, more concerned with the failure of early development theories to 'predict' or dictate effective economic policies in India, Latin America and (later) sub-Saharan Africa, wished to redefine the concept of 'development'. This time a camp took into consideration the historical context and also, in part, recognised that development goes beyond economic development. This camp would become the 'dependency' school of development.

2.3 Overview of the theory

For the purposes of this book, dependency is defined as Dos Santos's 'conditional' dependence. The reason for this is twofold. First, it is the definition most commonly cited in the literature as a departure point for dependency (O'Brien, 1975, p. 12; Roxborough, 1979, p. 66). Second, it is perhaps the most succinct definition, and one which is still very much relevant today, as will be seen in Section 2.7 (below). As noted in the Introduction, the literature in this area may seem, at first, outdated. However, the work of Dos Santos incorporates the idea of MNCs and indeed prophesises the increased power that such entities will have – making his work (in tandem with Frank's) a useful springboard into discussions for a wider and modified application of dependency. In addition to Do Santos, Frank's work is discussed throughout. It is through Frank's interpretation of Dos Santos's definition that dependency has been popularised; that is, it is his application that allows ideas of underdevelopment and development, together with core–peripheral exchanges, to be best understood. This application does provide the stimulus for a broader and more all-encompassing application of the idea of core–peripheral exchanges, which then act as a catalyst for modified dependency, as discussed in s2.7 and s3.5.

The basic hypothesis of the theory of dependency is that development and underdevelopment are partial, interdependent structures of one global system (O'Brien, 1975). Dos Santos expands on this:

> Dependence is a conditioning situation in which the economies of one group of countries are conditioned by the development and expansion of others. A relationship of interdependence between two or more economies, or between economies and the world trading system becomes a dependent relationship when some countries can expand through self-impulsion, while others, being in a dependent position, can only expand as a reflection of the expansion of the dominant countries, which may have positive or negative effects on their immediate development. (1970, p. 231)

References to underdevelopment abound in dependency literature. Underdevelopment is the result of dependence. In dependent countries there does exist development and progress. Underdevelopment merely suggests that an area has not been developed in a manner comparable to its full potential, or in all aspects of its economic activity. Underdevelopment does not indicate an absence of development. It is a status ascribed to a country that has not as yet reached economic maturity. Underdevelopment is the situation that occurs when resources are being actively used but in a manner that profits the *dominant* state's economy (the core) rather than the dependent (or peripheral) state. Central to Frank's (1967a) work is his attribution of the causes of underdevelopment to a series of contradictions exemplified in the capitalism/development notion. He suggests three paramount causes:

1. the hierarchal chain of core–peripheral relationships,
2. the exploitation of the surplus and its appropriation by the core,
3. historical continuity in change so that basic structures remain intact despite apparent transformations such as political independence.

What this suggests is the necessity of a fundamental change in core–peripheral relationships, if dependency issues can ever be resolved. Frank (1967a) seems to be of the view that a move to socialism is the only answer. This view was also perpetuated, to an extent, by the United Nations Economic Commission for Latin America (ECLA), which believed that new centres could occur only through a break with the existing centre. The ECLA did try to explain social inequality through core/periphery ideologies, but ultimately their status as a UN agency comes across in the tone of their work

(O'Brien, 1975; Warren, 1980). However, this book is less concerned with *solving* dependency and more with using it as way of measuring and understanding government – MNC relationships. Rodney (1981, s. 1.2) is of the belief that underdevelopment makes sense only as a means of comparing levels of development. It is, in his opinion, very much tied to the fact that human social development has been uneven, and if viewed from an economic standpoint alone, some humans (or human groups) have been producing more than others and, as a result, growing wealthier (Rodney, 1981, s. 1.2). It is through the discussion of underdevelopment that the idea of exploitation came to the fore. Rodney makes the claim that all those countries described as 'underdeveloped' in the world are being exploited by others, and the 'underdevelopment' with which the world is now preoccupied is a product of capitalist, imperialist and colonialist exploitation (1981, s. 1.2). Rodney was a keen supporter of Marxist ideologies, but that aside, his notion of exploitation is one which has elucidated commentary and criticism from people such as Kay (1975).

Dependency theory sees underdevelopment as purely the result of unequal power relationships between capitalist rich economies and developing countries (Valenzuela and Valenzuela, 1978). Underdevelopment is viewed as a consequence of imperialism, in contrast to Marxist theories that were focused on explaining the occurrence of imperialism (Roxborough, 1979, p. 43). Bodenheimer offers another way of thinking about underdevelopment, suggesting that dependency (and by extension underdevelopment) is the obverse side of imperialism (Bodenheimer, 1970). Developing countries, by this interpretation, are not poorer or less developed because they were/are behind in scientific discoveries. Rather, as can be illustrated by applying Dos Santos's definition noted above, it is as a by-product of being coercively integrated into a system (Dos Santos, 1973) (the European economic system usually), purely for the exploitation of their national resources and labour market, as opposed to any pioneering advances in industry or technology. Dependency is/was traditionally applied to the countries of Latin America and, to a somewhat lesser extent, those of sub-Saharan Africa. The pressure to conform to the European economic model of doing business may not have been the most efficient method of enhancing growth in these countries, where infrastructure, human capital, other structures and generally the economic makeup are considerably different from those of most European nations. It may be the case that the Latin American and African examples, traditionally used to illustrate dependency, prove Dos Santos's hypothesis that economies develop according to the needs and requirements of the dominant developed countries, suggesting that development was dependent or conditioned – to use Dos Santos's term – on the requirements of the core. From this, then, emerges the idea of dependent development. Dependent development suggests that a country or region could still develop, but this development would be dependent on other countries, supranational institutions (such as the IMF and World Bank), multinational corporations and other aid programmes leading to the underdevelopment of development (as development would be further exploited) and the development of underdevelopment (as underdevelopment would transcend development) (Angotti, 1981).

Just as there are different theories of development, there were different schools of thought within the dependency movement. These can be broadly divided into two parts. Early discussions in the same space as dependency originated with the ECLA and Prebisch. However, as O'Brien notes, the voice of the ECLA reflected that it was a UN agency: 'the highly paid officials of ECLA however radical in an international agency context, nevertheless conformed to the UN style of analysis with its bland, apolitical language of the international bureaucrat' (1975, p. 9). He continues by suggesting that the international bureaucrat tends to look for compromise and the lowest common denominator (O'Brien, 1975, p. 9). As a result, the role of the US in Latin America's underdevelopment and the effects of class struggle were not explored. The tone of this work was a subtler continuation of the anti-imperialism and anti-Marxist tradition. Regardless, the ECLA can be viewed as the starting point of dependency theories with particular relevance to the work of the structuralist school (although influence can also be traced to the work of Frank and Dos Santos) (Warren, 1980). The structuralist school are also regarded as the 'bourgeois' dependency theorists (Furtado, 1964; Sunkel, 1973); 'organic intellectuals chaffing at [their own national capitalist class'] subordination to the interests of foreign companies and the influence of the US state in domestic politics' (Leys, 1996, p. 12)

The structural features of an economy are paramount to structuralists when discussing an economy's development because they can, for example, highlight the external/internal equilibria arising from production structures and how these structures interact with the dependent relationship that developing countries have with the developed world (see Furtado, 1964). This manifestation of dependency is quite conservative, focusing on external relationships, and in doing so, it highlights dissatisfaction with the manner in which national interests are subordinated somewhat to the interests of foreign companies and governments investing large sums of capital into host nations (Leys, 1996, p. 12). They argue that regardless of the amount of money received, the consistent unequal core–periphery interrelationships of dominance and dependence continues to exist between component parts of a single world capitalist system (Furtado, 1964; Finger, Hall and Nelson, 1982).

Frank was critical of the structuralist school, as he believed the idea was insufficient to expand the internal market and to generate development. The school was also limited in its failure to incorporate social and political aspects of development into their theory. Frank believed these aspects to be paramount in the evolution of a theory which would consider the historical aspect (including political, social and economic factors) of a particular nation, and it was these criticisms that would help shape his formulations on dependency. This would become the 'other' approach to dependency. This approach is embedded in the work of Dos Santos (1970, 1973), Frank (1966, 1967a, 1967b, 1968, 1970, 1977a, 1977b, 1991) and Marini (1972). This is the more radical, left-wing side to dependence and has traditionally been linked to radical political parties in Latin America and labour movements across the continent. In this strand of dependency, the central emphasis is more on the nature and characteristics of internal structural relationships which both define and create dependency and the domestic infrastructure of dependency (Browett, 1980). Referring back to Dos Santos's conditions, dependence causes underdeveloped countries to be backward and exploited (O'Brien, 1975, p. 9, 12). Roxborough (1976) suggests that this type of dependency alters internal functioning and social formations.

Capitalism, then, leads to a combined and unequal development of its various parts (Dos Santos, 1970). Development is unequal because some countries develop at the expense of others (Dos Santos, 1970). Development is combined because it is the combination of inequalities plus the transfer of resources from underdeveloped to developed countries, which explains inequality and transforms it into a structural element of the economy (Dos Santos, 1970). In order to understand this and recognise the importance of the information, we must analyse economic relationships between the core and the periphery. In addition, we need to consider the compromises and collusions between the various elements in the global system which create, embed and develop the dependent situation so that we can have a deeper grasp of the key issues (O'Brien, 1975, p. 15). Despite disparity in the schools of thought on dependency, there are some key features that underpin the concept. After identifying these broad themes, it becomes easier to understand and appreciate the tenets of the theory before modifying it to adapt to the changes in the global economic system.

2.4 What then are the main features of dependence?

Despite numerous idiosyncratic differences among the plethora of dependency advocates, there are some broad similarities when it comes to outlining the main features of the theories. Angotti (1981) asserts that the common ground among this diverse grouping is the assumption that underdevelopment has causes external to the underdeveloped nation. There are four main theoretical perspectives on which all dependency theorists appear agreed.

First is that dependency represents a *critique of dualism*. A dual economy is one where two economies exist in the one region. One is intrinsically focused (i.e. a local economy), and the other is extrinsically focused (i.e. the global export market). Within Marxist-inspired theories, this was articulated as 'traditional' and 'modern' economies. Marxism, as well as modernisation theory, dictated that the main obstacle to development originated in the inherent sociocultural qualities of 'backward' countries, those that supposedly lacked the characteristics of the 'modern' Western capitalist economies (Marx, 1999; Hegel, 1953). Modernisation theory, suggested that underdevelopment was the status in between the transition from 'traditional' to 'modern'. Dependency theorists refuted this idea, citing underdevelopment as 'a special process due to the penetration of modern capitalistic enterprises into archaic structures' (Furtado, 1964, p. 138). Frank (1967a) also condemned this view of underdevelopment as a historical stage (Browett, 1980).

Second, the *relationship between core (affluent) countries and periphery (underdeveloped) countries* is found in all texts on dependency. Although there are different manifestations – such as the idea of exploitation of the periphery by the core – as well as issues of colonialism, all theorists broadly adhere to the idea of core/centre and peripheral exchanges.

The third common thread among dependency theorists is the *discussion of unequal exchange*. An imperialistic critique of capitalism, this common denominator in dependency literature promotes the idea that underdevelopment is related to the disadvantage of peripheral nations on the world market (Arghiri, 1972). Essentially, Arghiri (1972) is critiquing the Ricardian doctrine of comparative advantage, with its main implication being that the terms of trade and wages need revision in order to adequately compensate (in terms of labour and capital) in accordance with the value produced (see Dornbusch, Fischer and Samuelson, 1977; Golub and Hsieh, 2000; Leamer, 1984; Hunt and Morgan, 1995). This is linked in with discussions on exploitation, particularly the idea that those countries in the periphery are at a disadvantage in that their labour and production are dependent on the requirements of the core (Kohler and Tausch, 2002; Leys, 1977).

The final similarity in dependency literature suggests that the 'bourgeoisie' at the periphery is entirely dependent on external forces and, therefore, is unable to play a progressive anti-imperialist role (Cardoso, 1972; Leys, 1977). In addition to this, the literature in the traditional dependency space outlines the idea that dependency itself is a contrast between dominant and dependent forces and not a class struggle between imperialism and socialism (Angotti, 1981). Angotti suggests that domination refers to multinational corporations and international financial systems – that is, that it is a super-structural element whereby the powerful subdue the weak, the rich exploit the poor and so on.

Throughout this chapter, and this book, these broad themes will appear in relation to the interactions between governments and MNCs. There are significant nuances among dependency theorists, but there is significant similarity to warrant broad classification of the main features of the theory as outlined in this subsection. In the next subsection, further detail will be teased from these broad themes, focusing primarily on the work of Frank and Dos Santos.

2.5 Frank's dependency

Frank illustrated for the first time how development could not just *happen* in these former Third World nations as it had in Western civilisation at the time of the Industrial Revolution (1991). This is the effect of capitalism. Such is the scale of capitalism in the 'developed' world that the development policies for any particular country simply means finding 'one or more niches in which to carve out a temporary position of "comparative" monopoly advantage in the international division of labour' (Frank, 1991). This was one of the foremost criticisms of modernisation theories by dependency theorists. It has been Frank's condemnation of the modernisation paradigm and his incorporation of some of Prebisch's theses that has led to the dependency theory as we now know it. Frank was among the first to criticise modernisation theory, and it was this criticism, as such, that eventually manifested itself into his dependency theory. Indeed, Frank disputes the work of Gerschenkron (1962), who suggested that one of the advantages of 'underdevelopment' is that it can skip stages in technological development by importing relatively advanced technology without having to pay the costs of developing it.

But what then was Frank's dependency? Browett (1980), supplemented by Booth, suggests that Frank's perspective comes from several disparate sources: a 'synthesis' of the ideas of structuralism and Marxism (Booth, 1975, p. 52). Frank adopted some of the beliefs of the ECLA, together with their core–periphery approach, and was adamant in his view that it was not a historical stage, which was similar to views perpetuated by Furtado (structuralist school) at the time (Browett, 1980). To illustrate this, he referred to Britain. Prior to the industrial revolution, Britain was not underdeveloped, as per the terminology, but rather *un*developed in the manner in which resources had previously not been used or organised in a manner befitting profit accumulation. By undeveloped, Frank appears to mean that there is *no* development in a certain area or that the land is not being actively used in a manner befitting its potential. Instead, Frank echoes Furtado, arguing that underdevelopment has arisen from the 'penetration of modern capitalist enterprises into archaic structures' (Furtado, 1964, p. 135). In other words, Frank is saying that a country cannot hope to develop just by pumping new technological advances if the infrastructure and social framework of the country remains unchanged.

By 1977, Frank's dependence represented a reaction: first, against the previously dominant positivist diffusionist/modernisation theories of development (Frank, 1967b, 1977a, 1977b); second, to the strategies put forward by Prebisch (1950); and finally, against the theoretical approaches enunciated by Latin American Communist parties (Frank, 1968). In short, his theory of underdevelopment has been cited as representing an alternative to classic Marxist thought on imperialism and the American modernisation theory (Chew and Denmark, 1996; Frank, 1991). It criticised neoclassical, Keynesian, Marxist and Communist views all together (Frank, 1991) because, despite their widespread ideological differences, they all shared the view that underdevelopment was original or traditional. They all believed that development could emerge from reforms that would lead to the elimination of the traditional sector and the rise of the modern sector (Frank, 1991; Leys, 1996).

Most theoretical categories and guides to development policy have been distilled exclusively from the historical experience of the European and North American advanced capitalist nations (Frank, 1966), therefore failing to reflect the past of the underdeveloped world in its entirety (Frank, 1966). Arising from this ignorance has been the assumption that the past, and indeed the present, of underdeveloped nations resembles earlier stages of the history of developed countries (Frank, 1966), which in turn leads to misconceptions about contemporary underdevelopment and development. Underdevelopment is not original or traditional, and neither the past nor present of the underdeveloped countries resembles, in any important manner, the past of the now developed countries.

Frank suggested that national development, and not capitalism, was the 'solution' for promoting development. Whereas he did recognise the dangers of delinking with the global economy, he believed in radical democratisation because existing models of development were, in his opinion, inadequate (Frank, 1991). However, he was pragmatic, recognising that the debt culture negated the potential for the development of less-developed countries. Yet, we live in a capitalist, increasingly globalised society. With the deregulation of the financial markets and the rise in power (size and wealth) of many MNCs, national economic planning is no longer a viable option for developing (or even developed) nations.

Vital to any assessment of Frank's dependency was his insistence on a more egalitarian approach to *types* of development. He believed that political and social development were as important as economic issues (Frank, 1991). The idea of the interrelationship of political, social and economic factors in development suggests that a rounded policy incorporating all these aspects would be successful. However, the very presence of dependency suggests that states (or governments) may be limited in their capacity to influence political, social and economic development. Whereas this has the potential to be achieved via state influence in shaping CSR, a legacy of dependency may create a hierarchy of development needs for a state, of which economic tends to be at the fore. Indeed, this is something to which Frank alludes, noting that contemporary underdevelopment was actively created by progressive incorporation of Latin America from the 16th century towards the emergence of a single worldwide capitalist economy dominated by today's advanced capitalist nations (Frank, 1966). He also argues that the development of underdevelopment in the periphery was, and is, an indispensable condition for capital accumulation in the core – that is, their relationship is necessary (Frank, 1967). Using Chile as an example, Frank suggests that the idea of core–peripheral exchanges creates an inverse relationship between development and underdevelopment (Frank 1967). In other words, whenever development develops, underdevelopment underdevelops, splitting the two of them further apart and hence fuelling his proposal that a total break with capitalism is needed (Frank, 1967). Therefore, according to Frankian notions of development, the process of incorporations transformed the now underdeveloped nations immediately, totally and necessarily into dependent (rather than interdependent) peripheral capitalist economies under the monopolistic control of core nations (Frank, 1967).

So why Frank? As discussed above, Frank was merely one theorist situated within the more radical group of dependency. However, his work represents a departure from the work of others in the area. Whereas Dos Santos, Marini and others believed that peripheral countries could simply jump from develop*ing* to develop*ed*, Frank recognised that this might not be the case and that it may be that the best that could be achieved would be development within underdevelopment (Frank, 1991). This book is about the relationship between capital generated by MNCs and nation states, together with the broader role of the company (MNC) in society. Rhetoric on the global company's position in society has evolved beyond the economic contribution put forward by Friedman towards, at least in theory – a more holistic role for MNCs in the areas in which they operate. Echoing partly the enhanced role of MNCs in govern*ance*, this broadening of their role (again, at least in theory) appears cognisant of Frank's writings on dependency. Until the transition from economic development to egalitarian development is complete, both underdevelopment and development will continue to increase. In terms of the MNC, until the MNCs' role in society completely transitions from economic to holistic (not just in theory and practice but in how an MNC *thinks* about its function), the dependency of Frank will continue to best inform the inequalities of the global system. Therefore, it is his work on the interrelation of political, social and economic issues – together with his belief that underdevelopment/dependency could not be solved by capital infusion and interspersed with Dos Santos's definition/idea of dependency as a conditioning situation – that facilitates the emergence of a modified approach to dependence. This is an alternative means of understanding international relations that structures the second half of this chapter. Before outlining the potential and reach of a modified dependency, this chapter will look at the limitations of traditional dependency.

2.6 Criticisms of dependency

Dependency, from its very inception, and perhaps due in part to the timing of its inception, has engendered much criticism. This is attributed to a number of contentious issues within the theory, which serve to dilute the strength of the paradigm as an effective assessment of the current global system. This subsection highlights the main problems and criticisms associated with the concept, allowing consideration of the possibility of modifying some of the premises in order to overcome the perceived shortcomings below.

Whereas criticism of dependency and the idea of underdevelopment came from both the 'Right' and the 'Left' of the political spectrum, the continuing failure of the right to engage with the Marxist theories that inspired dependency limits the effectiveness of the criticism (Leys, 1996; Jackman, 1982). Key in the right's criticism of the concept is the failure to treat the market economy with the necessary respect (Jackman, 1982). As a result, the main camp of opposition has tended to be criticism from the Left; this criticism has highlighted a number of problems, or weaknesses, with the theory, which commentators argue explain the failure of dependency to thrive in mainstream economic circles; none of which are insurmountable in themselves.

First, Section 2.2 discussed the origins of dependency, citing the political climate and the requirement for a theory to emerge, which contradicted Rostovian policy and incorporated the historical aspect of individual nations. But whereas the global political climate enabled dependency's conception, it can be argued that the same global political climate prevented its long-term survival (Kay, 1975; Leys, 1996). Leys suggests that the 1950s and 1960s provided the ideal context for this theory to emerge, but out of which it would not survive (1996, p. 25). The demise of Bretton Woods and the deregulated economics system arguably support this (Eichengreen, 2004; Helleiner, 1994). Bretton Woods had a huge impact on the inception, application, evolution and desuetude of dependency theory (Leys, 1996), as it allowed governments to manage their economies. When this ended, governments' power to direct economic progress on a national level was considerably diminished. It seemed that with the dissolution of national borders in the economic climate, capitalism had overcome the last structures limiting its already notable success. The collapse of Bretton Woods, and with it the stability of the global market, was a terrible blow to developing countries (MacEwan and Tabb, 1989; Edwards and Santaella, 1993; Levy-Yeyati and Sturzenegger, 2001). With commodities and currencies floating freely on the market, international currency speculation abounded, resulting in high instability both with currency values and commodity prices. Aside from raising international debt to new heights, one has to appreciate the devastating effect on developing nations. Emerging into the global market, national regulation of capital was one of the few vices that ensured economic survival. More change was to come: the OECD adopted Keynesian economic policy at the end of the 1970s, yet another blow to developing countries. High interest rates became the order of the day as the United States deregulated and the UK (for example) embarked upon a strategy of deregulation and privatisation. By the mid 1980s, therefore, capital exports were universally deregulated. In Europe, the Maastricht Treaty further delimited domestic powers in the hope of achieving single-market superiority (Held, 2000; Strange, 2014); this was accompanied by the North American Free Trade Agreement (NAFTA) and the Uruguayan round of General Agreement on Tariffs and Trade, the latter of which stipulated the need for a further extension of free trade, including agriculture (which had previously been exempt) (Kobrin, 2015; Held, 2000; Spruyt, 2002). The impact of deregulated, and to some extent privatised, economies of many of the developed nations has had the effect of opening the global economy still wider and the limitations of the national governments are more widespread. Dependence on private entities for trade agreements has surely made developing nations feel more vulnerable now than they ever had.

Although valid arguments, and well supported by the demise of Bretton Woods, dependency emerged due to the *transformation* of the global system: specifically, nationalisation after World War II, as well as the climate of Cold War. It is the idea of transformation that is key here, as opposed to the specific circumstance. There still is room for dependency in today's global climate. The global system is continuously evolving, and the latest evolution is that of the exponential rise of multinational enterprise and the diminishing power of the nation state. Whereas some early corporations did exist in the form of the East India Company, the Hudson's Bay Company and Royal African Company, this latest evolution has proliferated the markets, state relations and the international governance agenda (Keay, 1991; Robins, 2006; Carlos and Nicholas, 1990; Carlos, 1994). In order to relate to the current evolution of the global system, dependency needs to evolve accordingly. This involves the rethinking of the typologies of 'core' and 'periphery', but it does – when re-evaluated – provide an alternative mechanism for assessing the current system.

With the fact that the paradigm emerged purely as a mirror image of modernisation, criticism has centred on the fact that it is not necessarily capable of standing on its own. Leys (1977), for instance, has commented that the theoretical framework behind underdevelopment still bears resonance to the diffusionist paradigm. So then the question needs to be asked if the diffusionist paradigm and dependency are the opposites of the one view/theory, or whether they are two unique concepts? Can dependency be effective if it exists only to contradict modernisation? Dependency, in contradicting modernisation – if indeed that is all that it can be said to do – still presents an alternative unit of analysis for assessing countries within the global system. Similarly, is anything that it brings *new* to different theories proposed as a response to the failure of the modernisation theory, and other neoclassical economic views? There have been considerable arguments over the perceived theoretical weakness of the theory, a confusion of the terminology and the debatably undue emphasis on market in the domestic and international economy (Cueva, Villamil and Fortín, 1976, Chilcote, 1978).

The failure to grasp the true meaning of underdevelopment is a recurring concept within the literature on critiquing dependency. If writers such as Frank (1966) are arguing that the underdeveloped nations of today can never catch up, then perhaps 'development' cannot be quantified. Leys defines development as that of capitalist development experienced by the capitalist metropoles (1977). But, if Frank is correct, and underdeveloped countries cannot follow a developmental path similar to the metropoles, then it is worrying if the analysis of how they became and are kept underdeveloped does not in itself disclose what 'development' can, or should, mean for them or how it is to be accomplished. This is notoriously obscure in dependency texts, and without a clear definition, it seems difficult to assume that dependency, as a theory, can expand. Aside from this, the failure to recognise the importance of Marx (and in particular his 'Law of Value') has suggested that the theory cannot get beyond the 'level of ideological critique' (Kay, 1975, p. 104) and rather, remains at best, an elaborate historical account.

To counteract the claims of dependency theorists, Kay (1975) uses the example of Canada. US firms dominate the Canadian manufacturing industry, and their agricultural sector is dependent upon a world market over which it has virtually no control (Kay, 1975). According to theory, therefore, Canada must be perceived as being underdeveloped (Kay, 1975). Kay, therefore, is arguing that dependency, in this instance, allows for the idea of rich countries being perceived as dependent. He suggests that this is a major flaw in the theory. But is it? As Section 2.7 suggests (which is further developed in Chapter 3), all states can be dependent – and this dependence can be reflected in the reliance on foreign investment. In the case of Canada, although it is wealthy, what would be the result of US firms based in Canada deciding to relocate elsewhere? Unemployment, market shock and insecurity would ensue (Titiroglu, Bhabra and Lei, 2004). Although addressing internal relocations between disputed Quebec and Toronto, Titiroglu et al. (2004) is useful in illustrating how business relocation has a 'shock' factor on the region's economy which it leaves behind. From this, inferences can be made – particularly that the shock factor would be much greater if business were to locate outside of Canada. Whereas today Canada may *seem* developed, upon closer inspection, heavy reliance upon US firms for employment and as a boost for GDP levels ensures that it can, in fact, be described as being underdeveloped. In addition to this, the typology of dependence proposed in Section 2.7 (below) does liken Canada more effectively to a dependent state. By shifting the core from the US to 'capital', Canada's dependence can be more effectively assessed. It may be the case, therefore, that Kay (1975, p. 104) was inadvertently proposing a 'modified' dependence and, in particular, the fact that those states perceived as being wealthy could still come within the definition of dependent.

O'Brien (1975) has also attempted to apply the formulations of dependency to Canada. It is his belief that in a world of increasing interdependence, it is important to know what makes a country dependent. He says that although Canada is an obvious example of a dependent country using the definitional gauge of dependency theorists, it also has a number of characteristics that would liken it to a developed country – for example, high per capita incomes, high levels of education, healthcare and welfare (O'Brien, 1975). He argues that if theories of dependency are to successfully replace the concept of underdevelopment, then it is important to answer why some dependent countries are rich and others are poor. Canada does have many problems, such as regional inequality, Québécoise nationalism and so on, and that these can be analysed through the dependency framework is not disputed. Nevertheless, if dependency is taken to be the conditioning structure of poverty, as Dos Santos (1970) suggests, then one has to question why some dependent countries are rich and some are poor.

According to Clement and Williams, 'comparisons between Canada and semi industrialised Latin America were rendered plausible by the considerable similarity in selected economic indicators, such as high levels of foreign investment, resource export specialisation and a technologically weak, and internationally uncompetitive, manufacturing sector' (1989, p. 121). In discussing 'modified' dependency in Section 2.7, the idea of 'rich' dependent nations will be paramount – in particular, how re-evaluating core–peripheral typologies can lead to a reimagining of dependency, one where 'rich' countries can quite succinctly fall within the definition of dependent. It is, however, the cyclical nature of capitalist economics which suggests that longevity and sustainability with regard to the economy may, in fact, be more important than the issue of 'rich' and 'poor' states – as, with the idea of 'race to the bottom' countries may experience periods of relative wealth, despite the fact that their economy remains underdeveloped and the 'countervailing' power of the government remains absent – or at least limited (Müller, 1973).

2.7 Modified dependency – dependency 2:0

Dependency has quite a chequered past. Despite internal fractions in the evolution of the theories, main features can and have been identified. Dependency represents a critique of dualism and focuses on the interplay between 'traditional' and 'modern' economies. It looks at the relationship between 'core' and 'peripheral' regions. From this, the idea of exploitation emerges. 'Core' countries were traditionally 'colonisers' with peripheral regions being traditionally the 'colonised', now newly independent regions. Due to this, exploitation and unequal exchange can be linked to the historical relationships between the core and periphery. The 'bourgeoisie' in the periphery are dependent and as a result are unable to play a progressive role. It is noted throughout dependency theory that this is a *structural* issue and not a class struggle. The definition of dependency that has been used throughout this book is the one from Dos Santos's (1970) 'conditions of dependence'. This is further developed through the lens of Frank's (1966, 1967, 1977a, 1977b, 1991) contribution to dependency. He was critical of diffusionist/modernisation theories for not recognising the importance of a country's history. He believed that capitalism was not the solution and 'national' development was required instead. He identified development as *more* than economic, noting the importance of political and social (and, at times, cultural) development. He also explored the relationship between development and underdevelopment. However, the theories around dependency are not without criticism. Key criticisms centred on the viability of the theory after Bretton Woods and, more generally, on his argument that the theory could work only in a transformation period, such as the shift from colonised to independent states after World War II. That it existed as an alternative of modernisation also prompted criticism. The failure to provide concrete definitions of development, developed, underdeveloped and so on, meant that it was hard to find a unified solution to dependency, and as an extension of this, the failure to produce concrete typologies of 'core' and 'periphery' caused confusion, with 'rich' countries like Canada falling within the dependency rhetoric. However, none of these criticisms or problems are insurmountable, and as the remainder of this chapter illustrates, the theory can be reworked, remaining viable and remaining true to the main features of the original theory. This is not a 'new' theory of dependence but rather, a 'modified' one, taking into consideration the advances in the global capitalist system since the theory's original inception after World War II.

Dependency emerged just as MNCs were beginning to have more of a role in the markets. At this time, the focus was on nationalism (newly independent countries identifying on the market), not globalisation. However, the theory, still subject to modifications, can offer guidance on our understanding of the inequalities within capitalism and indeed in the relationship between capital and state. These modifications must answer the criticisms and problems of the theory while also respecting the broad ideologies of its original manifestation. Two main problems can be identified with traditional dependency (in addition to the criticisms outlined above): one, the failure to identify key typologies and, two, the focus on nation-state relations. Modifications can be easily achieved in recognising power shifts in the global market (and incorporating the aforementioned shift from government to governance) (Hackett, 2016). If *capital* becomes the 'core' (with capital meaning the capital generated by MNCs), *all* nation states to varying extents become peripheral and, by extension, dependent insofar as they are all reliant to varying extents on capital investment for development (Hackett, 2016). Of course, in recognising the historical aspect of original dependency, a state's or region's past will play a role in considering just how dependent that state is thereby respecting the neo-Marxist underpinnings of the original theory and the importance of 'history' in understanding relationships within the market system (Leys, 1996). This would also explain why some states are comparatively 'rich' as well as dependent (see the Canada example above, referencing Kay, 1975). Under this modified approach, the idea would be that the UK and the US would also be considered to be dependent – given their historical strength, they would not necessarily be as dependent on capital generated by MNCs as the likes of small open economies (the example of Ireland is used later in this book), but they nonetheless require that capital to compete on the global market.

The recent financial crisis did highlight the fragility of the relationship between state and capital. Whereas the UK and the US were in a position to shore up their banking system, the fact that this was even necessary demonstrates a disconnect between the power of capital and the strength of the state to regulate and hold said capital accountable. In so doing, this facilitates the positioning of the US within the dependency framework. The US, similar to Canada, was an anomaly in the traditional dependency space. The US as a former colony had surpassed many other states (including the UK) in terms of development. As Chapter 5 explores (Section 5.4), the relationship between state and capital is also dependent on other features, such as resources and potential consumer size. The sheer population size of the US, in addition to the vast array of resources available, meant that the dependence, although still present, was less obvious than in other smaller, more open, economies.

It also becomes clear that the more 'globalised' a nation state is, the more 'dependent' it also becomes. By reimagining the actors in dependency, and incorporating recognition of the shift towards a more governance-oriented society, the value of this theory as a unit of analysis becomes clear (Hackett, 2016). Modified dependency has a wider, possibly universal application. By refining a modified dependency, and utilising Dos Santos's (1970) conditions of dependency, we can stipulate the following:

1. *Modified* dependency theory is a conditioning situation in which the economies of countries and trading blocs are *conditioned by the development and expansion of capital accumulation via MNCs.*
2. This accumulation may manifest *as investment within countries and trading blocs providing employment and services to the population.*
3. *A relationship of modified dependence exists when MNCs expand through self-impulsion while countries and trading blocs can only expand as a reflection of the MNCs investment in their region, which may have a positive or negative effect on their immediate and long-term development.* This development may be economic, political or social. (Hackett, 2014, emphasis added)

The nature of trade and indeed the structures which underpin global trade have changed somewhat since the inception of development theories generally and dependency theories in particular. However, the unequal relationships and exchanges that were noted in Section 2.4 as some of the main features of dependency remain, and it is these relationships that permeate the fabric of capitalism (Hackett, 2014). As we operate in a capitalist system, the nature of the system is such that equality is impossible. Development will therefore always be unequal – this does tie in with the conditions of dependency but also with Frank's claim that as development develops, underdevelopment also develops. This ensures that inequalities exist as a structural symptom of development. Equality becomes impossible, and the most that can be achieved is the alleviation of some of the symptoms or conditions of dependence.

2.7.1 Original dependency and MNCs

Even though the theory existed before the extent of MNC engagement with the global markets was realised, there are some indications in the literature of 'traditional' dependency theory that suggest that theorists recognised the importance of considering capital generated by MNCs within the dependency space. It is a fundamental basis of neoclassical economic thought that investment from MNCs promotes growth in the region of investment. However, within dependency, the suggestion would be that this investment actually promotes the development of underdevelopment (Jackman, 1982). As noted above, modernisation theorists believed that foreign investment promotes growth by providing external capital which either substitutes for or supplements local capital (Jackman, 1982, Bernstein, 1971). It is the presence, rather than the origin, of capital that is considered important (Jackman, 1982). Müller (1973) takes this further by stating that 'the central characteristic of a multinational corporation is that it seeks to maximise the profits not of its individual subsidiaries but rather of the centre parent company. This ... may even mean operating certain of its subsidiaries at an "official" loss' (p. 124). Within modernisation, therefore, capital fosters growth, and its benefits are spread throughout the economy. However, Biersteker (1987) notably suggests that modernisation theorists still recognise the potential for exploitation.

Within dependency, on the other hand, foreign direct investment (FDI), especially with regard to the multinational corporation, is viewed as the *anathema* of capitalist accumulation. Sunkel in the 1970s was arguing, for instance, that the key to present-day dependency is 'the penetration of the underdeveloped countries by the most powerful economic agent in the developed countries – the MNC' (O'Brien, 1975). By acting in the quasi-self-sufficient manner described by Baran and Sweezy (1966), multinational corporations are not as concerned with the internal structures of a country aside from their potential for capital accumulation. Müller (1973, pp. 124–151) also suggested that the MNC, when viewed through dependency theory, can and does exploit the national economy in its endeavour to accumulate profit. This is also reflected in the work of Dos Santos (1970), where he suggests that although MNC investment encouraged development of sorts (namely in the advancement of technological industries pertinent to the MNC), this development was conditioned by the exigencies of the international commodity and capital markets.

Baran (1957) and Frank (1966, 1967a) build on this, suggesting that foreign investment depresses national growth. The core–periphery relationship is considered exploitive in that profits are transferred back to the core rather than being reinvested in the periphery. They believe that investments made by multinational corporations are actually inhibiting growth since they are more than offset by excessive amounts of capitalist repatriation to the industrial core. Dos Santos (1970), too, focuses on the issue of profit repatriation. To this he adds for consideration the idea that in many cases foreign capital is given exemption from exchange controls for the importation of machinery and the financing for sites for the installation of industries, among other things, is provided. Jackman (1982), in his application of the 'Matthew Effect' to the debate (See, Merton, 1968, 1988, 1995), suggests that even what 'foreign investment hath giveth, it has taken it away' (see also Wade, 2004; Tausch, 2010). Economic dependency thereby contributes to the underdevelopment of the periphery (Jackman, 1982). At the same time, the external orientation of the periphery's economics encouraged by foreign investment is said to generate internal distortions and contradictions that retard growth (Jackman, 1982; Wade, 2004).

Politically, according to Jackman (1982), this has two main implications. First, it undermines the autonomy of the periphery. Through investment of capital into the region, it becomes apparent that MNCs and international lending agencies become major, if not dominant, forces in economic policymaking, a position they maintain by means of an implicit threat of withdrawal from, and consequent loss of capital by, the host country in the periphery (Smith, 1979). Müller (1973) suggests that the 'industrialisation of developing states is similar to that found in advanced capitalist nations of the West'. Therefore, 'the voluntary or involuntary institutionalisation of Western consumption values as the goal of economic growth has, in turn, brought about the need for a technology which can satisfy this pattern of consumption.' Using empirical data provided by the United Nations on patents granted, Müller makes the claim that underdeveloped countries are virtually entirely dependent upon foreign sources for their technology (1973, pp. 126–127). This supports the claim from Baran (1957) and Frank (1967) that foreign investment depresses domestic growth.

Second, it leads to the development of new class relations. What this then achieves is the acceleration of social inequality in the periphery; new groups emerge that are linked to the core, while the remainder of the periphery becomes increasingly marginal, in both economic and political terms (Jackman, 1982). Müller (1973) suggests that MNC activity and its impact can be judged as a contribution to development only if it results in an increase in the consumption potential of the poorest 60 per cent of the dependent country's population because, he asserts, dependency believes that unless economic growth brings some alleviation to those suffering most, such growth is a contribution not to development but rather to the continued underdevelopment of the nation in question (Müller, 1973).

2.7.2 Answering the criticisms and protecting the main features of dependency

As the above illustrates, early writers in the dependency space recognised the potential power of MNCs and their potential role within the dependency framework. Modified dependency appreciates just how powerful the MNC has become, or rather, capital generated by MNCs. Taking the approach that capital generated by MNCs is 'core' and nation states are 'peripheral' (with their historical relationships being used as a guide to ascertain just how peripheral they are), modified dependency has a more universal application.

In answering the criticisms of the original theory outlined above in Section 2.6, this subsection assuages fears of a dilution of the theory by ensuring that the main features of dependency are not only protected but also augmented. One of the key criticisms of the theory was that it emerged in a contextually unique era: post-WWII, post-decolonialisation, the system of national planning via Bretton Woods and so on. By expanding the typologies of core and periphery, modified dependency ensures that the theory need not be confined to a historical lens in order to explain underdevelopment. The fact that the theory exists as an alternative to modernisation is not a robust criticism; rather, it provides an alternative means of addressing the relationship between capital and states. Regarding definitions, it is important that these are pinned down somewhat, although it is also imperative that there is scope for reimagining their definitions to ensure the fluidity of the theory. The following conditions help in defining, understanding and applying the theory:

- 'Core' is capital, and specifically capital generated by MNCs.
- 'Periphery' comprises nation states. Some states can be said to be more 'peripheral' than others. In ascertaining degrees of periphery, the history of a state, including its interactions with other states and with capital, is imperative. It is anticipated that those states that fall within the traditional definition of 'dependent' may be perceived as being more dependent than traditional 'core' countries. This helps explain the phenomenon where 'rich' states like Canada were considered dependent under traditional definitions. 'Wealth' is not a symbol of being developed – sustainable wealth is. Where capital can withdraw at any stage, a state can still be dependent.
- 'Development' is economic, political, cultural and social advancement, which is independent of development in another state (Hackett, 2016).

- 'Developed' is the utopia. When full development has been achieved, put simply, all states are equally developed in all aspects (Hackett, 2016).
- 'Underdeveloped' suggests that development in a region is conditioned by the needs of another region – prompting an unequal development trajectory. True 'development' and being 'developed' are impossible in a capitalist society where inequality is a symptom of engaging with the system (Hackett, 2016).

With these definitions, and indeed the concept of modified dependency as a whole, it is important to clarify that the main features of dependency are being protected. Dependency still represents a critique of dualism and, in particular, the more refined capitalist service market today. The idea of core–peripheral exchanges is still protected by modified dependency, as is the idea of unequal exchange and exploitation. With regard to the limitations of the 'bourgeoisie' in the periphery, this does still exist. National governments are the bourgeoisie in a modified dependency – they are lacking in power to control, regulate or direct the activities of the core (capital). As with traditional dependency, at a national level this is a structural not a class issue. As all governments are now peripheral under the modified approach to dependency, it becomes clear that their power has diminished. Economic transactions are now at an increasingly global level. Governments remain at state level. The EU and entities like OPEC may be noted here as going beyond state level, but as discussed in Chapter 5, dependence is not limited to state transactions and may be viewed at a federal and international level also. With this in mind, it is necessary to explore the transition from government to governance on a global scale and the key actors in the relationship between core and periphery. If national governments are less powerful, their power of influence is diminished in accordance with the level of dependence on capital generated by MNCs for economic development, by that particular government. Frank's proposed solution of 'national' development (and not capitalism) remains true. Capitalism has caused the underdevelopment and therefore cannot be the solution. However, the potential of 'national' development is even less than it was during the work of Frank. There is the potential for CSR to be used to alleviate the conditions of dependence, allowing governments to become more effective stakeholders later; this however, centres on the role that capital wishes to have regarding social and political development. Although the consensus in the literature appears to be that the MNC is more consciously trying to pursue a holistic presence in society, the 'true' commitment of MNCs to more egalitarian development across economic, political and social development is questionable – again, think back to the McWilliams and Siegel commentary in Chapter 1 about the importance of 'appearance' and 'strategy'. As noted in Section 2.5, until this commitment to development beyond economic is inherent within the structures of the MNC, the value of CSR in solving underdevelopment is negligible. Rather, its role will simply be in alleviating the conditions of dependence, which may prompt (at a later stage) a more 'true' commitment to *all* types of development within the MNC remit. However, this supposes that the MNC wants to alleviate underdevelopment and dependency. The next chapter considers the emerging transnational class and the borderless nature of this class. As a result, this class has no loyalty to anything but capital, meaning that it would be difficult to ensure that a CSR policy could be pursued without effective legislation. However, such is the nature of modified dependence that those countries in most need of regulating MNCs' CSR policies are those that will be in the weakest position to do so, given the nature and extent of their dependence.

2.8 Conclusion

Traditional interpretations and understandings of relationships within capitalism would look at the interactions between MNCs and national governments as a natural evolution of capitalism on the development trajectory. This chapter challenges that assertion, noting that when viewed through an alternative lens, worrying trends begin to emerge. In reimagining relationships within the dependency space, a modified approach to the theory could have an almost universal application and be used as an alternative means to understand the relationship between capital and state and, in so doing, the power imbalances that exist in these relationships.

Given the shifts in the global system and the market generally, nation states are dependent on investment from MNCs to provide employment as well as other development (some of which may be articulated through an MNC's CSR policy), thus emphasising the importance of dependence and development within the scope of this book. With a dependence on MNC investment, the quality of the MNC's contribution to development in a particular region may be conditioned by the requirements of the MNC as opposed to the region – which does have implications for the effectiveness of a voluntary engagement within CSR. The importance of this shift in actors is imperative to the wider context of this book. If this book is looking at the capacity of CSR to develop regions, this is in keeping with the idea that MNCs are more powerful actors now than the governments of nation states. If MNCs are more powerful actors, the relevance of who makes decisions within MNCs on the direction of capital flows (towards economic investment and social contributions via CSR) is increasing.

3
The Rise of Governance and the Fall of Government: Capitalism 2.0

3.1 Introduction and overview

The global system has evolved. Today, we can see a move away from national governments towards a more transnational or global approach to governance. The MNC has a role to play in this shift. This chapter looks into this global shift and the relationships that underpin it in much greater detail. Addressing the TCC as described by Robinson and Harris (2000) and Sklair (2001), this chapter proposes that it is they who are the new dominant actors within the global system. The TCC exists solely for the accumulation of capital on a global scale with no loyalty to anything beyond capital accumulation. However, the reach of the TCC suggests that there is the *potential* for the CSR policies of MNCs (who are within the TCC) to contribute to the development of the areas in which they are based. Until this potential is realised and a true commitment to realising this potential is evident, the value of CSR in the development agenda (as proposed in Chapter 2) is compromised.

This chapter builds on Chapters 1 and 2 by recognising the challenges of constructing an effective CSR policy – one that leads to development as opposed to underdevelopment or dependent development. With the shift of power in the governance structure, it is the TCC that can act as leaders in a development agenda through CSR. With the purpose of corporations as the accumulation of profit, there needs to be a way to ensure that 'development' is achieved in a way which will 'develop' the communities in which the corporations may operate and not just develop the profits of those corporations.

3.2 Globalisation

The common explanations of 'globalisation' can be divided into three main themes. The first is the idea of globalisation as a *structural* process: 'globalisation has mostly been represented in terms of the duality of national–global where the global gains power and advantages at the expense of the national' (Sassen, 1998, p. xix); 'the deepening structural interdependence of the world economy' (Dunning, 1997, abstract (termed the classic definition of globalisation)); and 'globalisation is but a subset of the immense number of structural adjustments that the world is undergoing as a result of the evolution of a related group of new technologies usually referred to as information and communication technologies' (Lipsey, 1997, p. 73). The second comprises explanations which centre on the *economic* process, such as 'the increasing economic integration of the world' (BBC, 2008) and 'the mutual interconnectedness or cross border integration of national economic spaces' (Kobrin, 1997, p. 149). Third, some definitions factor in a more *holistic* understanding of the process, such as 'the coincidental effects of three major changes: the accelerated internationalisation of production; the sharply increased mobility of capital; and the greater mobility of knowledge' (Strange, 1997, p. 137); and 'globalisation is a complex set of processes, not a single one. And these operate in a contradictory or oppositional fashion' (Giddens, 2002, Lecture 1, p. 3).

These diverse approaches to defining globalisation resonate with the development theories discussed in Section 2.3. Globalisation as a *structural process* can be compared to the structuralist theorists within dependency (Furtado, 1964; Sunkel, 1973). With those who cite globalisation as an *economic process*, parallels can be drawn with modernisation theorists (Bernstein, 1971). For those who ascribe globalisation as an *all-encompassing* process, comparisons can be made with the work of Frank (1967a, 1967b, 1977a, 1977b, 1991). Indeed, it is interesting to refer back to Dos Santos's (1970) dependence (Section 2.3) and in particular dependence as a:

> conditioning situation in which the economies of one group of countries are conditioned by the development and expansion of others. A relationship of interdependence between two or more economies or between such economies and the world trading system becomes a dependent relationship when some countries can expand through self-impulsion while others, being in a dependent position can only expand as a reflection of the expansion of the dominant countries which may have positive or negative effects on their immediate development.

Looking at the rhetoric around globalisation, dependency sits quite nicely within the concept of globalisation (and particularly that third group of definitions), albeit as a precursor.

Regardless of the problems in defining the concept, it is possible to assess globalisation's role as involving the relationships between regions in the world. Perhaps this is best acknowledged by Ohmae: 'Today's global economy is genuinely borderless. Information, capital and innovation flow all over the world at top speed, enabled by technology and fuelled by consumers' desires for access to the best and least expensive products' (1995a, inside the front of the cover; see also Dicken, 2007; Ohmae, 1999; Ohmae, 1995b). This being the case, the alteration of the typologies of core and periphery as explained in Section 2.7 are fulfilled by the *extent* of globalisation. Krugman (1991) contends that globalisation has rendered obsolete any analysis of nations as cores. Instead, he promotes the idea of geographic trading regions – for example, the EU. As stated in Section 2.7, replacing the 'core' with MNCs (or rather capital generated by MNCs) and the idea of global capital suggests that the nation state in general has been relegated to a 'peripheral' region under the terminology of dependency theory. Section 3.5 will consider the impact of transnational capital and the evolving class on the dependency issue.

Within dependency theory, historical factors warrant consideration. As this is a defining issue for the concept, this paragraph and the next few paragraphs will consider how historical nuances can still have an impact on the modified version of the paradigm. With regard to the implications of the modified theory based on capital as the commodity, and corporation as the core, how do historical factors impact on the level of a nation's (or peripheral region's) dependence on capital? What is the relationship between globalisation and dependency?

Arguably, in answering the second question first, given the more tailored approach to dependency proposed in this book, the extent of a nation's globalisation reflects the level of dependence. If a country's position on the globalisation index is dependent on factors such as (inter alia) economic integration, personal contact, technological activity and political engagement, one can see how this is the case (KOF index, AT Kearney, Foreign Policy Magazine, 2006). By focusing on the factor of economic integration, this can be explained further. In order to address the extent of economic integration, the list takes into consideration levels of global integration, foreign direct investment (FDI) and taxation in a region (AT Kearney, 2006). This being the case, it can be assumed that those countries with the highest levels of FDI and global integration, combined with relatively low taxation, are more likely to appear higher up the list of 'globalised' nations. Can we then make the assumption that the more 'globalised' a nation is, the more dependent it is? It is possible, but perhaps without further research, it is a step too far to make this claim. Hypothetically, however, if this were to be the case, can one say that globalisation is the effect of dependence? Or has globalisation caused dependence? Arguably, both are the case. In order for globalisation to occur, this idea of interdependence needed to be initiated. This originated with interactions between imperial masters and their colonies. It could be argued, therefore, that globalisation is merely 'the most powerful manifestation of capitalism ever seen' (Business Week, 2000). As mass capitalism has become globalised, perhaps then it is the case that dependence today has evolved from the dependence on manufactured products, among other things, to a dependence on capital and investment (see Section 2.7).

Although further research may be required to more succinctly analyse the relationship between globalisation and dependency, the experience of Iceland before and during financial crisis does help to illustrate the point. Again, this is not a conclusion and merely illustrates the potential connection between measures of globalisation and indicators of dependence. Some reports would have suggested that Iceland was the most economically globalised country in the world prior to the global financial crisis (OECD Globalisation Report 2006, Globalisation 2007 index, Globalisation 2008 index). For the most part, the extent of this globalisation lay in the ability of the Icelandic banking sector to exploit the processes of globalisation, namely the carry trade (Habib and Stracca, 2012; Obstfeld, 2012; Ekholm, 2013). This was achieved by borrowing money from places such as Japan, where interest rates were around zero, for lending to institutions in high-interest-spending economies such as Iceland (Peston, 2008). Whereas, at the time, it appeared to be a no-lose arbitrage on differential interest rates in a globalised economy, the financial crisis accentuated this avenue as yet another manifestation of the difficulties surrounding financial capital (Peston, 2008). It resulted in the failure of a number of Icelandic banks including Kaupthing. However, this crisis had been predicted as early as February 2008 when an article in the Telegraph suggested that, 'based on the prices quoted in the credit markets, international investors reckon that Kaupthing, Iceland's biggest bank, is about seven times more likely to default than the typical European Bank' (Dey, 2008). The article continues with a reflection from Markit wherein the Icelandic banking sector is described as 'a classic example of plucky ambition or unrestraint, depending on one's attitude to risk' (Dey, 2008).

How then does this reflect on Iceland's dependence? Looking at the statistics around Iceland at the time of the financial crisis, it is clear just how much the country had come to rely on foreign banking relations in order to float the national economy. The value of Iceland's economic output (GDP) was around £20bn (Peston, 2008). However, the banking sector had borrowed approximately £120bn in foreign currencies, and thus the extent of the dependence on foreign capital is realised. The economy in Iceland was prospering as a result of the dependence on foreign capital. When crisis hit, loans could not be repaid. The extent of dependence on foreign capital to develop the economy, arguably at the expense of fostering home industry, effectively meant that the nation state could not service the debt. The case of Iceland has been one of the more extreme examples that emerged around the financial crisis.

The implications of a dependence on foreign capital can also be evidenced in the structural approach to corporate governance. In the example of Iceland, the country adopted the comply or explain model of governance similar to that in the UK. However, Iceland's population is only 330,000. In theory, it would appear that the comply or explain model would be more effective with a larger population, particularly when you consider the need for anonymity and disparate ownership. Perhaps of yet more interest to this book is the Icelandic approach to CSR, where it is considered that even though CSR is an important topic in Western Europe, little emphasis has been put on it in Iceland, in terms of voluntary corporate practices (Thorsteinsdottier, 2010). Although Thorsteinsdottier (2010) continues by citing a number of reasons for this, this book highlights another. Iceland is a dependent state. It is dependent on capital generated from MNCs. Therefore, Iceland systematically cannot have a comprehensive and effective CSR policy, as it is too dependent to regulate that capital which it is dependent on. That is not to say that CSR would afford benefits to Iceland insofar as it may provide an impetus to alleviate the conditions of dependence. The challenges of this are discussed more generally in Chapter 5. Iceland is used here simply to highlight that dependence, as a unit of analysis, can emphasise some of the shortcomings of the globalisation trend, in the manner in which it impacts on nation states' economies and development. Section 3.5 considers how the nation state is attempting to reinstate its role in the global market. However, this too is reliant on the level of the dependence of the state on foreign capital and, as a result, the ability of the nation state to shore up capital, where global capital has failed.

What then is the impact of a nation's history on the wider application of dependency theory? If the relationship between globalisation and dependence, as discussed above is true, and the evolution of capitalism and traditional dependence is the case, then the importance of a nation's history can be understood. Although globalisation and arguably by association dependence have become more ubiquitous in recent years, the roots of both lie in the early capitalist structures of the 17th century onwards. The early capitalist structures and relationships between imperial masters and their colonies formed the basis of globalisation due to the interdependence of different nations for commodities, employment and trade. However, if we also consider the history of dependence, parallels can be drawn. Frank (1991) argued that dependency has arisen from the exploitation of colonial states by their imperial masters. As a result, the colonies were unable to develop independently, and trade, manufacturing and even democratic processes developed only in the manner dictated by the needs and requirements of the imperial 'core'. As noted in Section 2.6, traditional dependency had anomalies like Canada and US which were perceived as wealthy but dependent under the definitions of the theory. By modifying the parameters of the theory, these anomalies are overcome. Being a dependent or an underdeveloped state does not necessarily mean a poor state. This is something that traditional dependency had failed to answer, but as Sections 2.6 and 2.7 demonstrate, these countries not only are dependent but in fact may be more dependent than many other states.

Today, with modified dependency, historical factors are still relevant, albeit in a slightly different format. Ex-colonial nations, although 'independent' today, still reflect their pasts in their home industrial sector and democratic processes. Ireland, for example, shows the lack of an effective indigenous industrial base due, in part, to its ex-colonial status as well as the fact that its democratic structure still bears resonance to those in place in the UK. Should this be the case on a more global scale, surely then it would be safe to assume that those countries, which in the past have been colonised and are dependent under 'traditional' definitions of the concept, would be more susceptible to the new dependence on global capital. These states have a weakened infrastructure due to their past as colonised nations. In addition, colonial 'peripheral' states would have been less developed in terms of wage levels (Hackett, 2014). Their history means that they may have a lower-wage infrastructure and less-developed regulatory regimes which can be used as modes of attracting investment. However, if this is the reason for capital investment in a region, can wages be subsequently raised or indeed a more robust regulatory regime developed? Thinking about globalisation through dependency, it would seem as though these cannot be brought about, because in so doing, the nation state is losing that which made it a competitive spot for investment in the first place.

As evidenced by the beginning of this section, a number of questions arise out of the implications of the definition of globalisation. These include, inter alia, whether globalisation is 'good' or 'bad'; the manner in which 'left' and 'right' ideologies should treat the concept and whether or not the consequences of globalisation are a deliberate attempt by multinational capital to emphasise the power of global capital over those states that depend on capital investment. Although not necessarily issues considered in this book, the importance of capital and more conversely global capital in today's economic climate warrants some consideration of the questions above.

Ravallion (2003) argues that the answer to the question on the 'value' of globalisation depends on how globalisation is measured (see also Giddens, 2002). Indeed, any assessment of the concept would have to accentuate the means of measurement. This does make sense. For example, depending on the measurement of area in answering this question, the answers would be different. Globalisation on a global scale is a 'good' development, in the manner in which it encourages integration of trade, among other things, on a supranational scale. Even in 'developing' countries, which attracts the greatest criticisms of globalisation, it is recognised that '[MNCs] spread wealth, work, technologies that raise living standards and better ways of doing business' (BBC, 2001). It is whenever globalisation is measured on an *inter*national scale that the problems become more inherent. It is then that issues of poverty, absolute and relative, and inequality overshadow the perceived advances of the ideology (Williamson, 2002). It is then that globalisation appears to be the 21st-century manifestation of the invade-and-conquer, subjugate-and-colonise paradigm.

Traditional economic thought would dictate that the reason behind the alleged problems of globalisation lie in the excessive regulation measures of the nation state (and in the European case, federal style level), thereby limiting the powers of the 'invisible hand' of the market economy. Deregulation is needed in order to overturn the protectionist type tariffs of the Western world, which in turn should invoke greater development in developing countries. This can be evidenced in the intellectual property issues that emerged out of the Uruguayan Round (Stiglitz, 2002, pp. 8–12). This example concerned the intellectual property rights of drugs. It meant that American and other Western drug companies could stop companies in India and Brazil from 'stealing' their intellectual property. However, if they had been allowed to do so, these Brazilian and Indian companies would have been able to make life-saving drugs at a fraction of the price of their Western counterparts. Stiglitz (2002) points to two repercussions: profits in the Western drug companies would soar, and in the developing world, thousands were condemned to death as governments and people could now not afford the excessive rates.

Viewing globalisation through an alternative lens gives a more pessimistic outlook. As with dependency, when viewed on a more global scale, globalisation can be illustrated as how 'pocket' nations in the global economy are condemned by the inequalities of said globalisation, regardless of tarriffs removed. Globalisation tends to look at processes and developments on a global as opposed to national or international scale. '[G]lobalisation is understood as the spread of transplanetary … and in recent times also increasingly supraterritorial connections between people' (Scholte, 2008, p. 1478). Specific nations, and their subsequent development, are not the focus of globalisation. Instead, it focuses on the cheap provision of services on a multinational level. The implications of this are similar to those of dependency. If the national economy is unable to cope without the influx of foreign capital, the long-term benefits of globalisation will be limited. A country will develop only in the manner in which capital dictates while capital is residing in their country. In the race to the bottom, capital can relocate, and the resultant casualties on a national level will not be considered. The country has further *underdeveloped* in the interim as national economic development was allowed to stagnate in endeavours to promote, attract and retain the foreign capital.

In short, globalisation in itself can be viewed as a 'good' or a 'bad' process depending on the metrics used. It can also be influenced by the manner in which it is assessed: from a traditional economic modernisation-style viewpoint or from a more critical theoretical approach. It can also depend on 'left' or 'right' ideologies. Marx, for example, foresaw the entanglement of all peoples in the net of the world market (Cammack, 2002). Today this, to a certain extent, has been realised by globalisation and the trends of the global market. However, what then are the implications for 'left' and 'right' ideologies? For the 'Left', globalisation presents as something of a contradiction. Milanovic (2003, p. 668) considers that the 'Left' perceives globalisation as a malignant force which culminates in child labour in the South and the loss of middle-class jobs in the North. This, however, presents a difficult situation for the 'Left'. As the Left is, by definition, internationalist, one can see the problems arising from this. Yet, despite being internationalist in nature, the problem arises out of the idea that today's globalisation, according to the 'Left' is led by a triumphant and often unbridled capitalism, and the results of this leadership dissatisfy the Left – specifically environmental degradation, obliteration of indigenous cultures and the exploitation of the weak (Milanovic, 2003, p. 668).

On the other side of the debate, approaches to globalisation are arguably more straightforward. Milanovic (2003) suggests that the more xenophobic approach to globalisation is particularly dominant in Europe. As he argues, globalisation in Europe engenders not only fear of losing jobs to the poor masses of the South but fear of losing the cultural homogeneity that has been attained by the more commonplace movement of people from different colours, cultures and ways of life. This has been evident more recently in the refugee crisis in Europe and the fears that have underpinned political rhetoric on this issue (Wolf, 2015; Withnall, 2015).

Parallels can then be drawn between the 'borderless' relationships within globalisation and those of core–peripheral exchanges considered in the previous chapter. The nature of globalisation complements the proposition that core regions have been replaced by MNCs as dependence today has evolved into a dependence on capital. However, as noted in this section, the historical aspect of dependency could not be ignored, as this was a fundamental aspect of both traditional and modified dependency. In recognising globalisation as a manifestation of capitalism, the historical consideration of a modified dependency is realised. By tying globalisation to capitalism, both dependency and globalisation can be seen to have evolved from the imperial conquests of the 17th century. This allows for 'degrees' of dependency, which take into account historical factors and, in so doing, respects the main features of dependency as outlined in Sections 2.4 and 2.7. Those nations that were colonised will arguably be more susceptible to influxes of foreign capital due to weaknesses in their respective infrastructures, which can be attributed to their past as colonies of various imperial empires. What remains is the idea that all states are dependent, but some are more dependent than others. Specifically, in factoring in the historical element as advocated first by Marx, but more specifically with regard to this by Frank, you begin to see not only how variations in capital can and do emerge but also how 'rich', 'developed', 'open' countries are perhaps more susceptible to shocks in the market. The next section looks at whether globalisation eliminates the inequalities or 'conditions' of dependency or whether dependency has actually become more embedded. This introduces the role of the TCC.

3.3 Has globalisation eliminated the inequalities of dependence?

Despite claims that globalisation is putting all people on the same level of development on a global scale, the conditions of dependence are still rife. Even with advances in communication and technology, there are some regions of the world that are considerably less developed than others. This is attributable to dependency: dependency today involves a dependence on foreign capital.

Mann (1997) suggests that global capitalism contains both state weakening and strengthening tendencies as well as an increase in the significance of international and transnational networks. He is of the opinion that capitalism is slightly weakening the nation states of the North, while economic development – as a result of globalisation – is strengthening the nation states in the Southern Hemisphere (Mann, 1997). Indeed, the work of Mann bears resonance to issues of modernisation within development theory. His idea that capital will eventually develop regions, until all are on a similar level, almost reflects issues within the diffusionist/modernisation paradigm, which suggested that infusing capital into a region could develop it extensively. Modernisation theorists would speak of the nation state diversifying in the wake of globalisation and developing (Milanovic, 2003). This idea of globalisation as a balancing act seems to suggest that it acts as a way of bringing the more underdeveloped regions in line with the traditionally developed West and North.

However, what this fails to acknowledge is the variation between nation states. Even aside from historical factors, such as those mentioned above, issues such as size, population and the location of a nation state are all going to be factors in the manner in which capital presents itself. Can contemporary capitalism, therefore, in the shape of globalisation, have the same effect on all countries? Or will variations in issues such as dependence on foreign capital, size and infrastructure and so on cause variations among these forces? Arguably, due to regional variations in almost all aspects, the idea of a truly equal global economy and infrastructure is almost impossible, as differences in certain areas will manifest themselves in some manner. Even Mann (1997) acknowledges that 'the vital issue for the nation state across most of the world is the level of development ... of the economy narrowly considered but also of the preconditions of this.... If world development stalls, then so will the extension of the nation state' (1997, pp. 487–488).

As the above indicates, globalisation may be viewed as diminishing the nation state. However, issues of inequality need to be mentioned here with regard to the possibility of dependence being eliminated by globalisation. Sklair (2001) acknowledges the contradictions of capitalism, whereby he considers a central crisis of capitalism: 'the simultaneous creation of increasing poverty and increasing wealth within and between communities and societies (the class polarization crisis)' (p. 6; see also Bradley, 1996; Berberoglu, 1992). He presents evidence to suggest that whereas global consumerism has increased a lot in some regions, in other cases the absolute numbers of the destitute and near destitute have also increased (Sklair, 2001, p. 6). Also, we have to consider the increasing gap between the rich and the poor in the world today (Korzeniewicz and Moran, 1997; Sheehy, 1996; Johnston, 1999; Emmenegger, 2012; Taylor-Gooby, 2013). Capitalism does not appear to be interested in 'balancing' inequalities; instead a capitalism-derived version of 'survival of the fittest' appears to be the order of the day.

Due to this, we have the emergence of a group of people who effectively control the *processes* of globalisation. Whereas some would suggest that the emergence of a transnational class would help *promote* equality, the emergence of such a class will serve to gloss over the problems described by dependency theory. The TCC is committed to the accumulation of capital on a global scale, and as such, loyalty lies with capital as opposed to a people, culture or state. The next section therefore, will be primarily concerned with the emergence of this new type of class. As a result of globalisation and the growth of the MNC, this new TCC presents a number of issues for the dependency debate and indeed bears some resonance to discussions on CSR, regulation and legislation in Chapter 5. Seemingly in recognition of the diminishing power of the nation state, how the TCC will impact dependent nations needs to be considered. Are the members of this class merely representatives of the 'see' of capital? If this is the case, then whether or not a borderless class is a positive aspect needs to be considered, even a means for global development. However, the attraction of capital could become the end for nation states. Should this be the case, compromises will be made with regard to social issues as countries become increasingly determined to attract capital at whatever the cost. The next section will address some of the discourse on the shifts in global governance and, in doing so, will concentrate on the TCC: its power, responsibilities and capacity to advance a global social agenda in areas such as CSR.

3.4 The transnational capitalist class

The structures that govern society have developed in tandem with advances in society. Numerous academics have, since the end of the last century discussed the demise of the nation state (Holton, 1998; Strange, 1996), with Stiglitz (2003) noting that globalisation (the most recent manifestation of capitalism) has prompted a transformation of society. As this chapter thus far has acknowledged, the 'territorial boundaries of states no longer coincide with the extent of the limits of political authority over economy and society' (Strange, 1996, p. xiii). Territorial boundaries are key points of discussion in the literature of Holton (1998) and Strange (1996 (above)) highlighting that states have power only within their borders. The emergence, then, of multinational corporations, which are *not* constrained by these territorial boundaries, does lend support to the claim that the nation state has declined. With the nation state's decline comes the corresponding rise of MNCs and the power associated with these organisations. The extent to which this power is 'organised' is still a point of debate, thus prompting the inclusion of this section in this book. In addition, the shifts in how our economy today operates by focusing less on manufacturing capital and more on financial capital.

Global capital can be divided into two main areas: manufacturing/industrial capital and financial capital. Whereas manufacturing capital is specific to materials and energy, this book is concerned primarily with financial capital. Finance capital was understood by Hilferding (1970) as the product of the interaction between universal banks; large manufacturing corporations; and a buoyant and dynamic industrial stock exchange and interaction structured by, for the circulation of, liquid fictitious capital. Two of the most commonly used markets within financial capital today are money markets and capital markets, both of which tend to go hand in hand, where money markets are considered to be less risky and are typically used for short-term investments and capital markets are more long term, riskier and therefore under a lot of scrutiny. Of specific interest here is the idea of 'capital markets'. Marx dedicated some work to what he termed 'money capital', which can have some relevance here, particularly his idea that '[m] oney capital engendering money capital is a mere anticipation of the real processes of accumulation' (Marx, 1863). Capital markets are more long term than money markets and house the stock market and the bond market. The idea of capital allows the generation of wealth through investment or at least the appearance or potential of wealth generation. A range of goods and services can come under the umbrella of financial capital, including things like brand names, software and patents. It can also be 'rented out' for a fee to create wealth. Since the work of Marx on money capital, financial capital has developed into a profitable yet risky enterprise to the point that today, 'financial logistics dominate technology in a way that creates new policy problems and increases the risk of system stability' (Feng, Froud, Johal, Haslan and Williams, 2001, p. 469). Many of the problems may be attributable to the fact that individuals or MNCs can claim ownership of their capital and use it as they please (including transferring the ownership of said capital to another individual/corporation and keeping the proceeds of the sale). As such, the nation state and relations with global actors have had to develop in order to encapsulate the change in the 'new' economy and the risk-averse culture. Typically, government regulations limit how capital can be used and try to limit its value – with the money in theory going back to society (for example, capital gains tax).

There has, as a result, been the emergence of a new class, which, like the capital that it peddles, is multinational in nature. Sklair describes this class as a TCC that is based on corporations and is more or less in control of the processes of globalisation (2001, p. 5). Sklair has identified what he terms as transnational practices (TNP) (Sklair, 2006, 2001, 2002b (see Chapter 5)). These he divides into three. First, the economic aspect (which is the institutional form of the multinational corporation); second, the political aspect (which he terms the TCC); and third, the cultural aspect (dubbed 'consumerism' by Sklair) (Sklair, 2006, p. 29). Together, these TNPs represent global capitalism. Thus far, this chapter has referred only to the MNC's power within the nation state while acknowledging the fact that the power of the MNC lies in its ability to cross borders. In assessing the power of the TCC, the manner in which transnational capital impacts upon, and beyond, the policies and legislation of the nation and supranational state can be illustrated. Any assessment of the role of transnational capital, therefore, needs to also consider the manner in which transnational capital is represented: through the global actors and institutions that operate at national and supranational levels. The TCC has been described as 'that segment of the world bourgeoisie that represents transnational capital, the owners of the leading worldwide means of production as embodied in the transnational corporations and private financial institutions' (Robinson and Harris, 2000, p. 11). Sklair defines the class as the 'identifiable actors working through institutions they own and or control that drive globalisation' (2001, p. 1). Hymer (1979) believes that the capitalist class increasingly look to the future growth of the world market, whereas Goldfrank (1977) looks to the fact that the growth of multinational enterprise has spawned a new corporate elite.

Globalisation has been described as the most recent manifestation of capitalism. Although the global systems approach to globalisation is not synonymous with global capitalism, the dominant forces in global capitalism are in fact the same forces prevalent in the global system (Sklair 2006; Hackett, 2012). With the emergence of transnational forces and the TCC, the nation-state approach to capitalism is out of date. Disillusionment with government seems to be a global phenomenon in recent decades, and if we consider the fact that borders of states are not as important, is it time to reconsider some of the assumptions of international political thought (Strange, 1996)? As Strange acknowledges, states are no long masters of the markets (1996). In many cases, it is the markets which are the masters of the states, '[a]nd the declining authority of states is reflected in a growing infusion of authority to other institutions and associations and to local and regional bodies and in a growing asymmetry between the larger states with structural power and the weaker ones without it' (2006, p. xiii). This quote seems to suggest that far from removing inequalities, by looking at a more global system, the problems go beyond the surface. This does link in somewhat with dependency as discussed in the previous chapter, especially when considered along with Wallerstein's (1974) world systems' analysis. But we still have the problems identified by dependency theory. By transplanting the role of governments with the role of MNCS, this more recent manipulation of the global system aligns with broader developments in global capitalism (Wallerstein, 1974).

As I have noted elsewhere (Hackett, 2012), Backer (2007–2008) arrives at a similar place to Sklair. Focusing on the role of regulations and their relationship with the MNC, he notes that those individuals that govern the MNC have an emerging role on the global stage and thus have assumed responsibilities to society (see also Teubner, 2012; Davis, 1973). As noted in the beginning of this subsection traditional global leaders, with the advancements in society, have become disenfranchised from the global agenda. The territorial boundaries that Strange (1997) and Holton (1998) reference above have diminished nation states' capacity as key actors. This extends to Chimni's (2007) work where he considers that international law has disenfranchised lesser-developed countries from developed countries, which in itself can be seen as a version of Frank's dependency discussed at length in Section 2.5. By removing national governments as main actors, their powers as enforcers are constrained considerably. In extending this premise, the distinctions between 'developed' and 'less developed' (or underdeveloped) are less relevant on a macro level, due to the role of the MNC (and the class which governs it) in the power stakes of global exchanges (Hackett, 2010). Today, the TCC is in fact the 'core' actor in governance discourse, and states now operate a peripheral role, with some being more 'peripheral' than others (see Chapter 2; Dos Santos, 1973; Frank, 1966, 1967a, 1967b.). I have used the example of the UN Guiding Principles on Business and Human Rights elsewhere to show this trend where, by example, it states that:

> [t]he issue of business and human rights became permanently implanted on the global policy agenda in the 1990s, reflecting the dramatic worldwide expansion of the private sector at the time, coupled with a corresponding rise in transnational economic activity.

This suggests recognition by such bodies that there is another player in the global capitalist hierarchy (UN Guiding Principles on Business and Human Rights).[1]

As capital as evolved, so too has the quest for capital. Whereas once states competed for territory in order to assert their power, today that competition is replaced by competition for investment, market shares and natural-resource territory (Stopford and Strange, 1991). Bargaining power could be the new military power in that the state with the most investment would, theoretically, be the most powerful state. This reasoning fails to acknowledge the fact that capital owes no allegiance to a particular region when under the MNC, but governments' attempts to attract said capital are understandable. Old alliances of national capital have mutated into a transnational bourgeoisie, and today, this class is the one with hegemonic capabilities (Robinson and Harris, 2000). What then distinguishes the TCC from these local and national capitalists is the fact that it is involved in *globalised* production and manages 'globalised circuits of accumulation that give it an objective class existence and identity ... above any local territories and politics' (Robinson and Harris, 2000, p. 19). Whether or not the TCC is the pinnacle of the rise of the world capitalist system or indeed represents the actual demise of the system is something to be considered at another

1 See also, Norms on the Responsibilities of Transnational Corporations and other business enterprise with regard to Human Rights; Global Reporting Initiative; Global Sullivan Principles of Social Responsibility; Principles for Global Responsibility Benchmark; Social Accountability 8000 (SA 8000); United Nations Global Compact; Sethi and Williams, 2000.

date. Regardless of terminology, however, the approach outlined primarily by Sklair represents something of a departure from what has preceded it – namely the positioning of national governments within the global system.

Critics of the idea of a transnational approach to capital have argued that until the social relations between members of the capitalist class in different nation states are as important as social relations between members in the same states, there cannot be a TCC (See, Scott, 1997). In response, Sklair (2001) argues that it is only specific relations that need to be considered such as those that a TCC has with national actors, agencies and institutions in separate countries, as well as actors, agencies and institutions that cannot sensibly be described as national. References in the literature focuses particularly on the European Roundtable of Industrialists (ERT) and, specifically, how the mobilisation of MNCs in the EU has had a role within legislative advances and governance mechanisms (Cowles, 1998). Issues around separation of powers seem less important than accommodating the needs of big business – this influence is not extended to national industries. The ERT reflects the new European order, which Van Apeldoorn (2000, 2003a, 2003b) believes provides the landscape by which governance is situated to serve the interests of a globalising transnational capitalist elite (Bohle, 2006; Sklair, 2002a and 2002b; Heemskerk, 2013; Amin, 2014). Sklair (2002a) raises the point that groups such as the ERT do have implications for democracy. The ERT are not elected to their positions by the public or even national agencies. It is a type of cronyism whereby members of the industrialist group can elect their own members to the group. If this group is able to be highly influential in legislative matters one can see just how far the nation state has been undermined by the power of the TCC.

Sklair's (2006) work supports this debate, particularly where he suggests that the TCC have a vast influence in global economic and social agenda in a global capitalist world. The TCC, he surmises, is comprised of corporate executives, bureaucrats, politicians, globalising professionals and the media (2006, p. 32), and in defining transnational as 'forces, processes, and institutions that cross borders but do not derive their power and authority from the state' (2001, p. 2), appears to differentiate transnational from international. Critics of Sklair's approach might suggest that these individuals are the same people that comprise national governments. The difference here is defined in terms of objective. A member of the TCC has no loyalty to a particular region, class or race. Rather, their objectives are determined by corporate viability, profit maximisation and those policies that can help sustain, and attain, said profit maximisation. This presents as a challenge for defining a social agenda for the TCC insofar as it must be tied into the primary role of the MNC – that is, profit maximisation.

*Inter*national seems to suggest that power and authority is still derived from state or at least interstate relations. In apparent agreement with this view, Chimni cites the TCC as 'constituted by the transnational fractions of the national capitalist classes' (2007, p. 499). The purpose of such a class is to 'create ideal and local conditions not only for their own interests but also for the interests of the capitalist system as a whole' (Sklair, 2006, p. 32). Under this ideology therefore, the TCC are making system wide decisions, suggesting some degree of uniformity. Chimni (2007) expands on this by claiming that the TCC seeks to unify the world market through the instrument of international law. The manner in which Sklair speaks of 'ideal and local conditions' indicates recognition of country specific intricacies, but at the same time ensuring a focus on the 'big picture' as opposed to national trends (2006). Harvey (2003) recognises the problems of this new type of governance. In his theory of new imperialism, he looks at leaders and analyses how different backgrounds (political, economic, etc.) impact on their understanding of their role in society. His theory opens with the notion that 'the fundamental point is to see the territorial and capitalist logic of power as distinct from each other...the relation between these two logics should be seen therefore as problematic and often contradictory rather than as functional or one sided. This dialectical relation sets the stage for an analysis of capitalist imperialism in terms of the intersection of these two distinctive but intertwined logics of power' (Harvey, 2003, pp. 29–30). What this seems to suggest is that governments and business leaders have different goals – it is in *uniting* these roles, or at least intertwining them, that capitalism can truly evolve to the advantage of not only these leaders but also society as a whole. Theories of new imperialism such as that espoused by Harvey have come under criticism from academics writing in the area of the TCC. Robinson, for instance argued that new imperialism theorists tend to ignore 'empirical evidence on the transnationalisation of capital and the increasing role of transnational state apparatuses in imposing capitalist domination beyond the logic of the inter-state system' (Robinson, 2007, p. 12).

The benefits of the TCC over traditional leaders (i.e. national and even federal governments) lie in how the economic interests of its members are increasingly globally linked rather than exclusively local or even national in origin. Added to this, is the limitation of the regulatory power of a state. In failing to extend further than its boundaries, regulatory reach is severely constrained for state actors. The TCC are not subject to such constraints. These people, according to Sklair (2001, 2006) proclaim to be citizens of the world and the property, shares and corporation with which they work are increasingly globalised. In short, the TCC are outward oriented and have global perspectives rather than the inward oriented and local perspectives advocated by the traditional leaders. The TCC in exerting economic control in the workplace, political control in international politics and cultural control in everyday life has cemented its position as a global leader – 'it is hardly a controversial proposition that global capitalism, driven by [M]NCs, organized politically through the TCC and fuelled by the culture ideology of consumerism, is the most potent force for change in the world today' (2006, p. 34). Indeed, with the rise of the TCC, there are some problems for governance structures, which shall frame some of the latter sections of this article. Padfield, for example notes that, 'corporations... are increasingly taking on roles as pseudo-governmental actors' – highlighting their rise in the global leadership stakes, but, offsetting this with the idea that they fail to '[incur] the accountability to the people generally associated with state action' (Padfield, 2009–2010, p. 703). Using the example above of the UN Framework for Business and Human Rights, it would appear that this pseudo-governmental role has been accepted with business being described as 'specialised organs of society'. Also of relevance here then are democratic deficit concerns. If a non-elected entity (by the public at least) is engaging as pseudo-governmental actors, questions need to be asked in relation to their mandate to make such decisions. This raises a number of questions as to whether organisations should have these pseudo-governmental roles – and, if it is decided that they should – whether there needs to be some reform to ensure that they are held accountable to the public or at least to stakeholders beyond notions of public legitimacy and licence to operate.

If it is the case that the TCC has undermined the power of the nation state in legislative and influential aspects, how does the dependent nation state cope with this mutation of democracy? Not presupposed to strong influential infrastructures due to dependence, and the likelihood of the deep seated-ness of this dependence, it can be supposed that the dependent state is the state most adversely affected by this evolution of capital. Dependence on capital, as stated throughout this book, is ubiquitous. However, the level of dependence is very much related to the strength of internal infrastructures, population size as a consumer base and so on. As such, whereas all states are for the most part affected in some way by this mutation of democracy, the degree to which they are able to claw back some benefits from the situation is related to the extent of their dependence. The next section will therefore look at the role of the dependent state within the TCC and the implications for the dependent state within the TCC.

In considering the rise in dominance of the Multinational Corporation (MNC), and indeed the force that controls this on a political scale (the TCC), Sklair's proposition of the existence, and increasing power of the TCC can be accepted. Shaped by national class structures, but based on a global level, members of this class have the ability and foresight to make 'global' decisions and disengage from some of the more fragmented policy directives shaped by nation states. Subsequently, the next point of consideration must centre round the harnessing of such power and shaping it to advance a global CSR agenda. Issues of governance will be discussed in

Chapter 5, as well as the fact that if an organisation like an MNC is established for the purposes of profit, and the members within the organisation are driven by capital accumulation and profit maximisation, the inevitable challenge is in embedding a CSR agenda on a global scale by those who are driven by profit; not people or planet.

3.5 The role of the dependent nation state in the TCC

Dos Santos (1970) has described dependency as being 'a conditioning situation in which the economies of one group of countries are conditioned by the development and expansion of others. A relationship of interdependence between two or more economies or between such economies and the world trading system becomes a dependent relationship when some countries can expand through self-impulsion while others, being in a dependent position can only expand as a reflection of the expansion of the dominant countries which may have positive or negative effects on their immediate development'.

Bearing in mind proposed alterations to dependency theory due to developments in the global system, Dos Santos's definition, although still applicable, needs to be considered in light of these developments. As a result, dependency today, is a conditioning situation in which the economies of nation states are conditioned by the movement of capital. A relationship of dependence therefore emerges between economies and transnational capital when nations can only expand as a reflection of capital investment, which, may have a positive effect on immediate development but have negative consequences for long-term development. This definition (and the expanded version of this definition as outlined in Chapter 2, s. 2.7) needs to be considered when discussing the manner in which the TCC has impacted on the dependent state.

Under mainstream development theory (modernisation theory) it is assumed that capital infusion into a region can balance out global inequalities by developing 'less-developed' nations (Bernstein, 1971). Globalisation advocates this view. Theorists such as Mann (1997) proposed that development of the South, (traditionally less-developed, dependent regions), occurs at the expense of the North and West, (traditionally 'developed'). To arguments such as this, comparisons can be drawn between modernisation and globalisation. Modernisation was to traditional dependency as globalisation is to a tailored dependency theory. In short, modified dependency represents a critique of globalisation.

Just as modernisation claims of capital infusion failed to result in development, the influx of global capital into a dependent state today will not only fail to develop the region, but, will also aid its underdevelopment. Measures of development are accrued using GDP levels. A country will strive to produce high GDPs in order to gain more influence and credit on the global market. The attraction of foreign capital provides a means for this figure to be raised. Being global does not necessarily mean being everywhere. In an endeavour to attract the elusive capital, nations, especially those increasingly dependent on foreign investment, can compromise on issues in order to secure the capital. But, capital has no roots, no cultural preference and no national loyalty. Capital moves in order to accrue the greatest profit and in order to do so, there is little consideration of the implications on others of its achievement.

What then are the costs of attracting this capital? In the case of Ireland in the 1980s in particular, capital was attracted due to a number of features, including a lenient tax regime and a perceived lack of regulatory framework (Cairncross, 1988). The reason for this was that prolonged dependence in Ireland (under both traditional and modified measures) meant that a strong home industry could not, and had not, ever been developed. This benefited the case for inward FDI at the time – but today Ireland is paying the price. In advertising a low tax regime and a lenient regulatory system to attract capital in the 1980s, Ireland is now being held hostage to that capital (Collings, Gunnigle and Morley, 2005; Killian, 2009). If it imposes stricter regulation, or raises taxes, capital will leave (to illustrate this, look at the pathway of the Director's Compliance Statement (s. 45) in Companies (Auditing and Accounting) Act 2003, Hackett, 2011)[2]. This is due to the fact that capital today is promiscuous – it owes no allegiance to any

2 The Director's Compliance Statement (DCS) arose from a specific recommendation of the Review Group on Auditing. It refers to a proposed amendment to the 1990 Company Law Act with particular reference to the inclusion of s. 45 in the Companies (Auditing and Accounting) Act 2003. Companies falling within the scope of the act had to produce a compliance statement that set out: its policies respecting compliance with its relevant obligations; its internal financial and other procedures for securing compliance with its relevant obligations and its arrangements for implementing and reviewing the effectiveness of the policies and procedures referred to above, as well as any other relevant enactments that could materially affect company performance. Added to this, auditors were to publicly state if, in their opinion, the directors' compliance statements were fair and reasonable. As such, whereas it did predate Enron, it has been described by Appleby (2005) as a conservative version of s. 404 of the Sarbanes Oxley Act. It had been an attempt to reform the sector post a number of banking scandals. Business reaction was predictable – high costs of compliance and the harsh nature of the legislation would result in business relocations – and so on. The adverse reaction from business led to the establishment of a Company Law Review Group (CLRG) to discuss the contentious issue of the DCS, which ultimately decided that it was not feasible to commence section 45 because of cost, the impact on national competitiveness, and the likelihood of companies registering outside Ireland. In essence the government backed down. The fear of the removal of capital outweighed the desire to innovate. Dependence on foreign capital had become so severe that the government could not dictate the direction of compliance. Yes, a watered down version of s. 45 emerged (Article X) but this removed the more innovative clauses of the proposed legislation for example, the role of auditors in assessing the fairness and reasonableness of the DCS.

nation due to its transnational, increasingly global nature. The host country that provides the greatest benefits will succeed in getting the capital, seemingly regardless of the consequences on other nations.

The costs of capital attraction can be high. With the example of Ireland, FDI meant that the government lacked the impetus to develop the home industrial sector, as it was assumed that foreign capital would provide enough stability for the Irish economy (Jacobsen, 1994). As a result, Ireland is arguably more dependent today than it was twenty-five years ago. The reason for this is that although there have been no significant developments in the home industry, costs of living, standards of living and global consumerism have all increased. This too can be said to be the case in all nations to a varying extent.

Today, the effects of globalisation are becoming increasingly evident. Early manifestations of globalisation theory considered the phenomenon of global reach (Barnet and Müller, 1974; Ghoshal and Bartlett, 1986; more recent discussion can be found in Norbäck and Persson, 2014). A primary stage of globalisation, 'global reach' incorporates the theories of dependency as proposed in the 1960s and 1970s. Due to the fact that the state-centrism tendencies of this theory, and others, appeared to negate the power of globalisation, a theoretical shift has been evidenced in the form of Dicken's (1998, 2007, 2015) global shift which considers investment strategies and theories and the role of the state, concluding that it still represents a key influence on the global economy today (See also Bourne, 2009). This has been evidenced in the recent global financial crisis, including in the UK and the US.

The recent financial crisis has been global in nature. Most countries have in some manner, either directly or indirectly, been affected by the liquidity dilemma. However, the attitudes of governments in responding to the crisis have differed considerably, reflecting the level of dependence of some countries on foreign capital investment, in combination with historical factors, all of which have had a lasting effect on the national infrastructure of some nations.

For example, let us look at the UK (for a good overview of the US, see Swagel, 2015) with regard to national initiatives. The UK was affected quite badly by the crisis with problems for inter alia, Bradford and Bingley, Lloyds TSB and, most conversely perhaps, Northern Rock. In September 2007, the government provided a guarantee to existing retail deposits (that were not covered by the Financial Services Compensation Scheme). This was subsequently extended to cover new deposits and some wholesale funding. In addition, the government nationalised Northern Rock in 2008 (National Audit Office, 2009, p. 8. Para. 24), and restructured it in 2010. It was subsequently merged with Bradford and Bingley plc. in 2010 to form

UK Asset Resolution Limited (equity owed by the HM Treasury). (For details on Lloyds Banking Group plc. and Royal Bank of Scotland see Baber, 2014). The UK introduced a taxpayer-funded bailout to shore up the banking industry. Add to this the recent publication of *The Turner Review* (2009) and the extent of the commitment to addressing the issues arising out of the current situation can be realised. Evidence of this can be found in the regulatory responses to the financial crisis in the UK. The Financial Services Act (2010) introduced 'financial stability' as a new regulatory objective into the Financial Services and Markets Act (2000) (FSA, 2010, Part 3, Section 1 (3)). The previous regulatory objectives had been market confidence, protecting consumers and protection from financial crime, protection of consumers being paramount. Post 2010, all regulatory objectives were to be treated on an equal footing. In addition to this, structural changes were introduced in the Financial Services Act 2012, with more responsibility for the stability and protection of the UK financial system being given to the Bank of England (2012, Part 2, Section 2 (2)). The FSA 2012 also introduced the Financial Conduct Authority (replacing the Financial Services Authority) and the Prudential Regulation Authority (PRA). Again, one of the key objectives of these authorities is protecting the stability of the markets (for a good overview, see Baber, 2012, 2014).

Regardless of the success, or otherwise, of these measures, their very initiation speaks volumes. It seems that, within the UK (and to a lesser extent the US) and others, the nation state has stepped in to protect and restructure the economy where global capital has failed. Does this mean that globalisation has failed in its capacity to diminish the power of the nation state? Has protectionism superseded free trade? Not necessarily. Instead, this move by states such as the UK reflects how historical factors, and issues of colonial dependence can affect decisions today. What is now generally the UK was once the base for the imperial British Empire. It was a 'core' country in colonial quests. As a result, the domestic infrastructure is secure enough to pass measures such as those implemented in the wake of the Northern Rock scandal. Regulation is effective as areas such as the London Financial Centre are globally recognised institutions, and MNCs will be willing to adhere to the principles-based approach to governance due to the strength of the infrastructure and arguably its ability to withstand crisis.

What then can we say about other states, more dependent on foreign capital – historically peripheral regions? What is the impact of global financial crises on these regions? In Section 3.2 the Icelandic banking crisis (2008–2011) was considered, a crisis that sparked debate on a global scale especially with the failure of Landsbanki, Kaupthing and others. Prior to the crisis, the Icelandic government had taken a rather laissez-faire approach to regulation (Thorhallsson and Kattel, 2013, p. 84). Iceland's response to the crisis differed from that of the UK: obtaining a loan from Russia and one from the IMF to stabilise the economy (Iovine, 2009; BBC Business, 2008). (Note that Thorhallson and Kattell attribute this to systemic differences with small open economies like Iceland, totally abandoning the corporatist model (even the weak UK corporatist model) in favour of moving straight to a neoliberal economy). Iceland also began negotiations to join the EU and in turn the Euro given the then almost complete demise of the national currency (Charlemagne, 2009; Traynor, 2009). However, this was not followed through, because the kroner stabilised, and indeed the Icelandic economy has improved significantly since 2011. For the purposes of this book, the almost national economic planning approach that the government took to recovery in Iceland has rejuvenated the economy – arguably fulfilling Frank's (1977b) suggestion that national planning was the only solution to dependency. In fact, it may be that Iceland's failure to fully join the EU actually facilitated a recovery much quicker than could otherwise have happened (as it allowed for the more national planning measures to proceed) (Thorhallsson and Kattel, 2013).

Also of note is Ukraine and indeed Greece, which had to ask the IMF for funding with regard to their banking crisis (Marson, 2009; MacKenzie, 2015). How do the states of Iceland, Ukraine and Greece differ from the likes of the UK and the US? First, and in keeping with the narrative of this book as a whole, these nations have histories that could fall under the remit of 'traditional' dependence. Greece was part of the Ottoman Empire; Ukraine was part of communist USSR; and Iceland had been colonised by both Norwegian and Danish monarchies. Today, these nations rely heavily on foreign investment for their economy. Unlike the British government, domestic infrastructure does not enable these countries to shore up their economy in the wake of crisis. This is arguably due to the fact that they are more dependent than past 'core' nations such as the UK and, as such, do not have the facilities with which to protect their economy in light of the failure of global capital to do so.

As the last number of paragraphs illustrate, the historical aspect of dependence has been realised by the most recent financial crisis. If foreign capital was to relocate away from a country depending on it, the national economy would at the least suffer irreparable damage and, at most collapse. Above, the ability of the London Financial Centre to retain capital due to its reputation and, arguably, the fact that the infrastructure is comparably sound in the face of crisis was mentioned (Clark, 2002; Wójcik and MacDonald-Korth, 2015). Dublin, for example, does not have this security. Capital is attracted to Dublin for the English-speaking populace and the tax and regulation benefits to MNCs. Yet the requirements of a global society means that technological, communication and other consumerism products would still be needed by consumers even in the light of capital flight. This can be applied on a more global scale. Removal of capital from any nation is going to incur job losses, problems for the economy, debt, and so on. However, the global consumerist society will not have changed, as the goods will still be available and may even be at a lower price. As a result, capital will still be spent by the population, yet the nation would not be receiving the capital, resulting in more national debt and the further underdevelopment of the nation, fulfilling Frank's theory, where he states that whenever development develops, underdevelopment underdevelops, splitting the two of them further apart and hence fuelling his proposal that a total break with capitalism is needed (Frank, 1967, 1977b, 1991).

This chapter aimed to consider the relationship between dependency and global relations. Dependency posits that a state's development is conditioned by other factors. Within a modified dependency, this factor is the transnational capital generated by the MNC. Therefore, the state is dependent on the MNC. However, the TCC has no loyalties to states. Instead, loyalty lies with capital. How then can a TCC, intent only on profit maximisation, have an effective CSR policy designed to meet the specific needs and requirements of a particular state or region? It cannot, without regulation. But, if the state 'regulating' the CSR policy of the MNC is so dependent on the capital generated by the MNC, how can it be effective or even implemented? It cannot, because some capital is better than no capital, and it will be the case that a dependent nation will compromise on CSR policy to avoid capital flight. Systematically, dependent states cannot have a national CSR policy.

Therefore, if it is the case that underdevelopment develops in 'dependent' regions, how can the nation state attempt to regulate the TCC and MNC or even impose CSR legislation of any type? As capital is not stationary, can, or will, a nation state attempt to regulate the CSR of the MNC in order to develop their region, which holds the temporary status of 'host nation'? The state cannot effectively impose such measures on the MNC and TCC as the fear of capital flight supersedes any plans for development as a result of capital investment. It is the case that nation states, so indebted to capital injection, will accept development of any type, regardless of whether it correlates with the requirements of the host capital. The reason for this is that capital with restrictions on development is still better than no capital at all.

3.6 Conclusion

Modified dependency does fulfil its role as an alternative assessment of the economy. However, more questions have been raised. Dependent states are beholden to capital injection. This being the case, can the government of a nation state effectively require an MNC to implement CSR in the region in order to promote development? Is the fear of capital flight greater than the need for development? Attracting capital can have negative implications for home development and for how the removal of capital will adversely affect the economy.

If it is the case, that the TCC has superseded democratic structures, then it is fair to assume that pre-existing domestic infrastructures and modes of governance are ill-equipped to govern this new borderless class. Does this necessarily mean a crisis for governance? On the face of it, no. As the financial crisis illustrated, nation-state responses to ongoing problems have had varying degrees of success. However, attributable to levels of dependence on foreign capital, this crisis has also aided the identification of the ability of domestic infrastructure in some nations, to perhaps, in some cases, direct MNC policy. With other countries, the liquidity crisis has served to highlight that dependence has become so ingrained that they cannot do so. Even with the stronger nations, with their ability to direct MNC policy, it is clear that investment, in addition to stability, is a key priority in governments' economic policies. This in itself poses a further dilemma: how can the borderless MNC (and the emerging TCC, which arguably has loyalties to capital, and capital alone) and, in turn, global capital, be regulated by an inferior – by comparison – domestic state which is, on some level, dependent on said global capital for prosperity.

Global capital's answer to this is to use methods of self-regulation, such as CSR, as a means to regulate companies and people themselves, as well as to ensure some return to external stakeholders and society. In order to ensure that the proposed CSR initiatives in a region are sufficient, input is needed from stakeholders to assist in the shaping and directing of said CSR policy. Using the terminology of corporate governance (of which CSR is a part), then, governments can be categorised (or downgraded) to the status of external stakeholders, and their role as external stakeholders is to guide the direction of CSR policy in the best interests of the area in which they go. However, if the TCC exists solely to accumulate capital and has loyalties only to capital, designs on CSR seem paradoxical in nature. Therefore, CSR appears cosmetic in the TCC's endeavour to accumulate still more capital. CSR will be effective in attracting more capital in areas with a wider consumer base (see Chapter 5) and in states where the TCC is competing for a slice of the market. The dependent state loses out because in order to retain capital generated by the TCC, states like Ireland (see the Director's Compliance Example) are making more compromises to capital, as opposed to influencing capital to make compromises in the shape of CSR – such as in the UK – in order for the TCC to remain in the country and therefore to retain an elusive piece of the economy.

4
The Changing of the Guard: Government to Gatekeeper

4.1 Introduction

Changes in the governance structures, which have coincided with shifts in the global system, have contributed to the changing relationship between business and government. Corporate social responsibility (CSR), a key focus of this book, has become much more embedded since early manifestations of the concept. The value of CSR has become increasingly important as states' power has diminished with the changing world order. As states have become less powerful and 'smaller', they have increasingly become dependent on capital generated by MNCs for development within their borders.

And so, a new role for government has emerged. No longer 'global leaders' in the sense that they once were, governments today now act as quasi-gatekeepers for regional and national development by trying to persuade MNCs to think long-term about investment *within the particular government's region* as opposed to short-term profit gain. But the question then becomes, why should MNCs listen to them? MNCs think in the language of corporate governance and consider relationships and influences within business exchanges in this way. Governments' power lies in their role as external stakeholders of an MNC and the influence that this can have on company policy and indeed on consumers interested in the products of the MNCs. Chapter 1 considered the role that governments have had in shaping CSR policies in the US and the UK in particular. This chapter is more concerned with this role within a dependency framework and from the perspective of government as a diminished player in the world system.

Mitchell, Agle and Wood (1997) defined the role of stakeholders and the idea of a stake. Modifying this approach slightly, this chapter operates from the premise that a stakeholder is someone who is influenced by or can influence a corporation's policy direction. As an external stakeholder, governments can still play an effective role in shaping CSR policy. As well as national government, CSR is increasingly on the agenda in the EU and at an international level (for example, the United Nations Guidelines on

Business and Human Rights). In keeping with the language used throughout this book, this chapter considers government as an important and powerful (depending on the extent of state dependence) external stakeholder of a corporation and, in addition, as a quasi-gatekeeper, to the corporation to ensure best return for the particular region in the regulation of economic activity.

4.2 Stakeholders

The words 'stakes' and 'stakeholders' have amassed considerable debate in academic and business literature. Even as literature in the area has accumulated and evolved considerably, with new directions looking at social identity in interpreting the term (Crane and Ruebottom, 2011), in addition to the more traditional prominence in the management literature (Parmar, Freeman et al., 2010), the two broad camps that have been around since the concept's inception appear to remain: those that give a broad interpretation of the term and those that exercise a more conservative approach.

Addressing the narrower approach first, the literature of the Stanford Research Institute referenced by Freeman (1984) presents a definition that ascribes to this more restricted interpretation, describing stakeholders as those groups 'in which the organisation is dependent for its continued survival'. Freeman (2001) suggests that the narrow definition is focused on those groups vital to the success and survival of the corporation, a view augmented by Mitchell, Agle and Woods' (1997) idea that the narrower interpretation experiences a more direct correlation with the economic interests of the firm and therefore is something that can only be lost. This more economic approach (which bears resonance with the shareholder-value approach to the firm (Hillman and Keim, 2001; Eisenhardt, 1989; Fontrodona and Sison, 2006; Donaldson and Davies, 1991)), has been followed by Clarkson (1994), who frames stakeholders in terms of risk. Voluntary stakeholders, under Clarkson's interpretation, have invested something in the company and have therefore *assumed* risk, whereas involuntary stakeholders have risk *imposed* upon them by virtue of the activities of the firm. This is an approach which is later refined somewhat by Post, Preston and Sach, where they define stakeholders as 'the individuals and constituencies that contribute, either voluntarily or involuntarily to [the firm's] wealth creating capacity and activities and that are therefore its potential beneficiaries and or risk bearers' (2002, p. 8).

Contrast this then with the classic Freeman definition whereby a stakeholder in an organisation is classified as 'any group or individual who can affect, or is affected by, the achievement of the organisation's objective' (Freeman, 1984, p. 46). Under this interpretation, a stake is anything that can be affected, or is affected, by the actions of the company – which in a way reflects Taylor's (1989) ethical stance, opining that fundamentally, everyone ought to count, and count in the same way. Building on Taylor, Cragg (2002) pursues the idea that all legitimate interests of stakeholders are equitably addressed (but, conversely, refutes the idea that every stakeholder should have equal footing in corporate decision making).

Advancing this position, then, Mitchell et al. (1997) consider the attributes of a stakeholder. In so doing, they identify three key features: (1) the *power* to influence, (2) the *legitimacy* of the stakeholder's relationship with the firm and (3) the *urgency* of the claim (p. 854). Those taking a similar approach include Alkhafaji, who looks at the interest–support relationship between stakeholders and the corporation (1989, p. 36), and Sternberg, who identifies 'stakeholders' within a similar space (2000, p. 95). Also advocating the broader interpretation are Savage, Nix, Whitehead and Blair, who expand on both Alkahfaji and Sternberg (and also offer a more developed interpretation than Sternberg) by identifying the requirements of a claim and an ability to influence (1991). In so doing, they are making a valid point. By determining a stakeholder as someone/something who has been influenced by a firm, or someone/something who has an influence on the firm's decisions, the reality of global competition is both recognised and accounted for.

Moving towards the broader application of the stakeholder debate, then, a stake is something which is affected by or affects the firm. In this way, both the idea of claim (usually affected by) and the ability to influence (effects) as proposed by Savage et al. (1991) are incorporated. In addition, the power, urgency and legitimacy of the claim are also recognised, in accordance with the Mitchell et al. (1997) identification criteria. A stakeholder, therefore, can be defined as *a person, or group of persons, whose existence, quality of life and/or everyday routine is or will be impacted in some way, either positively or negatively, by the actions (or inactions) of a firm.* Some may argue that this definition of a stakeholder cannot be correct, as it does not include the environment as a stakeholder. There are two ways of addressing this. A stakeholder can be a stakeholder only if they can personally defend their rights as a stakeholder. They may not realise that they are stakeholders, but once they do, they are in a position to defend that right. The environment is not a person. It has no personal attributes, unlike a group or government. Therefore, it relies on non-governmental organisations, not-for-profits and charities to defend its status as a stakeholder. By eliminating the environment as a stakeholder, and instead widening the scope of the stakeholder definition in other ways – for example 'existence, quality of life/and or every day routine is or will be impacted in some way, either positively or negatively, by the actions (or inactions) of a firm' – the protection of the environment is considered in assessing a person's right. Pollution of the water, killing of fish *will* impact stakeholders at some point. It is not then necessary to consider the environment as a unique stakeholder as it is a social issue – something that affects everyone.

4.2.1 External stakeholders

When recognising the existence of stakeholders, it is necessary to categorise them. Starting broadly, then, stakeholders can be identified as either 'internal' or 'external'. Precise definitions are for the most part limited to business dictionary definitions. Having noted this, Donaldson and Preston (1995, p. 67) make the comment that although stakeholder theory goes beyond descriptive observations such as 'organisations have stakeholders', a lot of the literature is implicit rather than explicit. This is particularly the case for external stakeholders (also termed 'public stakeholders' in Clarkson, 1995). An external stakeholder appears to be anyone outside the company, who were, are or could be affected by its actions, methods and results. This tends to encompass groups like consumers, suppliers (who can also be internal stakeholders), lenders, local communities and governments. Therefore, in applying the above definition of stakeholders, external stakeholders become those who have a claim over the organisation's activities or influence them but are not themselves an internal part of the organisation.

4.2.2 Government as an external stakeholder

Governments, therefore, can be captured as external stakeholders. They can ensure that MNCs meet particular standards. Evidence of this influence can be found in the literature (Duanmu, 2014; Holtbrugge, Berg and Puck, 2007), and indeed with the government of a host nation, one can see how this can be realised. The flip side is also understandable. A government's 'claim' is influenced by the firm, the size of the firm, the type of firm, employment, investment and so on due to the effects on the economy and employment. But in being so influenced, the government's role in society is somewhat diminished. As an external stakeholder, the government's main role should be its capacity to influence others. This influence could be created through a role in influencing company policy; regulating an industry in most cases as a democratic representative of other stakeholders, such as local communities; and ensuring that any detrimental effects of company actions on the resources or indigenous industry to people of a community are more than remedied and are offset by clear benefits for the state, the region and the community in which the MNC operates.

External stakeholders do not operate within a vacuum. Therefore, government's capacity to influence and be influenced does not operate within a vacuum either. As the Introduction to this book has noted, we have recently emerged from a global financial crisis. This crisis (if indeed it can be deemed as such) served to highlight the inadequacies of the system in which the global market operates, the power of non-state actors (in this case MNCs) and the limitations of the accountability mechanisms in place to ensure that MNCs behaved in a responsible manner. In responding to the fallout from the liquidity crisis, the response of governments varied, with some being seen as more successful than others. In line with modified dependency as discussed in Section 2.7, governments are now dependent on MNCs for capital investment, jobs and services. However, when the historical element is taken into consideration, some governments may be less dependent than others (e.g. the US or the UK) and therefore may able to introduce laws, regulations and systemic changes which may not be possible with smaller governments. And thus, an observation can be made, namely that some governments are more effective external stakeholders than others. Their effectiveness is dependent on how dependent the government is on MNC investment as well as other factors: the history of the state, the population size and so on.

Savage et al. are mentioned above in relation to stakeholder definition and purpose, specifically on the idea of a claim, and the ability to influence. Admirable and pivotal to stakeholder identification as this may be, it does not necessarily reflect reality. They operate on a somewhat utopian level, so with regard to governments as stakeholders, for example, do not incorporate the reality of dependence on capital and how this might impact on the ability of governments to influence the behaviour of the MNC in question. This book is interested in the 'influence' that governments have, particularly in their ability to shape the CSR policies of MNCs operating within their borders. The ability to influence is compromised by dependence on capital generated by MNCs. Fear of capital flight may be enough to curb a national government's ability and wish to influence capital's decisions. Granted, this fear may be more real in small, open and traditionally dependent economies such as Ireland, as mentioned in Chapter 3 (Section 3.5), in comparison to a perceived stronger state like the UK, with historical strength and a reputable stock exchange on its side. However, Chapter 3 developed on Chapter 2's proposition of the ubiquitous existence of dependence. That being the case, a key question emerges: Is the government's ability to influence affected by its nation's dependence on foreign capital? It may be the case that whereas CSR (and the power to direct CSR) is symptomatic of a dependent state, other factors such as population size, natural resources and so on may give some countries a significant bargaining tool, and as a result, CSR becomes MNCs' way of legitimising their existence within a region. For small open economies, factors such as population size may actually negate their potential to direct the course of capital – especially where the MNC operates on a global level. For a state like Ireland, for example, with a population of 4.6 million (2013 statistics) or Iceland, with a population of 323,000 (2013 statistics), how can the population size help when the population of the UK is 64.1 million (2013 statistics) and the city of London has a population of 8.63 million? This will be discussed in more detail in Chapter 5, but of note for this chapter is the idea that for smaller open economies, the role of the government as an external stakeholder may be limited to disciplining the state to expect nothing from capital other than it remaining within state borders and how, in doing so, it provides jobs. That being the case, for small open economies, development within the state may be left to the will of capital within its borders, and the nature of its relationship with capital could suggest that capital retention may be paramount to the small open economy's design for capital.

4.3 What is the relationship of between stakeholder theories and CSR?

Justifying the relationship between stakeholder theories and CSR is necessary. Although Friedman (1962, 1970) argues that the efficient functioning of the markets and effective government regulations would ensure that the pursuit of profits would coincide with society's interests and, as a result, the business of business would be business, developments have been made since the 1970s. Today, governments and MNCs are increasingly recognising the rights of others as well as stockholders/shareholders. This is usually articulated through the CSR policies of the MNCs at a corporate level and through norms, policies and legislative expectations of governments. Indeed, as Section 1.2 demonstrated, stakeholder management became one of the prevalent themes of CSR by the 1980s and 1990s as academic literature on CSR began to diversify (Carroll, 1991). Add to this the manner in which MNCs have relieved some of the burdens on governments with regard to the provision of, and support in, the delivery of services that were previously regarded as the core business of government – for example, youth job training and employment schemes – thereby weakening the previously defined boundaries between the two entities. Different manifestations of this relationship have permeated the literature, with perhaps the most common being Giddens' Third Way (1998, 1999, 2001, 2013). It centres on a belief in the *value* of community, a *commitment* to equality of opportunity, an *emphasis* on responsibility and a *belief* in accountability. In this way, then, it represents a response to the change in the social and environmental space. In rejecting profit led, 'hard capitalism' and extreme socialism, it occupies the middle – recognising the benefit of private enterprise for public betterment. In sum, the Third Way is an ideology that bridges the economic strength of the 'right' with the social elements of the 'Left' promoting growth, entrepreneurship, wealth creation and enterprise, balanced with a strong social-justice element (Giddens, 1998, 1999, 2001, 2013; Wheeler, 2001). With the relationship between state and MNCs becoming more consolidated, the economic arguments of Friedman have less relevance today. Whereas the rationale for MNC involvement in social issues *may* be questioned, it does exist and is increasingly more embedded in the business model of the MNC and the social element of the state, suggesting that the business of business is very much business but with an added element of promoting responsibility.

In the past, stakeholder theories of the firm were considered a description of how a firm *ought* to be managed, and not necessarily describing how a firm *is* managed. Globally, with the advent of legislation in different countries, it may appear (on the surface at least) that the distinction between ought and is has been blurred almost beyond recognition. In part, this can be attributed to the increased focus on stakeholder rights by the judiciary and legislative advances since the 1990s; Donaldson and Preston (1995) note that 'court decisions and new legislation have weakened the so-called "business judgment" rule, which vests management with exclusive authority over the conduct of a company's affairs' (p. 75). Albeit written in 1995, this has continued to be the case in more recent years. At an EU level, for example, developments in the realm of disclosure (Article 19 a (1), Directive 2014/95/EU (amending Accounting Directive 2013/34/EU)) have ensured that environmental issues, and increasingly respect for human rights (Global Compact, UN Guidelines), are (or will be) recognised within national legislation (see in general Kinderman, 2013; Parker and Alemanno, 2014)). For example, in the UK, the provision of an enhanced business review in Companies Act 2006 (s. 417, Companies Act 2006) requires a statement from MNCs of a certain size to produce information on, inter alia, environmental matters and social and community issues (see also s. 172 Companies Act 2006). Although this does display some genuinely similar characteristics to the operating financial review (in relation to environmental and community issues in particular) (Companies Act 2006 (Strategic Report and Director's Report) Regulations 2013; Rowbottom and Schroder, 2014), the development of these types of provisions indicate the relationship between stakeholder theories and the rhetoric around CSR.

Within the US, a similar story unfolds. Thus far in the US, the courts have been willing to implement legislation requiring corporations to consider the impact of their actions on others: stakeholders in addition to shareholders. In *Unocal v Mesa Petroleum* (493 A.2d. 946 (Del. 1985)), the decision by the Delaware Supreme Court on defensive tactics against takeover bids presents something of a departure from the more traditional approach. Although requiring corporate directors to demonstrate the existence of a 'reasonable threat' in hostile takeover situations, the discussion around 'reasonableness' recognised the importance of the impact of the takeover on 'constituencies' other than shareholders. This decision was further expanded in *Paramount Communications Inc. v Time Inc.* (571, A.2d. 1140, (Del. 1990)) to include factors such as the long-term business plan, in a director's consideration. In addition to these examples in the US, evidence from other jurisdictions, such as the codetermination provisions in Germany (Mitbestimmungsgesetz 1976 (Codetermination Act 1976); Baums and Frick, 1997; Kraft et al., 2011), together with the dual board structure, indicate the more ubiquitous departure from the Friedman ethos towards a more stakeholder-oriented mode of analysis. With society seemingly recognising the role and value of other interest groups within the business framework, a description of the firm that mirrors this recognition is required. Although not of particular reference here, the increase of global communications, the broad acknowledgement of the harm that MNCs have done in the past in relation to the environment, for example, is relevant. This acknowledgement appeals to a global social conscience, which in turn encourages, and even may require, MNCs to consider these aspects as well in their business decisions. In addition, the 'rights' revolution of the past 60 years regarding workers' rights and human rights legislation indicate that business for the sake of profits is no longer enough (Mosley and Uno, 2007). At a minimum, consideration of other groups is necessary for an MNC to fulfil its legal responsibilities, never mind social requirements.

But, thinking about the context in which this book is situated, in an era of post-financial crisis, the challenge for government when considered as an external stakeholder is to continue to champion stakeholder rights. Of course, the government has an impact on MNC activities regardless of whether we consider their role as 'external stakeholder' or not, but in thinking about the relationship in this way, I think that the hierarchy of relationships between government and MNCs may be more realistic and more consistent with the narrative of this piece. As discussion unfolds in Chapter 5, it may be that given the structure of the global system together with the nature of MNC's economic practice, such endeavours (i.e. the promotion of stakeholders' rights) will be fruitful only where capital (generated by MNCs) has something to gain by remaining in the region. With smaller, very open economies, capital legitimacy is at best unfocused and at worst absent, as it is in the current economic climate, where capital retention is a more important mandate than 'influencing' corporate policy. Evidence of this in action can be found in the example of the proposed DCS in the Republic of Ireland (s. 45 Companies (Auditing and Accounting) Act 2003 (see s. 3.5, fn. 2)), where rather than 'influencing' capital in its role as an external stakeholder, the Irish government was influenced *by* capital from a fear of capital flight, which resulted in a volte-face in proposed government policy (Suiter, 2003; Appleby, 2005). In the UK, a similar scenario emerged with the Operating and Financial Review (OFR) (Rowbottom and Schroder, 2014).

Regardless of the economic environment, the popularity of the Third Way ideology and the recognition of the diminishing role of the nation state (due to the processes of globalisation) have led to social duties and expectations being placed on MNCs. Due to this shift, together with the discussion above on social and environmental issues in particular, Friedman's opinions on the responsibility and role of business are no longer viable in such an evolving business climate. Naturally, profit maximisation is still key to the business practice of MNCs, but this ethos is intertwined with CSR – representing a more tactical approach to profit maximisation, echoing the strategic tones of CSR definitions today (McWilliams and Siegel, 2001). CSR as a self-regulating mechanism adopted by MNCs for businesses' commitment to especially social and environmental issues serves to legitimise MNC behaviour within a region and provide the corporation with relatively free rein over the direction of their CSR activity (Du and Vieira, 2012). However, for small open, capital-investment-dependent countries, where bargaining tools such as a large consumer base are absent, MNCs do not *have* to legitimise themselves within their business model, as such countries appear to have accepted that any attempts to regulate capital in an innovative manner will be thwarted by threats of capital flight as noted above in relation to the DCS in ROI and the OFR in the UK (Newell, 2008).

Freeman poses an alternative to Friedman, and under his viewpoint, the relationship between CSR and stakeholding can be realised by how stakeholding is used as a means to interpret corporate responsibility (Freeman, 2001). CSR and stakeholding today, and interactions between the two, have developed considerably as illustrated by advancements in legislation such as those examples discussed above. This is despite the fact that Clarkson (1995) observed that it is necessary to distinguish between stakeholder issues and social issues, because, in his line of reasoning, corporations and their managers manage relationships with their stakeholders and not with society.

Today, external stakeholder issues increasingly overlap with social issues, and due to the change in attitude with regard to governmental legislation in some jurisdictions, stakeholder issues are ever more encompassing than those issues previously considered solely within the remit of CSR. The relationship between the two can be somewhat confusing, and their difference has been overshadowed by their similarities with the onslaught of legislation, such as the constituency statutes in the US and Section 172 of the Company Law Act 2006 in the UK. What this legislation suggests is that stakeholder considerations have evolved into social issues and therefore warrant treatment by a CSR policy.

4.4 Role of government within CSR

The government of a state represents the state and implements legislation *as* the state. Due to the development of business practice in recent decades, the government of a state finds itself increasingly situated within the general environment of business operation. With the fading of the lines between state and business, government finds itself confronted with an increasingly more important role to play – that of an external stakeholder.

The strength of the government's power to implement legislation in the realm of CSR corresponds with the strength of its role as an external stakeholder. The sheer representative power of a government may correspond with the strength of its role as a stakeholder. Sternberg (2000) considers that corporations are not like governments and that stakeholders are not like citizens. This being the case, she reasons that all stakeholders do not have equal footing with corporations. However, as a democratic representative of the nation state (in most instances), the government can arguably command significant power as an external stakeholder of a corporation. In applying the Mitchell et al. (1997) definition of a stakeholder, governments (as external stakeholders) sit quite comfortably within the stakeholding concept because they do come with (a) the power to influence, (b) a legitimate relationship with the firm (if the firm operates within their borders, they have a legitimate claim) and (c) the urgency of the claim (p. 854). This has been realised in the manner in which governments are increasingly using their power as stakeholders to drive CSR – at least in perceived 'strong' economic regions (i.e. the UK and the US). Despite the apparent confusion in ascertaining the relationship between stakeholding and CSR, it can be said that CSR has advocated stakeholder theory and vice versa: 'the CSR movement has been a major factor in moving corporate governance theory in the stakeholder direction by demanding that companies go beyond the creation of short-term shareholder wealth in pursuit of broader objectives such as sustainable growth, equitable employment practices and long-term social and environmental well being' (Williams and Corley, 2005, p. 495).

4.4.1 CSR and dependency

Chapters 1–3 considered the idea of dependency and primarily the existence of a 'modified' dependence: a dependence on capital generated by the

TCC (see Section 2.7 and Section 3.4). This section considers specifically the implications of dependence on the concept of CSR. Chapter 1 considered in detail the role of CSR in society today and how there has been an increase on the focus of the rights of external stakeholders – in this case, national governments, and, their ability to act as influencers of MNC CSR policy. However, this section focuses specifically on how the government's ability to influence is challenged by the nature of its dependence on transnational capital (Mosley, 2003, p. 102; Robinson, 2012). Whereas Chapter 1 did highlight how the UK has begun to supplement CSR policy with legislation, arguably such interventions occur only because capital is willing to allow it.

CSR is a symptom of dependence and, in particular, a symptom of a dependence on a more 'lightweight' style of financial capital advocated within the Anglo and American systems. This being the case, a nation-state's approach to CSR is another means by which countries can attract capital and encourage capital to remain within its borders (Detomasi, 2008; Scherer and Palazzo, 2011; Lee, Fooks, Gilmore et al., 2012; Adelopo, Yekini and Raimi, 2015; Kinderman, 2011; Midttun, Gautesen and Gjølberg, 2006). A voluntary national approach to CSR is an attractive incentive to capital. By ceding to capital in this way, national governments allow capital to shape their own interventions. At the same time, the existence of an MNC CSR policy allows capital to legitimise its existence in the nation state. The strength of the legitimacy exercise depends on the state in which the MNC is operating. With states like the UK, where capital is more inclined to compete for a niche in the market (for more, see Section 3.5), brand marketing to the substantial potential consumer base necessitates a more robust approach to CSR and indeed enables states to engage to a limited extent with capital, to supplement the voluntary approach to CSR, such as that which has occurred in the UK (Frankental, 2001; Lewis, 2003).

What about small open economies? For states like Ireland, there is an even greater compromise to capital. Although Ireland has made similar economic choices to the UK – albeit for path-dependent reasons – the character of the Irish economy, with its limited indigenous industrial sector, means that Ireland is not in as advantageous a position as the UK (Coffee, 2000; Mahoney, 2000; Cooke, 2005, pp. 53–59). Capital does not need to legitimise its existence in a small open economy like Ireland's as strenuously as it does elsewhere. As will be discussed in Chapter 5, the limitations in the size of the potential consumer base in Ireland will impact its ability to engage with MNCs for supplementary legislation. Capital is attracted to regions for different reasons. With a more established state like the UK, it may be a niche in the market (Frankental, 2001). For a small open economy like Ireland, it may be advertising tax concessions for profit maximisation.

Therefore, in states like Ireland, legitimising capital is not an option; capital can, and will, leave if state governments attempt to act as 'influencers' in directing CSR beyond what the company expects, because in accordance with Section 3.5 in particular, capital has no loyalty to states, and where there are no further benefits to capital, capital will leave. That is not to say that MNCs operating in Ireland will not have a CSR policy. They will - CSR departments and the publication of a CSR report have become as integral to business in recent years as the publication of the annual report. But it is the content of the CSR policy where the important discussion lies. It may be enough for the MNC to pay homage to CSR, without robustly engaging with CSR activities in Ireland. In other countries, specifically where the population is larger, the government is stronger and the natural resources are more marketable, so CSR is more of a bargaining tool.

This book has established that all states are dependent but that some are more dependent than others. Looking at how states have approached the concept of CSR may give an indication on the extent of the dependence within that particular state. For 'outsider' modes of governance, the UK is the most advanced in the manner in which legislation and government policy supplement the CSR landscape (Ward and Smith, 2006, p. 5). However, in even ascribing to the term CSR, countries are committing to their dependence on capital in order to legitimise its existence through CSR policy. Of note, therefore, are those states in which the contract with capital is traditionally configured in a very different way – rather than being a voluntary requirement, it is embedded in the societal requirements of those regions. Instances of this are to be found in the more 'insider' modes of governance, such as that which operates in Germany where 'CSR ... goes hand in hand with the national economic and social framework and is considered a fundamental part of their highly regulated and institutionalised industrial relations system' (CSR in France, Germany, Hungary and the UK, 2014; Townsley and Stohl, 2003; Silberhorn and Warren, 2007). However, as corporate governance converges, there are implications regarding dependency (for convergence, see Stilpon and Thompson, OECD; Coffee, 1999; Goergen, Matynova and Renneboog, 2005; Gilson, 2001; Haxhi and Aguilera, 2012; Clark and Wójcik, 2007; Schmidt and Spindler, 2002). Within the European Union, as will be discussed in Section 5.3, there is a move towards voluntary CSR within EU policy and communications. This is as a result of dependence on transnational capital and the desire to retain capital. This being the case, the EU has embarked on the Anglo-style approach regarding CSR, and as such, there is a definite shift towards voluntary CSR in the EU, one that is challenged in Sections 5.3–5.5.

As competitiveness for capital intensifies, so too does dependence on the said capital, as regions are committed to more compromises in order to attract and retain such capital. Regardless of apparent 'successes' in CSR literature, advances in CSR practice can be considered implications of a further dependence on capital, with CSR being symptomatic of that dependency. As CSR becomes the tool by which capital legitimises its existence, the small open economy loses out. Design to attract capital in the short term – especially given its small size and population, among other things – disciplines such economies to expect nothing from transnational capital other than continued employment. Ireland illustrates this, and as Chapter 5 considers, unless change comes from beyond the nation-state level, CSR policies in states like Ireland are destined to be wholly designed by transnational capital. Therefore, regardless of apparent advances in the CSR paradigm and literature, the national governments are conditioned by dependence, which makes it *influenced by*, as opposed to influencing, transnational capital within its borders. What does this mean then for the role of government within the CSR/dependency infrastructure?

4.5 Role of government as a gatekeeper of society

A national government is an external stakeholder of a corporation. Using the Mitchell, Agle and Wood (1997) identification framework outlined above (see Section 4.2 and 4.4), it is clear that the government is influenced by, and theoretically has the power to influence, the activities of the MNC. However, as the last section demonstrated, the existence of a ubiquitous dependence on capital has somewhat constrained the capacity of national governments to maintain the balance between being influenced by and influencing MNC behaviour. Thinking about the role of government within a wider governance perspective then, the idea of the government as a quasi-gatekeeper begins to emerge.

Literature on gatekeeping is well established (Coffee, 2002, 2006; Kirkbride and Letza, 2003), and on considering the functions of gatekeepers of the firm, some are particularly relevant in the context of governments. The idea of gatekeepers and gatekeeping is key to discussions within corporate governance. Gatekeepers are intermediaries who keep a check on the managers of a company in order to benefit shareholders and investors (Coffee, 2006). In short, they have been viewed as a solution to the agency problem – that is, the idea of the firm being owned by shareholders but controlled by managers (Berle, 1931; Dodd, 1932; Sommer, 1991). The structure of the firm may lead to a problem where managers will seek to pursue short-term profit gains for their own interests at the expense of the owners (i.e. shareholders) of the firm. Extending this premise then to the broader governance agenda, the government is a type of quasi-gatekeeper in the CSR framework. MNCs are in control of the CSR policies that might have benefits to society. The government acts in a gatekeeping role (as external stakeholder) to keep a check on the quality of the CSR policies – to ensure that it is not an exercise in capital legitimisation but rather something that can provide true development to society. Therefore, rather than acting as an intermediary between the MNC and its shareholders as per corporate governance articulations of gatekeeping, governments act as intermediaries between the MNC and stakeholders (specifically society) in ensuring that the MNC is not attracted to short-term profit maximisation over the long-term value of investing in a region and assisting development within said region. National governments do want to promote sustainable business activity in the region, as this benefits the state in which the business is based.

However, like gatekeeping within corporate governance, problems can arise. Gatekeepers within the corporate governance sphere are typically paid by the party that they are supposed to be watching, but their credibility comes from reputation, and in theory, reputation is not going to be compromised for a single client (Coffee, 2006). Of course, this has not always been the case with credit rating agencies coming under scrutiny in the most recent financial crisis (Hunt, 2009; Pagano and Volpin, 2010) and auditors being ascribed blame after Enron (Coffee, 2002, 2006; Benston and Hartgraves, 2002). Within this wider context, a similar problem can arise. The government is receiving investment from the MNC into the region. The government also wants to keep a check on the quality of the CSR policies of the MNC for that region. However, a government's time in power is finite. What does a government want to be remembered for – being an effective check on CSR policy or attracting and retaining capital for the region (thus providing employment, among other things)? The challenge is in ensuring that the national government maintains independence and recognises the value of a robust and tailored CSR policy for the region. CSR is the vehicle by which the government can ensure a more sustainable business practice. But, the previous section has already concluded that CSR is a symptom of dependence. Therefore, we need to consider how effective the government can be as an external stakeholder and quasi-gatekeeper for stakeholders if said government is dependent on the MNC to invest in the region, provide employment and so on. With the shifts in the governance system, the MNC has new responsibilities. The government, as an external stakeholder of the company, or a gatekeeper, has to ensure that these responsibilities are met. However, with the government being dependent on investment from the MNC for employment, this relationship may not be equal. Thus, it is important to look at how to balance these responsibilities.

4.5.1 Balancing responsibilities

As I outlined in Chapter 1, case law and academic discourse initially indicated that the only obligation that business owed was to increase profits for their shareholders (*Hutton v West Cork Railway Co* (1883) 23 Ch. D 654; *Dodge v Ford Motor Company* 204 Mich 459, 170 NW 668. (Mich. 1919); Friedman, 1970). As literature and, in tandem, case law and practice expanded and consolidated, the notion that business owed a wider duty to society became more commonplace (Freeman, 1984, 2001; *AP Smith Manufacturing Co v. Barlow*, 13 NJ 145, 98 A2d 581, (NJ 1953); Carroll, 1999; Mitchell et al., 1997). Although the profit-maximisation ideology retained support ('the business of business is business' (Friedman, 1970)), focus shifted to long-term maximisation via the pursuit of CSR. CSR today is characterised as 'instrumental, strategic rationalizations' (Carroll, 2015, p. 89) and remains 'the benchmark and centre-piece of the socially conscious business movement' (Carroll, 2015, p. 87). Today, these additional responsibilities are generally accepted beyond academic literature – with government policies, MNC's corporate strategy publications and international obligations emphasising that corporations need to make a social contribution, as well as contributions of an economic nature.

As MNCs have become more powerful within the global system, government power has diminished somewhat. And to an extent, this is understandable. As we have become more globalised, the value of an MNC not constrained by national borders can be seen. On the other hand, states that hold MNCs to account (should they fail to meet their responsibilities) can do so only within their national borders. Therefore, far from being on an equal partnership with business, government has been relegated to an external stakeholder, performing a gatekeeping role to ensure that the state receives the best value from their CSR policy. The relationship is not equal; therefore, can exchanges between the two be advantageous to the government's constituents? I fear that whereas exchanges may have the *appearance* of advantage or value to the region in which the MNC operates, it will in fact be the MNC that will ultimately benefit. Such is the nature of strategic CSR today, and when one of the key external stakeholders may be considered weaker – such as the government in a small open economy – it is the local community that loses out.

Whereas the literature on CSR has consolidated somewhat over recent years, there is fragmentation as to the accepted approach to CSR application and enforcement at a national level. This fragmentation seems to be linked to the diversity in governance structures at a national level. Within the more Anglo-American systems, CSR is perceived as 'value added' to everyday business. Although this outlook is beginning to change in some jurisdictions (see Chapter 1 for more discussion on this – with particular references to advancements in the UK), CSR is for the most part not embedded in business practice. This can be contrasted with the Scandinavian approach, where social issues were always part of the business transaction. Today, however, CSR has nearly negated traditional business practice in Scandinavia by imposing this Anglo-American ideology on a structure that had managed to consider social issues so well without characterising it as CSR. Perhaps, in using the language of Matten and Moon (2008), the approach to social issues in Scandinavia was 'implicit' CSR in contrast to 'explicit' CSR within the Anglo-American model (Carson, Hagen and Sethi, 2015). Albareda et al. argue that the movement towards CSR in Scandinavia and the Netherlands is a partnership model and a model which involves a change in attitude by social actors to assume a 'co-responsibility' for an inclusive society and the creation of a shared area of welfare (2007, pp. 400–401).

This is interesting from a dependency perspective because it suggests that the landscape for CSR-influenced activities has become more fragmented, as governments try to maintain their national identity as well as align with both EU directives and global trends on CSR (Carson, Hagen and Sethi, 2015; Vallentin, 2013). Requirements outlined at the level of EU, OECD and so on add yet another layer to a complex web of policies, regulations and statements of best practice. EU communications on CSR have led to a CSR landscape that is difficult to navigate (A renewed EU strategy 2011–2014 for CSR, Commission White Paper on CSR, 2002; Green Paper promoting a European Framework for CSR COM, 2001, 366). In addition, within European national governments, for example, approaches to CSR differ (Lozano, Albareda and Ysa, 2008). As the Scandinavian example suggests, governments are also trying to reimagine their approach in order to align with EU and global trends. Although Albareda et al. (2007) argue that this transition to a more Anglo-American approach to CSR is an heir to the Scandinavian political culture, I fear that the partnerships between government and business have lost something in the process. By characterising social partnerships as CSR, in keeping with EU trends, the history of business and state interaction on social issues has diminished. In requiring business to consciously outline their CSR practice, it may be that it is the communities in which the MNCs operate that are losing out. Similar to imposing a particular type of development plan on countries that had been colonised, this artificial adoption of CSR may actually detract from business and government interaction as opposed to strengthening the partnership. Indeed, this presents a deeper challenge. If we see CSR as a symptom of modified dependency, the shift towards CSR (and voluntary CSR at that) is evidence of the development of underdevelopment, with any CSR policies on the ground being examples of dependent development (Frank, 1967a, 1967b, 1977, 1991).

Although there has been an attempt to harmonise approaches to CSR at an EU level, there is a global disparity in national approaches to CSR. Even at an international level, where guidelines and standards have been introduced, national interpretations of the guidelines have varied considerably. Whereas some of this may be due to national understandings of the role of business in society, some too can be attributed to dependence – both of the traditional and the modified type. As such, some perceived 'stronger' jurisdictions, such as the UK, have been increasingly able to embed CSR practice within the business agenda (supplementing 'voluntary' CSR as well as principles and standards with soft and increasingly harder law), others are more willing to maintain the voluntary approach to CSR. Therefore, a disjointed global landscape of CSR national approaches remains.

Chapter 3 discussed the processes of globalisation (Section 3.2) and the emergence of the TCC as global leaders (Section 3.4). As global leaders, the TCC can overcome some of the problems associated with CSR and, in consolidating the position at a global level, ensure that equality on CSR provisions is an obtainable goal. In a leadership role on the global stage, the TCC has a responsibility to a wider range of stakeholders – the best manner in which this responsibility can be met is through a CSR standard based on equality and borderlessness. However, in imposing a global approach to CSR, there is a challenge in articulating effective CSR at a micro or local level. If the TCC is genuinely concerned with equality and equality of opportunity globally, then national governments as external stakeholders/gatekeepers are ideally positioned to direct CSR activities at this local level – educating the MNC on local idiosyncrasies therefore facilitating a workable partnership to emerge. This partnership, however, presupposes two conditions: one, the TCC is genuinely committed to the CSR agenda and; two, all states are equal and have an equal voice in directing CSR at their national levels. First, the TCC is loyal only to profit; therefore, CSR can be at best 'strategic' (McWilliams and Siegel, 2001) and at worst an exercise in capital legitimisation. Second, states are not equal; as Chapters 2 and 3 explored, inequality has always existed between states. Although generally today, inequality exists between states and capital, inequalities between states remain – due to historical relationships. Add to this population size, natural resources and so on. Comparing the US to Ireland illustrates this point. The US government has a mandate of a huge population and extensive natural resources, and it remains a global political power. The US could be extremely effective in mandating CSR initiatives and directing CSR. Ireland in comparison has a small population and limited natural resources and is not considered a leading political power. As a result, the relationship between government and MNC in Ireland is less likely to be seen as a partnership.

The MNC owes a responsibility to a wider range of stakeholders, and because the governance landscape has changed, the TCC (as the political 'wing' of global capital) are now global leaders and, as such, *have societal responsibilities beyond profit maximisation.* National governments, although decidedly less powerful, still have responsibilities to their constituents, and these responsibilities make up a mixture: economic (job provision), social (services) and political (freedom from corruption). As the governance landscape has shifted and the TCC are acquiring more of the societal responsibilities, *it is the task of the national government to ensure that these responsibilities have been met and, if not, to hold the MNC to account for failing to meet said responsibilities*. For the most part, societal responsibilities are articulated via the CSR policies of the MNC and supplemented by national guidelines and requirements together with international codes.

Although national government is an external stakeholder of the MNC, I see their role as increasingly one of a gatekeeper. Gatekeeping is acting as a check on the MNC, in this case, to ensure that they have the long-term interests of stakeholders (in particular, the local community and society) at the heart of their operations within the region. But as Enron and the recent financial crisis have illustrated, gatekeepers can be ineffective. Couple this with a state's dependence on capital generated by the MNC to provide employment for the region, and we can see that a government's effectiveness as a gatekeeper or indeed a stakeholder may be constrained by fears of capital relocation. However, government is assisted in this endeavour by guidelines, principles and best practice on CSR. Some initiatives do exist at a national level – the effectiveness of these are dependent on the history of the state and its status (dependent under traditional and modified dependence, or dependent only under modified dependence). Others, though, exist at a global level, with states having some flexibility in relation to implementation and enforcement. However, far from being a solution, this presents further problems for a dependent government and the community that it represents.

4.6 Situating the government as external stakeholder/gatekeeper within the TCC and CSR framework

In addition to national initiatives on CSR and the EU communications as discussed in the last section, a lot of codes exist on an international level that relate to CSR and its implementation on an international level. With international codes and standards, international bodies have advanced the principles. They apply to the MNC and, in theory, should be more effective given their wider reach. With the TCC having an almost global reach, standards that apply beyond national boundaries would be advantageous.

In this way, national governments are there to ensure that standards are being met, allowing them to direct CSR initiatives without having to design and implement them. Above, I noted that the TCC, if it assumed its social responsibility as a global leader, could address inequalities in CSR policy and practice and embed a global standard into business objectives. But dependence on capital investment from MNCs has weakened the capacity of governments to act as effective stakeholders or gatekeepers. Therefore, their ability to direct and shape CSR has been compromised – the TCC are not being pushed by government to direct a global CSR standard.

Although discussed in greater detail in Chapter 5 (Section 5.2), the OECD guidelines characterise the challenge of relying on international or transnational codes where national initiatives are limited by government dependence. The OECD guidelines on multinational enterprise do have the ability to cross borders, and this power is recognised by Backer (2007) and Kita (2010–2011). I have discussed elsewhere (Hackett, 2012) whether the OECD is transnational, thereby challenging Kita's definition of it as a 'transregional group' (Kita, 2010–2011, p. 359). Instead, I favour Sklair (2001), who suggests that to be truly transnational, an entity needs to be able to cross borders without deriving power from any state (2001, p. 2). Although the OECD loosely falls within this definition, it is still informed by state practices, thus challenging its ability to act as an autonomous overseeing organisation. The OECD would, then, in my opinion, be better characterised as being inter- or at least intra-national in scope. Even if we are to be persuaded by the potential transnational nature of the OECD, the reach of the entity is limited. Some statistics would suggest that non-OECD countries are attracting an increasing share of world investment, which coupled with the recent financial crisis underpins fears of capital flight from OECD countries (OECD Economic Outlook, 2015, p. 7). This symptom of dependence as outlined in Section 2.5 does constrain the effectiveness of regulations, enforcement and sanctions on MNCs, even at OECD level. The bland nature of the language in the OECD guidelines as they relate to the NCPs also fails to impress:

> The NCP is a government office responsible for encouraging observance of the guidelines in a national context and for ensuring that the guidelines are well known and understood by national business communities and by other interested parties. ... When issues arise in relation to specific instances of business conduct, the NCP is expected to help resolve them. (2011 Update on the OECD Guidelines for Multinational Enterprises)

This does not suggest that punitive sanctions should in this instance be a failure to comply with the requirements of this particular code. The discretion levied at individual governments in implementing the NCP supports the 'intra-state' as opposed to transregional nature of the OECD (National Contact Points for the OECD Guidelines for Multinational Enterprises). Again, the government as a stakeholder should be able to direct CSR to comply with the OECD guidelines. In its role as a gatekeeper, government should be able to ensure that the CSR policy proposed is valuable to the community that the government represents. But a government weakened by dependence on capital may be less likely to utilise the discretion levied at individual governments to be proactive in directing best practice.

Going beyond even international codes and standards, MNCs' self-regulation has been cited as a means to alleviate fears of capital flight (Backer, 2007). Although MNCs increasingly accept a responsibility for social change, social issues and CSR practice, the sheer global reach of MNCs and MNC practice necessitates a consideration of a potential crisis of accountability if self-regulation were to be the only enforcement mechanism (Hackett, 2012). Indeed, recent reform in the US in particular would suggest that self-regulation has been diminished in a reactionary reform of the financial sector (which typically advocated self-regulation) (Omarova, 2010–2011). Historically, there has always been an inclination to attack the US model of self-regulation (McKenna, 1983; Coffee and Sale, 2009; Fisch, 2009). (These articles are best read in tandem as Fisch extends the analysis of Coffee and Sale.) More recently, the rationale for criticism on the US system has stemmed from the financial crisis, which rose through the US system and was spread then to other countries via US-based financial intermediaries. This crisis has shown that the market is no longer the self-correcting system that it was thought to be in the 1980s and that the idea of securities regulation sitting outside broader financial regulation does not necessarily create an ideal environment for business transactions. Perhaps the criticism then of the US model of self-regulation is well founded; on the other hand, it may be that the scale of the financial crisis was required to clearly identify once and for all that deregulation should no longer be the presumptive policy prescription (Coffee and Sale, 2009).

Even at an international level, then, holding MNCs and the TCC to account does pose a challenge. This challenge is intensified for the weaker government: a weaker stakeholder and a weaker gatekeeper. Diverse approaches to CSR at a national level as well as the measures in place in regulating corporate behaviour all are predicated on national policy objectives and driven by a national political agenda. (See, for example, the Dodds–Frank Act; also of relevance here is Sarbanes Oxley). In the Dodd Frank Act, the power of self-regulation seems to be negated as the US attempts to reform the financial centre with a series of reforms. The problem with this reform is that it fails to recognise the increasingly global nature of the world economy, thereby limiting the effectiveness of the measures proposed (Omarova, 2010–2011). This re-emphasises the point about the state-centric approach to regulating CSR and the fact that the entities which they are regulating are not bound by territorial boundaries. However, on another level, it shows that the US is not afraid to regulate – and be innovative in their regulation. For a weaker government, the reach of Dodd Frank (regardless of criticism) is not a possibility.

Going further, it is interesting to compare the approaches to MNCs by the UK and US governments. Despite both having a similar corporate governance structure, the gap between the two jurisdictions in their approach to engaging with transnational capital has perhaps widened still further in the aftermath of the recent global financial crisis. The US has advanced the Dodds–Frank legislation, which seems to alienate MNCs from national governance infrastructure – an apparent contradiction to global trends given the power of the MNC. In contrast, the UK approach still indicates the shift towards a tertiary governance structure with David Cameron's Big Society seemingly cementing the relationship between government, business and society (see also the Public Services (Social Value) Act 2012) (Lowndes and Pratchett, 2012; Ishkanian and Szreter, 2012; McKee, 2015; Sullivan, 2012; Bach, 2012; Teasdale, Alcock and Smith, 2012). This is not to say that the US have not made shifts in this direction, with the most obvious one being the constituency statutes referenced in Chapter 1. Disparity in approach however, is not limited to the UK and the US. Compare the position of the UK and Section 172 (1) (d) of the 2006 Companies Act, where a director of a company is obliged to consider 'the impact of the company's operations on the community and the environment' with the Irish position on CSR – there was a provision in the Companies Consolidation and Reform Bill 2011 regarding director's duties. This is Section 222 (3) (a), where it suggests that the director has a duty to '[draw up] a statement ... setting out the company's policies (that in the director's opinion, are appropriate to the company) respecting compliance by the company with the relevant obligations' (see also s. 223 Companies Act 2014). Although this is not in relation to CSR, it is included to highlight regional diversity in issues under the umbrella of corporate governance. The UK imposes a *positive obligation* on the director, whereas in the Irish provision (which interestingly is a watered-down version of proposed (and rejected) section 45 of the Companies (Auditing and Accounting) Act 2003), inclusion is at the *discretion* of the director.

Guidelines and codes in the area of CSR allow for national discretion, and it is a discretion that has allowed for some refinement of CSR practice in different jurisdictions. Studies note that EU member states, for example, organise their approaches to CSR in very different ways, citing both institutionalised approaches and decentralised approaches (Berger, Steurer, Konrad and Martinuzzi, 2007). This same study also notes the diverging national interests concluding that 'CSR is a politically contested topic, and actual CSR policies are determined by the socio-political history of a country as well as by government majorities (and related ideologies)' (Berger et al., 2007). In the UK, the guidelines have been supplemented by the Business in the Community organisation together with a new company-law requirement (s. 172 (1) (d) Companies Act 2006), ensuring that directors take the needs and requirements of stakeholders into account when making decisions (BitC, www.bitc.org.uk).

I have previously referenced Chimni and his work on capitalism as a divided self and society (Chimni, 2007, p. 505 in Hackett, 2012). As I interpret this, then, governments cannot comfortably *regulate* capital, operating through the TCC on social issues. Whereas they may not be able to effectively regulate, governments should ideally be able to inform or direct capital on best practice to ensure that they are protecting their constituents. Approaches to regulation are still firmly grounded in national and international approaches. If we have accepted a new hierarchy of leadership, as outlined in Chapter 3 of this piece, there is surely a requirement for this leadership to assume responsibility for filling the democratic deficit and aligning government approaches to CSR to a globally recognised standard. However, while having notable limitations, such as the need to have a CSR policy tailored to the particular needs of the region, the idea of a transnational standard would help solve a lot of the concerns about national CSR standards and capital flight.

Further, there is a relationship between responsibility and accountability. Corporations (and by extension the TCC) have a responsibility to stakeholders beyond shareholders and society generally. This has been discussed at length in this book. This responsibility is tied in with the shifting focus of the firm from short-term profit maximisation to a more long-term engagement. It is also related to the shifts in governance structures; globalisation has precipitated the rise of the MNC and the corresponding decline in global power of state governments. The responsibilities of the firm are in part articulated in the MNC's CSR policy. The role of the government is then to hold the MNC to account where it fails to meet its responsibilities. Acting as a quasi-gatekeeper, as this chapter has suggested throughout, the government is encouraging the MNC to remain focused on the long-term benefits of the firm (and as such an engagement with societal issues) and not to be distracted by the thrill of short-term profit maximisation. In the same way that MNC responsibilities can be said to be articulated through CSR policies, the government's accountability mechanisms lie in the various laws and regulations in place to ensure that MNCs meet their responsibilities. These standards are subjective, ranging from the constituency statutes in the US and legal obligations under statute in the UK (e.g. s. 172 (1) (d), Companies Act 2006) to suggestions of best practices (BitC, www.bitc.org.uk). Regardless of the subjectivity of these accountability mechanisms, they do provide national governments with an individual means to ensure that MNCs meet their responsibilities.

However, as this book has noted, the global market does not operate within a vacuum. In an ideal world, governments *can* influence and *are* influenced by the MNC in their status as external stakeholders. As the recent financial crisis has demonstrated, the MNC is in control, and when faced with crisis, governments do feel the full force – due to a dependence on capital generated by MNCs for employment, services and so on. Therefore, government still faces the challenge of engaging with MNCs within a system dependent on MNCs for growth, prosperity and other development. If a government is dependent on MNC investment for development, how effective can their accountability mechanisms really be? The borderless nature of trade and the idea outlined in Chapter 3 about the TCC having no loyalty to a country or culture does add to concerns over the effectiveness of accountability mechanisms. The power of CSR, if harnessed correctly, could assist development, which in turn could alleviate the systems of dependency. However, if the TCC has no loyalty beyond profit maximisation, some additional influence needs to be there to direct the CSR policies of MNCs. This would be most successfully achieved through a robust regulatory regime – but as we have seen throughout this book, the states that would benefit most from this (i.e. the most dependent (typically, small open economies)) are those that are least likely to be able to implement it. In theory, the idea of hard law requirements would ensure that the MNC *had* to abide by commitments to the social life of the corporation beyond profit accumulation. This is explored in Chapter 5 in greater detail, but suffice to say, the countries which have had relative success in this regard (at a national level) are those which were traditionally *not* dependent or within a modified dependence, considerably *less* dependent than others given their historical development. This makes them more effective at bargaining with capital (discussed in Chapter 5) as many of the infrastructures for regulating capital, together with an established trading base, such as the FTSE and so on, are well established, have a solid reputation and are deemed 'safe' for investors. They are the most effective external stakeholders among governments. Taking a hard law approach, or indeed adopting a more robust regulatory stance on scrutinising MNC behaviour, would ensure that state governments, in their capacity as external stakeholders could influence or shape MNC activity within their borders. The real loser here, however, is the more dependent state/government, both in terms of their effectiveness as an external stakeholder and what they can cede from capital investment. Their dependence on investment by MNCs for growth may mean that national governments in small open economies are resigned to investment solely for jobs. That is the nature of capitalism, and the result of this would mean that the desire for investment overrides any national commitment to innovate on CSR regulation.

4.7 Conclusion

As an external stakeholder, or indeed a gatekeeper, government should be able to direct the CSR activities of an MNC to ensure that it protects the interests of stakeholders – facilitating sustainable business practice but also providing a valuable CSR landscape. CSR if properly articulated, implemented and practised could be a useful tool in developing a region and alleviating the symptoms of a modified dependence on capital. However, for CSR to be this effective, government needs to be a robust stakeholder. Whereas this is possible for some states – and, as Chapter 1 noted, the developments in the UK CSR landscape have been much lauded – it is not possible for all, due to an historical as well as modified dependence together with issues such as population size and natural resources. Whereas some initiatives do exist at an international level, these are still to be implemented and enforced at a national level. The weaker government – that is, the government in a small, open and dependent economy – cannot rely on international guidelines to strengthen their position as a stakeholder. Government initiatives are not the only means of engaging with business CSR activities. The next chapter considers how CSR is shaped at an international and European level and how this supra-engagement with business can surpass the symptoms of national dependence on capital as articulated throughout this book.

5

Regulating CSR: A Precursor to 'Complete' Globalisation

5.1 Introduction

This chapter posits that in an ideal world, regulation of CSR policy would alleviate many issues. Although the idea of regulating CSR seems paradoxical in nature, the evolution of CSR is such that there is an ideological shift with regard to CSR quasi-regulation in some jurisdictions – for example, in the constituency statutes in the US (state level); s. 172 of the Companies Act 2006 in the UK; s. 223 of the Companies Act 2014 in Ireland; and, perhaps most far reaching, s. 135 Companies Act 2013 in India. Regulation would be ideal to ensure that true 'development' occurs beyond dependence on capital investment. It would also ensure that governments' value as an external stakeholder is realised and, indeed, cement their role within a more globalised market system. However, the challenge lies in the economic climate in which we are currently situated. Not only do states need development via CSR, but also injections of investment are paramount to ensuring growth. This chapter makes the argument that faced with a choice, national governments are less likely to enforce a mandatory CSR agenda if it means losing out on capital investment. Perhaps the solution lies elsewhere.

Suggesting that the current trend towards a quasi-regulation of CSR is at state level (and rather inward facing), this chapter poses that, despite the benefits that a dedicated CSR policy could bring to nation states, it is unlikely that this would occur given the nature of state dependence and the shifting market structures and relationships today. It proposes an alternative for dependent states, in Europe at least. Suggesting that a prime factor in directing CSR is potential consumer base, the chapter notes the inability of some economies to strive for long-term investment due to the limitations in population size. By proposing that CSR be legislated upon from a federal level (i.e. the EU), the chapter considers that the sheer size of the potential consumer base in the EU should ensure that the TCC would be more flexible with regard to proposed CSR policies, because failure to do so could result in capital loss for the TCC.

For small open economies, dependence on foreign capital negates their ability to develop effective legislation which would both promote CSR and protect stakeholders. This will then allow for a discussion on the possibility of legislation, regarding CSR, to be implemented at a supra- or even international level.

5.2 CSR at an international level

CSR has engendered considerable debate and publication at all levels (local, national and international, as well as academia, management, business, etc.). This section is concerned with international advances in the realm of CSR – especially with the development of the OECD Guidelines for Multinational Enterprise (hereafter, the OECD guidelines) and the United Nations Guiding Principles on Business and Human Rights (Ruggie Principles). There do exist a number of 'inter'-national guidelines, proposals and so on, on CSR and sustainable development.[1] However, as with supranational directives within the EU – as will be discussed in detail below – these are, for the most part, 'voluntary' in nature. Added to this, despite the fact that there does exist a number of business codes of conduct, the OECD guidelines were (prior to the Ruggie Principles) the 'only multilaterally endorsed and comprehensive code that governments are committed to promoting' (OECD Observer Policy Brief).

5.2.1 OECD Guidelines for Multinational Enterprises

The OECD Guidelines for Multinational Enterprises are recommendations made by governments to MNCs operating within their borders. They provide the principles and standards which aim to encourage responsible business conduct in a variety of areas, including 'social' issues considered under the realm of CSR (OECD Observer Policy Brief). The OECD guidelines express the shared values of governments of countries that are the origin of most of the world's direct investment flows and that are home to most MNCs. They aim to promote the positive contributions that MNCs can make to economic, environmental and social progress (OECD Observer Policy Brief).

Adherence to the OECD guidelines is voluntary. This does not necessarily imply any less commitment, by adhering governments to encourage their observance. In fact, the OECD Observer Policy Brief suggests that

---

1 The OECD Guidelines for Multinational Enterprise, the Caux Principles for Business, Global Reporting Initiative, the Global Sullivan Principles, the Principles for Global Corporate Responsibility: Benchmark, the Social Accountability 8000 (SA8000) and the United Nations Global Compact, the UN Guiding Principles on Business and Human Rights. For detailed discussion on these, see Gordon, 2001; Leipziger, 2010; Levis, 2006.

'[t]he active system under which the Guidelines are promoted attests to the importance adhering countries give to the Guidelines' (OECD Guidelines Policy Brief, www.oecd.org/investment/mne/1903291.pdf). Of primary importance here is the existence of the NCP. The National Contact Point (NCP) is defined as 'a government office responsible for encouraging observance of the guidelines in a national context and for ensuring that the guidelines are well known and understood by the national business community and by other interested parties' (NCPs for the OECD Guidelines for Multinational Enterprises). The website continues by saying that 'The NCP gathers information on national experiences with the Guidelines, handles enquiries, discusses matters related to the Guidelines and assists in solving problems that may arise in this connection. When issues arise concerning implementation of the Guidelines in relation to specific instances of business conduct, the NCP is expected to help resolve them' (National Contact Points for the OECD Guidelines for Multinational Enterprises).

Again, however, this supposes that countries operate within a vacuum and that all countries are starting from the same position. A country's individual needs, in reality, will affect the manner in which they can 'commit' to the guidelines. Factoring in the themes of inequality and dependence that are threaded through the book's narrative (see Chapter 2 and Frank, 1967a, 1967b, 1977a, 1977b), the starting positions of each country vary considerably. This level of commitment, of course, is difficult to gauge, especially given the nonbinding nature of the OECD guidelines. However, some reports suggest that the process implemented by the OECD guidelines is simply not working (Aaronson and Reeves, 2002; Letnar Cernic, 2008; Oshionebo, 2013). Reasons for this derive from the language, which, it can be argued, is unclear on implementation (Aaronson and Reeves, 2002). In addition, criticisms have included the fact that NCPs have been created more to publicise the standard than ensure compliance (De La Cuesta González and Valor Martinez, 2004). As a result, the guidelines leave much to the discretion of governments and multinational enterprises (Aaronson and Reeves, 2002). How effective can the NCP be?

In Ireland, for example, the National Contact Point lies within the remit of the Department of Jobs, Enterprise and Investment (DJEI, www.djei.ie/en/ (note that even finding this information is incredibly difficult, suggesting a sense of inaccessibility to the information and protections offered within.)). The language concerning the National Contact Point is in fact rather vague in nature – 'one of the aims of the Committee (the OECD Investment Unit) is to promote implementation of the OECD Guidelines on Multinational Enterprise' (www.entemp.ie), and it speaks volumes that even this vague language has not made the transition from the Department of Enterprise, Trade and Investment to the new Department of

Jobs, Enterprise and Innovation. As such, the positioning of the National Contact Framework itself seems very much like an afterthought. Today, the National Contact Point in Ireland is based within the Bilateral Trade Promotions Unit, but no material has been added since July 2014. It is difficult to access any material on the OECD guidelines beyond the Bilateral Group on Trade and Corruption (www.anticorruption.ie/), suggesting that the National Contact Point, despite its potential on promoting corporate engagement with responsibility initiatives, has not really had a role to play in Irish affairs (aside from the Corrib oil dispute in 2008 which involved the Irish and Dutch NCPs and produced a report in 2010 (Final Statement of the Irish and Netherlands NCPs on the notification date 21 August 2008; Siggins, 2009). Of interest in this report is the use of language more pertinent to the UN Guidelines on Business and Human Rights, suggesting that this might be the preferred vehicle for these issues in future – that is, in the final remarks and conclusions, the report states that 'enterprises have a responsibility to respect the rights of those people on which their activities have an impact – echoing the second pillar of the UN guidelines and even citing John Ruggie on p. 16 of the report'.

More generally, in the case of the National Contact Points, the OECD Committee on International Investment and Multinational Enterprises (CIME) is charged with the role of overseeing the actions of the National Contact Points. Yet, given the nature of the guidelines (voluntary), the CIME is precluded from acting as a judicial or quas-judicial body (OECD Guidelines Policy Brief, www.oecd.org/investment/mne/1903291.pdf p. 4). What this presupposes, therefore, is that the National Contact Points could theoretically *not* implement the OECD guidelines and yet *not* face recrimination. Again, the concern is the impact of 'light-touch' regulation, in the form of CIME, on the dependent nation. Whereas CIME possesses admirable qualities, the nonbinding nature of the OECD guidelines could limit its effectiveness, especially with regard to nations dependent on an influx of capital and governments striving, particularly in the current global climate, to retain the said capital.[2] Yet another point of note, with regard to this lack of enforcement from the OECD, is the potential difficulty of such 'voluntary' international guidelines successfully and effectively permeating national economies. Especially given the more volatile nature of the global

2 Also of relevance (if only on a tangential point) is the role of NGOs, the Business and Industry Advisory Committee, and the Trade Union Advisory Committee. Although not pertinent to the discussion at hand, it is important to recognise that because the OECD Guidelines are addressed to enterprises, business and labour, it is crucial to acknowledge their consultative role to the CIME. The degree of their effectiveness, however, is limited, once more, by the voluntary nature of the guidelines, the limitations in the role of the CIME and the fact that national governments are allowed to be flexible in their approach to the National Contact Points.

economy after the financial crisis, it is perhaps plausible to suggest that implementing voluntary codes – which may or may not disenchant capital investment – may not be considered of primary importance (in general, see Gordon, 2001; Letnar Cernic, 2008; Schuler, 2010).

What does this mean then for CSR? CSR is by its nature voluntary and a form of self-regulation by the particular MNC (albeit with some shaping from industry standards). However, as a later section (Section 5.4) discusses, for the dependent state – as defined in Chapter 2 – a 'voluntary' approach to CSR will not inspire development in a manner best suited to the nation's needs and requirements. What may then be required is a change in the thinking around CSR – what it means, what it contributes and how it is managed within the MNC, the industry and the area in which the business operates. In changing the thinking, there should be a move away from the company-defined CSR contribution to something more formal with a regulatory undertone. Of course, as will be discussed later, the challenge of dependence limits the potential of any such regulation at a national level, and so, it may be that EU or global-level regulation is required. With the likes of the OECD guidelines, their potential to assist dependent states in driving a robust CSR agenda is restrained by implementation failures and the failure to challenge those implementation failures.

The limitations of CSR as an inspiration for development is accentuated by the vagueness of language used by MNCs, which is grounded in a Public Relations exercise rather than a concrete desire to do good. Looking at a small, open and dependent state like Ireland, you can see this vagueness emerge in communications from MNCs based in the region: for example, 'Building a Legacy for Good' (Dell); 'AIB made good progress on energy and environmental issues in 2014' (Allied Irish Bank). If CSR is allowed to develop at the discretion of governments and MNCs, it would appear that the dependent nation would lose out. If, as Aaronson and Reeves (2002) claims, the US has done virtually nothing to implement the OECD guidelines, for example, without recrimination, what hope is there for a dependent nation (see also Francoise, 2007)? The failure to initiate specific rules and procedures enables compromises to be ceded in order that capital will remain within a nation's borders. For dependent nations usually characterised as small open economies, such as Ireland, 'commitment' to the guidelines is perhaps dependent on the inclinations of foreign capital. Commitment to the guidelines can perhaps succeed and be implemented only insofar as it does not interfere with or compromise the wishes of foreign capital. Ultimately, it is the dependent nation state that is missing out. Unable to implement effectively, let alone enforce, legislation, the nation is further acquiescing to the demands of capital, and what ensues is yet deeper stagnation of development potential. Recently, another vehicle to assist in the direction of CSR has emerged in the shape of the United Nations Principles on Business and Human Rights (the Ruggie Principles).

5.2.2 United Nations Principles on Business and Human Rights (the 'Ruggie' Principles)

This book has, from the outset, bemoaned the global system as it exists today due to the rising power of the MNC but also the corresponding diminishing of power of the government. This has, as outlined in Chapter 4 (Section 4.5), led to a struggle in achieving the balance between the responsibilities owed by the MNC to its stakeholders and the government's role in holding MNCs to account should they fail to meet those responsibilities. The reliance of governments on MNC investment for development (albeit dependent) within their borders compromised the capacity of the state's ability to hold MNCs to account. As some states were, and continue to be, more powerful than others – the extent to which rights are enforced is subjective, due in part to the inadequacy of the state-centric system – a theme that has permeated this book.

At an international level, little had been achieved in attempting to regulate MNCs' contribution to society – in particular, there has been little attempt to make MNCs more socially responsible. Initial attempts were made with the UN Norms on the Responsibilities of Transnational Corporations and Other Business Enterprises with regard to Human Rights (2003 UN Norms). These norms recognised the MNC as being an 'organ of society' '[r]ecognizing that even though States have the primary responsibility to promote, secure the fulfilment of, respect, ensure respect of and protect human rights, transnational corporations and other business enterprises, as organs of society, are also responsible for promoting and securing the human rights set forth in the Universal Declaration of Human Rights' (Preamble, 2003). Had these remained, the scope for CSR development and indeed alleviating the symptoms of dependency would have been boundless. However, there was a huge backlash from business, which delimited the potential of the Norms to make any meaningful change. This backlash again highlights the apparent legal vacuum in which MNCs operate and the lack of accountability mechanisms for failing to meet their responsibilities, the desire for self-regulation of CSR and the disproportionate power that MNCs have over nation-state governments – perhaps even extending as far as the UN.

After the attempts in the Norms, embedding corporate responsibilities within international law has largely been the task of the United Nation's Guiding Principles on Business and Human Rights (Ruggie Principles, 2011). These principles are said to build on the 2003 Norms and advocate a three-pillar approach: protecting human rights (the state duty to protect human rights); respecting rights (the corporate responsibility to respect human rights); and remedies (the provision of remedies where business have not met their responsibilities or where states have failed in their duty to protect human rights). As such, the Ruggie principles, as they have come to be known, have sought to achieve a common ground between corporate responsibilities and state obligations – in a way attempting to bridge the gap outlined in Chapter 4. In seeking to do so, they have diluted the strength of the principles, with the winners undoubtedly being the MNCs. In a sense, the language of the Ruggie Principles, has managed to dilute human rights' protections to market level language, making the Principles more akin to the language of MNC CSR ideology. Specifically, the use of *should* over *must* or *shall* suggests that the Principles (and by extension human rights) are something that can simply be ignored should more pressing issues come to the fore. It also shows how rights have been diluted at UN level since the abandoned Norms. For example, Principle 11 (Ruggie Principles, 2011) states that 'Business Enterprises should respect human rights' can be contrasted with the equivalent part of the Norms, which states that:

> [t]ransnational corporations and other business enterprises *shall* respect economic, social and cultural rights as well as civil and political rights and contribute to their realization, in particular the rights to development, adequate food and drinking water, the highest attainable standard of physical and mental health, adequate housing, privacy, education, freedom of thought, conscience, and religion and freedom of opinion and expression, and shall refrain from actions which obstruct or impede the realization of those rights. (UN Norms, E, 12)

In any criticism of Ruggie is the use of the NCP to enforce the principles. Above, the limitations of the NCP are explored in great detail. With a flawed enforcement mechanism to begin with, it is important to note again that the individual needs of a state will impact on the manner in which they are able to commit to the deadlines. This is difficult to gauge, but in short, the value of the NCP is in publicising the standard, not in its enforcement capacity (Aaronson and Reeves, 2002). In situating the principles within the framework of the NCP, the Ruggie Principles have diluted the potential of the Principles themselves. Designed with compromise in mind, the Ruggie Principles have stagnated the potential of the discourse in this area and again highlighted the vacuum in which corporations operate along with the worrying limitations of mechanisms for accountability. In sum, when the Ruggie Principles were unveiled in 2011, they were heralded as the future – the future potential for holding states and corporate entities accountable.

They looked not just at *why* states should ensure corporate responsibility for human rights, but also in the operational principles, provided some guidelines about *how* this could be achieved. But as with a lot of the discussion throughout this book, much depends on the strength of the government. The Ruggie Principles are only as effective as the particular national government allows them to be. Since the adoption of the Principles, the excitement for their potential within civil society seems to have waned considerably. As with other initiatives in this area, it seems as though, despite public commitments and grand gestures, effective implementation of Ruggie and development beyond Ruggie, is not a key issue for national governments or indeed the EU. Instead, what remains is the rhetoric of responsibility and an insufficient and poorly planned implementation/enforcement system, which in itself relies on a deeply flawed enforcement initiative from yet another imperfect international instrument.

What this section endeavoured to explore was the ability (or inability) of international codes and principles to inspire, or foster, CSR. Considering that the OECD Guidelines for Multinational Enterprises and the UN Guiding Principles on Business and Human Rights are the only guidelines/principles that take into account government and government roles within the CSR spectrum, it is important to discuss their value within any broader discussion of state–MNC relations, CSR and development. While recognising the role of the OECD guidelines at an international level, the voluntary nature of the guidelines, the vague language with regard to its implementation and the fact that it does not include non-OECD nations suggest that at the minute these guidelines are insufficient in incorporating CSR issues, without being supplemented by various codes and practices at supranational and domestic level. With regard to the Ruggie Principles, similar issues arise; the market language of the principles, the voluntary nature, the vagueness in language and the ambiguity around enforcement and the provision of remedy all suggest a ceding to capital as opposed to a genuine attempt to create a partnership between state and corporations in fostering, directing and accounting for CSR protections. If the UN is seen to be compromising on this issue, what hope can there be for state-level initiatives? The next section therefore considers CSR at an EU level. This addresses the aims and objectives of current EU CSR policy as well as some of the problems – especially for more dependent states – in existing policies and recommendations.

5.3 CSR on a European level

CSR within the EU has prompted a number of recent developments. In 2001, the European Commission (EC) published its Green Paper 'Promoting a European Framework for Corporate Social Responsibility'

(Commission of the European Communities (CEC), COM (2001) 366 final). In this, the EC addressed all the social actors – companies, governments, social organisations and so on – to highlight the need for and the importance of CSR (Lozano, Albareda and Ysa, 2008, p. 51). The EC sought to 'promote and energise CSR in the framework of political action, introducing the issue into government agenda, in accordance with the Community policies and international standards' (Lozano et al., 2008, p. 52). It is within this context that the European approach to CSR can be understood. CSR within the EU seems to be not so much an end in itself, but more a means to achieving one of the strategic objectives established in the final declaration of the Lisbon European Council (2000), wherein the EU aimed to, by 2010, 'become the most competitive and dynamic knowledge-based economy in the world, capable of sustainable growth with more and more better jobs and greater social cohesion' (Report of the Presidency Conclusions of the Lisbon European Council 23 & 24 March 2000: www.europarl.europa.eu/summits/lis1_en.htm#b). This objective can be highlighted in the documents pertaining to CSR within the EU, which have been considered a response to this more pertinent, 'sustainable development' agenda (Hunt, 2003).

So, CSR in Europe is directly linked to the strategic objectives established in the final declaration of the Lisbon European Council (Report of the Presidency Conclusions of the Lisbon European Council 23 & 24 March 2000: www.europarl.europa.eu/summits/lis1_en.htm#b). Arising from this, four main publications (with two recent additions subsequent to these) dictate the path of CSR within the European Union. The first, the Green Paper 'Promoting a European Framework for Corporate Social Responsibility' (Commission of the European Communities (CEC), COM (2001) 366 final), highlights the voluntary approach to CSR as advocated by the European Union, describing it as 'a concept whereby companies decide voluntarily to contribute to a better society and cleaner environment' (COM (2001) 366 final) and 'investing "more" into human capital, the environment and the relations with stakeholders' (COM (2001) 366 final).

This approach was augmented with the publication of a communication concerning 'CSR: a business contribution to sustainable development' (Communication: COM (2002) 347 – final, Brussels) and the final report of the European Multistakeholder Forum on CSR (2004), which cemented the voluntary nature of CSR within the EU – for example, 'behaviour by business over and above legal requirement, voluntarily adopted because business deem it in their long-term best interest' (COM, 2002). Finally, the Communication, 'Implementing the Partnership for Growth and Jobs: Making Europe a Pole of Excellence on Corporate Social Responsibility' (2006), clarifies the Commission's position on CSR and establishes 'a firm political direction, which will give a new impetus for actions and serve as a basis for continued dialogue among all stakeholders' (http://eur-lex.europa.eu/LexUriServ/LexUriServ.do?uri=COM:2006:0136:FIN:en:PDF) More recently still have been the 2015 CSR forum and the communications arising from the CSR Strategy 2011–2014. The first report, 'Corporate Social Responsibility: promoting society's interests and a route to sustainable and inclusive recovery' (2013a), is very much the product of its timing. Emerging from the financial crisis (see, in particular, 22–30 inclusive, Motion for a European Parliament Resolution), it comes perhaps as no surprise that the voluntary tone of CSR remains key to the EU strategy (as well as an apparent awe of capital – see, for example, H, Motion for a European Parliament Resolution), but it does suggest concrete ideas for the application of CSR. The second report to emerge, entitled 'Corporate Social Responsibility: accountable transparent and responsible business behaviour and sustainable growth' (2013b), offers a bit more hope. Although again highlighting the voluntary nature of CSR (this time through disclosure mechanisms), it does suggest that this could be done alongside regulatory measures (point 4, Motion for a European Parliament Resolution). This could provide a lifeline for small open economies that may be incapable of driving a robust and effective CSR agenda at state level. Also of interest in this report is the adoption of a new Commission definition of CSR: 'the responsibility of enterprises for their impact on society'. This wider definition, and the explanation of the definition in the report, suggests the adoption of a Carroll-influenced approach to CSR, but it also seems aligned with the Ruggie Principles, which appear to be heavily promoted in recent EU communications on this issue. Evidence of the interrelation between the publications can be found not only in their approach to CSR (voluntary) but also in the manner in which they correspond with the Lisbon Council's desire to develop a competitive and dynamic base. However, the EU response to CSR does not exist within a vacuum: it cites the UN Global Compact, the Ruggie Principles, the ISO 26000 Guidance Standard on Social Responsibility, the ILO Tripartite Declaration of Principles concerning Multinational Enterprises on Social Policy and the OECD Guidelines for Multinational Enterprises as influences on the Commission's CSR strategy. Today the European approach to CSR is somewhat disjointed, with focus being divided among Europe 2020, Business and Human Rights, CSR reporting and Socially Responsible Public Procurement.

It is claimed that through these publications, the EC has played a fundamental role in the driving of political initiatives and strategies adopted by governments for the promotion of CSR (Lozano et al., 2008, p. 52). Its action has become 'a catalyst for government action through the promotion of a common reference framework for national CSR-related activity' (Lozano et al., 2008, p. 52). And indeed to a certain extent, this is the case. Its influence can be documented in the relatively recent peer review of EU member states' activities on CSR during 2013–2014 (note that only seven member states engaged in this process, with the seven states that engaged being states that would traditionally have been known as 'core' states within the 'traditional' dependency framework) and in the Compendium of Member States' CSR Policies (Williamson, Stampe-Knippel & Weber, 2014).

Pioneering governments within the EU, such as the UK, have consolidated EU recommendations, together with their own initiatives, in order to foster a vibrant CSR culture. The UK is arguably a global leader in the field in its approach in initiating some of the infrastructure that supports CSR, for example the manner in which it was the first country to institutionalise CSR in a governmental ministerial capacity (although this ministerial office has since been rescinded). Nonetheless, the UK has made some inroads (for more detail, refer to Chapter 1, Section 1.3.1.2) when taking into consideration the change of direction in approaches to governance to attain even a 'cosmetic' relationship with CSR if this is, indeed, what it actually is. What of the rest of the countries in the EU? Does their history in some way play a part in their CSR agenda or indeed provision of CSR at government level? Member states' individual histories may be reflected in national interpretations of the EU recommendations, specifically in the manner that those recommendations are both interpreted and realised (Lozano et al., 2009).

There are a number of issues with the CSR agenda adopted by the EU. In an endeavour to be everything for everyone, the attitude towards CSR is such that it can be adapted to the varying interpretations of the role of the firm: for example, both the Anglo 'profit-maximisation-enlightened shareholder-value' firm (Williams and Corley, 2005) and the German 'stakeholder-oriented two-tier' firm approach (Clarke and Bostock, 1997) can come within the definitions of CSR as postulated by the EC (Cernat, 2004; Steurer, 2010). This is, in turn, transcribed into the recognition of numerous approaches to fostering CSR within national boundaries. However, is the potential of an EU-wide CSR policy diminished by attempts to be all-encompassing? Although CSR policy needs to be EU wide, attempting to incorporate all interpretations of the role of the firm, for example, does diminish attempts to write legislation on CSR. However, the challenge is understandable. In the endeavour to become more competitive, there has been a significant shift towards 'light-touch' regulation. This being the case, can it be said that there is a marked shift towards *Anglo* forms of corporate governance? Although it may be too soon to make such a statement as this, it can be acknowledged that the drive towards achieving competitive superiority seems to encourage the light-touch-regulation approach favoured by Anglo models of corporate governance. Indeed, the communications coming from the EU seem to be very much grounded in this corporate model, using market language such as 'stakeholder' to situate CSR within the broader regulatory and governance landscape. As Baker (2006, Chapter 29) notes, 'New Labour has pushed for a reconfiguration of the regional (European) ... orders in accordance with the imperatives of the Anglo-Saxon model.' On this point, the status quo has prevailed, with both the Con-Lib Dem coalition government and the now Conservative government not diverging from this approach.

'Light-touch' approaches to regulation within the EU can be evidenced in the voluntary nature of CSR policies. Ascribing generally to deregulation (although the most recent European Parliament Communication (2013b) suggests that regulating CSR activities may become an issue in the future) in order to promote competitiveness may have the side-effect of inducing even deeper ingrained dependence among some member states – namely the small open economies that are member states, such as Ireland. This is a disadvantage of the European approach to CSR, and one that will be referenced in Sections 5.4 and 5.5. Even the ambiguous language in the 2013b communication from the European Parliament makes it unclear whether any supplementary CSR regulation is to be state or EU level ('4. Believes that the debate on CSR should be placed in a broader setting which, while ensuring that CSR remains primarily a voluntary policy, also leaves room for a dialogue on regulatory measures whenever appropriate').

Existing CSR recommendations within the EU are a means to achieving the 'dynamic' and 'competitive' regime, as outlined in the Lisbon objectives (Report of the Presidency Conclusions of the Lisbon European Council, 2000). What this in turn suggests is that perhaps CSR is only perceived as a way of attaining competitiveness through 'light-touch' regulation and, as a result, could indicate a lack of commitment to the concept beyond a means for accomplishing sustainable development. If this is the case, can the EU's drive for CSR be taken seriously? Or can the criteria of an EU CSR scheme be met in a 'tick-box' manner?

5.4 The domestic approach to CSR: from a small open economy perspective

The 'Corporate Responsibility: accountable, transparent and responsible business behaviour' (2013b) report does suggest that the characterisation of CSR as voluntary could be accompanied by regulatory measures. As noted in the previous section, a vagueness surrounds whether these regulatory measures should stem from the EU or national level. Disparity exists within the EU both in terms of governance and in the perceived dependence of member states on capital. These two measures of disparity suggest that national responses to requirements such as that potentially outlined in the 2013(b) report may differ quite markedly. The UK is considered a global leader in promoting CSR both historically (the concept evolved there along with in the US) and in practice. The UK is an advocate of the business-in-the-community (BitC) model. It is not, however, the only member state that ascribes to this model. The other advocate of the BitC approach is Ireland, a small open economy that has an ingrained dependence on capital. With similar approaches to *characterising* CSR (and indeed their corporate governance systems) does the difference in size and extent of dependence have any impact on how they *experience* CSR?

Chapter 1 (Section 1.3.1.2) considered the character of CSR in the UK today. In advancing the 'Third Way', the accession of the New Labour government has inspired a new era of government and business interaction, which has culminated in the recognition of the UK as a global leader in CSR (Ward and Smith, 2006; Giddens, 1998, 1999, 2001, 2013). Ministerial advances were made to CSR under New Labour. Although this has waned considerably, with rhetoric such as 'Big Society' becoming more the norm under the Conservative government (notably this initiative has been disbanded under the Conservative government, despite being a Conservative policy), under the command of BitC, social issues are considered by welfare state services and business alike. The profile of the 'Third Way' has also been enhanced by improvements in disclosure legislation, among other things. (Moon, 2004; Companies Act 2006; UKLA's Disclosure and Transparency Rules; etc.). Later, this chapter considers the practical implications for the UK governance structure and whether disclosure legislation is a means for companies to engage with CSR, rather than having a rules-based system like the US.

Unlike the UK, Ireland has not, as yet, supplemented the BitC model with 'discretionary' legislation or indeed situated the CSR brief specifically within any government policy or agenda. Some recent attempts have been made to articulate the Irish position on CSR, with the publication of 'Good for Business, Good for the Community: Ireland's National Plan on Corporate Social Responsibility 2014–2016' (2014). This publication was a response to the EU peer review of member-states' CSR activities. It echoes the EU requirements for CSR and emphasises the importance of voluntary approaches to CSR (notably, the continued adoption of the CSR definition in the EC Green Paper (2000) – even though this had been changed in 2013 by the EU). Where it discusses national legislation on CSR, this is extremely vague, noting things like 'employment legislation' and 'health and safety legislation' (p. 7). In sum, it enhances the argument throughout this book that Irish dependence on foreign capital is such that innovation is limited to the retention of capital, as opposed to fostering social development beyond the requirements of standard legislation (i.e. employment law, health and safety law, etc.). The Irish government can never implement legislation in the field of CSR under the current status quo. Ireland, like the UK, does follow the BitC model, yet whether or not BitC can meet Irish requirements from CSR without supplementary legislation or ambitious policy changes (i.e. beyond the core EU requirements) is questionable. The somewhat stagnant approach to CSR within Ireland is attributable in part to the failures of the EU system to enforce mandatory CSR. However, there is a solution of sorts to the Irish problem, but this would mean changing the very ethos of the CSR approach within the EU.

Irish innovation is limited to the retention of capital, as opposed to the long-term development of the country via capital. Furthermore, evidence suggests that facing the prospect of capital relocation, the Irish government has, in the past, backed down rather than lose capital (for example, the DCS, proposed section 45 of the Companies (Auditing and Accounting) Act 2003 – see fn.2 and Section 3.5). This does not present as a positive approach to CSR.

What the DCS highlighted was the inability of the Irish government to effectively implement regulatory policy, due to fears of business relocation and capital flight. The DCS showed that Ireland is dependent on inward FDI (for a general discussion, see Conroy, 2009). The response to the DCS served to emphasise Irish dependence and emphasise the power that capital and the retention of capital has on the Irish government. It appears unlikely that the Irish government will pursue a robust CSR legislative framework due to dependence. It is not that Ireland does not *wish* to innovate; it systematically cannot. This is the legacy of dependence, a legacy that was emphasised in the fallout from the DCS. Innovation is limited to that which is the design of the MNCs operating in Ireland. Irish concerns are limited to strategically 'keeping' capital without intense regulation, among other things.

If legislation at domestic level is not currently an option, due to Irish dependence on foreign capital, how is CSR promoted in Ireland? The answer lies in the Irish BitC model. Is 'business-in-the-community Ireland' the best approach to CSR for a small open economy? Or is it merely the easiest method of submitting to the EU plans for CSR? This is not to say that there have been no articulations of CSR in Ireland. Socially responsible investment (SRI) is pursued in a number of areas, such as the National Pension Reserve Fund (www.nprf.ie/ResponsibleInvesting/responsibleInvesting.htm). However, SRI is more of a pre-empting of CSR in the manner in which it fosters responsible practice (Sparkes and Cowton, 2004). It is a starting point, but with Irish dependence on foreign capital, the practical reality of SRI evolving into an effective CSR policy for a state remains unlikely.

The concept of the BitC model to which Ireland subscribes refers to the way that governments and societies understand the role of enterprise in society, especially with regard to the resolution of social challenges and the part played by business in community development (Lozano et al., 2008). Lozano et al. acknowledge nine key elements of this model, ranging from the use of CSR to solve the problems of social governance, to support for social-action initiatives by enterprise through employee volunteering and secondment of staff.

The key elements of the BitC model are what follows: the promotion of CSR from government-originated programmes to solve problems of social governance in the face of economic crisis; CSR linked to the involvement of enterprise in the development of society: job creation schemes, social cohesion and so on; the direct link between CSR and sustainable development (which is broadly reflective of the EU rhetoric on CSR); contributions from corporations to sustainable development; the importance of pressure exerted by civil society on the role of business in relation to sustainable development; the importance of public–private partnerships; the partnership relations between local government and companies on concrete projects; public initiatives; non-interventionism; the importance of voluntary initiative and corporate self-regulation; support for social-action initiatives by enterprise: employee volunteering and secondment of staff, as well as a policy of facilitating and soft interventions, tax subsidies and business initiatives (Lozano et al., 2008, p. 93; in general, see Matten and Moon, 2008; Jenkins, 2006).

Within BitC, governments operate under the 'voluntary' approach to CSR, thus echoing the communications coming from the EU and from the global arena. But that is not to say that the BitC model precludes a robust CSR landscape. As considered in Chapter 1 (Section 1.3.1.2), the UK government is moulding the BitC model and supplementing it with advances in soft and more direct legislation (Lozano et al., 2008, pp. 93–114) creating a more focused approach to CSR engagement. This, in total, is augmenting the benefits of the BitC system to the point where the UK model is considered to have 'comparatively well-developed and institutionalised CSR' standards (Moon, 2004). Ireland has not displayed the same enthusiasm for complementing the pre-existing BitC model with legislation and the centralisation of services (2008, pp. 93–114). The Irish government is traditionally viewed as being *particularly* welcoming to the voluntary CSR approach (Lozano et al., 2008). Whereas the Irish government is, and has been, supportive of EU initiatives on CSR (such as the EC's Green Paper attaining the objectives outlined by the Lisbon European Council), it is less enthusiastic in developing and enforcing a national CSR framework beyond the requirements of the EU recommendations as most recently outlined in the 'Good for Business, Good for the Community' publication (2014). This again can be attributed to the systematic failures in the Irish case. Irish dependence on capital generated by MNCs has inhibited, or perhaps even prohibited, the potential for robust and innovative CSR legislation/regulation.

Therefore, is it the case that CSR in Ireland is restricted to what those multinational corporations (MNCs) operating within its borders will permit? What then is the approach to CSR adopted by the BitC Ireland model? BitC advocates for the corporate community involvement (CCI) mechanism for fostering CSR in Ireland. It has been an appropriate expression of CSR in Ireland to date due to the manner in which it encourages interaction with local community and input from governmental bodies. A successful CCI programme *could* help combat the problems faced in specific regions which can be attributed to Irish dependence on foreign capital, a dependence discussed in detail in Chapter 2. Ireland's needs are particular. Ireland does not present with the same requirements as many 'underdeveloped regions', in that it is an example of a comparatively wealthy yet dependent state. Therefore, her needs are more akin to issues such as ensuring job security – especially in the trend towards relocation to low-cost economies and regional development – that is, the manner in which areas of Ireland remain rather underdeveloped, with little industrial or financial capital investment – such as the west and northwest. For example, the need to develop local business in such areas could perhaps be aided by technical scholarships in education, software donations to local schools and financial advice being offered to those interested in starting up their own business. This is not uncommon. If we look at Intel and the way in which in the past they have provided science education to elementary and high school students in the Philippines, together with the donation of computers and software, then the potential for such CSR policies in Ireland can be best understood (Hess, Rogovsky and Dunfee, 2002). Ireland is used here as an example of a small open economy. Dependence on foreign capital creates a unique scale of need in each nation state, a need that is framed by numerous influences, such as the historical legacy within the country, the traditional industries and so on. What these all suggest is that corporations cannot have one all-encompassing CSR policy that will cater to the needs of every individual state in which the MNC operates. Instead, an approach to CSR, such as the CCI approach advocated by BitC Ireland, *would* recognise the importance of a tailored CSR policy. In so doing, the symptoms of dependence could be alleviated. But to have a tailored CCI approach, a level of negotiation between MNCs and government is required. Government, if wanting to robustly promote CSR, cannot fear repercussions from capital in forcing a required approach to CSR. This may not be possible for the small, open and dependent country. Kanter (1999) has said that firms 'view community needs as opportunities to develop ideas and demonstrate business technologies, to find and serve new markets, to solve longstanding business problems' (p. 124). It is not to say that this type of interaction with the community has a negative effect on company profits, among other things. As Moore (1995) acknowledges, working with the community could actually have a very positive effect in the manner that it raises the profile of the firm, obtains a measure of general goodwill and increases the loyalty of employees.

Turning back to dependency, this can be applied more generally and can show hypothetically how initiatives such as CCI could work to the benefit of both the MNC and the nation state. Much of the repatriation of profits in a country may come from large corporations outsourcing for parts. This will have a negative effect on that country's GDP. However, it may also have a negative effect on MNCs operating in that country. By contributing technology and training to local businesses as well as the education sector, component parts, for example, could be produced at home rather than being imported from abroad. The benefits would be threefold. First, there would be benefits to the company, with a reduction in transport costs and an increase in reputation value in the local community. With regard to reputation value in the local community, a company that is educating and training members of the community with a view to employment is going to be valued as an intricate component in the creation of a vibrant local economy. Second, benefits would be evidenced among local business through an increase in job security (although once again this job security is highly dependent on foreign capital). There would also be some benefits accrued in the development of the limited indigenous business structure, together with the fostering of relationships. Third, with regard to national benefits, by allowing some of the MNC's profits to be invested in local enterprise for parts, the 'real' story of that country's GDP could be improved due to a smaller amount of profit being repatriated. However, this impact on national development will *still* be dependent, but given the circumstances of many small open economies today, all development is likely to be dependent, and perhaps utilising this 'dependent' development in a way that will foster local business objectives may eventually inspire some non-dependent development. While the community benefits from the donation of the employee's time and talent, the company will benefit from more loyal employees, aid in recruitment and the teaching of teamwork skills to the employees (Hess, Rogovsky and Dunfee, 2002).

However, whether or not the promises of CCI are met in Ireland, for example, remains to be seen. This approach to CSR is potentially ideal for the Irish case and indeed for small open economies generally – but not without legislation promoting this process. I understand that this goes beyond the basic tenets of CSR and particularly the idea that CSR initiatives are, and should be, voluntary. This may be the case in an ideal world, but when different regions are on a different development trajectory (and under the spectre of dependence), the voluntary nature of CSR may need to be reimagined. Whereas the 'other' BitC advocate that the UK has, on the face of it, been effective in this area, it may be that the UK has merely been effective in implementing the infrastructure which supplements CSR – that is, the initial institutionalisation of CSR in a ministerial capacity (albeit this role has been subsumed into wider ministerial roles today), the drive from discretionary regulation towards more direct regulation in the shape of s. 176 (Companies Act 2006) and so on – but that the UK government's designs on CSR are cosmetic in nature.

Although the potential of s. 176 (Companies Act 2006) has not yet been realised, it does point to significant advancements in the UK's CSR landscape (Sadler and Lloyd, 2009; Wynn-Evans, 2007; Williams and Conley, 2006; Ashraf, 2012). The UK has advanced considerably since the advent of the Bullock Report (1977), wherein attempts to respond to the EU's Fifth Directive called for the harmonisation of worker participation in companies across Europe (Conlon, 1975). Of primary note here is how the Bullock Report seemed to represent the misconceptions of the interactions between state and capital. Has it been the case that the UK has become more Europeanised in the interim?[3] This is possibly so. Also of relevance is the almost global shift towards more stakeholder-oriented views of the firm, as considered in detail in Chapter 4 (Sections 4.2 and 4.3). Even in a more 'shareholder-oriented' model of the firm – as traditionally advocated in Anglo governance – there has been a marked compromise with regard to the increasing importance of the role of the stakeholder, especially the environment. This has culminated in a number of advances in the UK sphere, most notably s. 176 of the Companies Act 2006.

For the UK even to advance to this level of CSR is quite remarkable given its history as an industrialist economy (Holmes, 1986; Lord Carr, Bullock Report, cc. 181–182.) unwilling to engage in the social chapter and – as some of the arguments proposed with the advent of the Bullock Report (1977) would suggest – totally opposed to legislating on, and around, the structure of the company, rights of shareholders and so on, considering it to be 'based on false principles which are both fundamentally undemocratic and contrary to the requirements for making British industry more

3 Although perhaps not the most politically welcoming statement at the moment, some points of interest can be found in Featherstone, 2012; Favell and Reimer, 2013.

productive' (Lord Carr, Bullock Report, cc. 181). Yet, whether or not the UK government's commitment to CSR is cosmetic or a committed attempt to foster CSR within its borders is unclear. One should consider the Cadbury Report (Report of the Committee on the Financial Aspects of Corporate Governance, 1992) and specifically that '[t]he country's economy depends on the drive and efficiency of its companies. Thus the effectiveness with which their boards discharge their responsibilities determines Britain's competitive position', so we can see how the UK government's approach to CSR within corporate governance may be an attempt to accommodate capital while retaining competitiveness – the price of low regulation. Fear of disenchanting capital can further be evidenced in former Prime Minister Tony Blair's volte-face on the evolution of a 'stakeholder society' (Richards, 2000). Speaking in Singapore in 1996, Tony Blair unveiled this new political philosophy of a 'stakeholder society' (Richards, 2000). However, within a week, Tony Blair retracted his 'philosophy', watering it down to a 'slogan' stating that he was not contemplating tying companies up in red tape, bureaucracy and regulation (Sealy, Alexander and Rider, 1998, p. 69). Perhaps parallels can be drawn in the demise of the Big Society and the manner in which the government wound up the Big Society Network when problems emerged (Slocock, 2015; Wright, 2014).

What this indicates is that even within the 'model' BitC region, even a perceived 'strong', 'independent' state like the UK compromises with capital, in order to retain investment and global competitiveness. It may have been the case that the calls for a 'stakeholding society' were simply a step too far for business in the UK to contemplate, and following the media attention at the time may have contributed in part to what was, in effect, a retraction by Blair. (For instances regarding government compromise on collective bargaining in the workplace, see Wheeler, 2007. In this case, it was suggested that in attempts to provide a 'low-cost', 'low-regulation' economy, 'organised labour has seen its position undercut either by direct state intervention or by the state absenting itself as a negotiating party' (Wheeler, 2007, p. 2))

The UK's use of CSR as a bargaining tool can also be reflected in the perceived failure of the light-touch approach to corporate governance, as it is considered that 'disappointment is inevitable because procedural rules cannot control the self-serving behaviour of social and political elites' (Erturk, Froud, Johal and Williams, 2004). Is CSR, therefore, merely a way to avoid intense regulation of business behaviour and thereby thwart the UK's competitiveness on a global stage? It may be the case that disappointment is inevitable, but it is a price the UK government is willing to pay for a low-regulation, competitive model of governance. CSR may be nothing more than a concession – a window-dressing exercise that hides the inadequacies of the corporate governance regime in the UK. Regardless of how one considers the reasoning for the UK's readjustments of political views on corporate issues, the fact remains that the UK has – for whatever reason – 'comparatively well-developed and institutionalised CSR structures' (Moon, 2004). Even if this is an attempt to maintain public acquiesce to the capitalist regime, or to ensure competitiveness, it remains significantly more than small open economies like Ireland has achieved or is likely to achieve.

This may be because the UK has developed legislation in order to supplement the BitC model. Ireland has not much in this regard. Furthermore, the systematic failures of the Irish system, as a result of a more ingrained dependence, suggest that Ireland could be exploited because of its inability to implement and enforce an effective CSR policy. As the last section considered, there is a shift in Europe towards the Anglo 'light-touch' system of regulation. By being based in Ireland and benefiting from its dependence on capital investment, will engagement with CSR projects serve merely as a cosmetic exercise for MNCs in order to cash in on the European light-touch regime and the corresponding lack of national requirements? It may be the case that CSR projects established via BitC Ireland serve to meet the demands of European business at this moment in time.

This is not to say that Ireland has not benefited from European integration. Indeed, Ireland's status as the gateway to Europe, the only English-speaking economy in the Eurozone and so on, has favourably advanced the Irish economy. However, the question remains as to whether Ireland is prepared – or even able – to embark on the next stage of this integration – that of a deeper commitment to CSR policy. Such are the constraints of capital: Ireland has maximised the benefits of European integration at this stage (without further advances on an EU level) and must now be content with a profit-maximisation approach to the economy, as opposed to a long-term investment in community development. With this in mind, Ireland may be in an even more favourable position than other small open economies referred to throughout this book. Some general questions though do emerge relating to CSR.

Chief among these is if CSR is designed to be of long-term benefit to the corporation as well as the community, then why is there not a more committed desire to it in corporations' investing in states? Why is it reliant on goodwill from business as opposed to the realisation of the potential benefits of CSR? McBarnet (2007) addresses the benefits for business when she considers the business case for CSR, suggesting that even the poorest regions add up to a market. It is in meeting the needs of the poorest region that a profitable market can also emerge, which also suggests the role of consumers in influencing the activities of MNCs (McBarnet, 2007). McBarnet (2007) cites the Vodafone provision of services in sub-Saharan Africa as an example of providing social contract, which facilitates entrepreneurship in an area lacking adequate communications.

Why has this idea of an eye-catching, low-cost intervention, as discussed by McBarnet, not been realised in small open economies like Ireland? The answer to this question lies in the concept of the small open globalised economy. Being a small economy has disadvantages in the manner in which it attracts capital. Investing in the US or the UK – with a large potential product consumption base – would suggest the need to interrelate business with socially responsible acts. Competing for a slice of the larger economy would theoretically instigate a need for embracing the local needs and requirements, and incorporating these needs and requirements into company policy. The UK, for example, has an estimated population of 64.1m – in comparison to Ireland, for example, which has an estimated population of 4.6m. There is a significant difference, and this difference corresponds also to the potential consumer base in each nation. It is understandable, therefore, that an MNC operating in both the UK and Ireland – hypothetically speaking – would be more inclined to foster a vibrant CSR policy in the UK, due to the potential benefits in brand recognition (among other things) in accordance with the larger population. Ireland, it seems, is once again at a disadvantage. What this could also suggest is that businesses seek to operate in such states for different reasons. Within small open economies such as Ireland, short-term profit maximisation could be the main goal due to the small potential consumer base. With larger economies – like the UK – endeavouring to establish a niche in the market and in doing so compete in a much larger potential consumer base could mean a more committed desire to incorporate community demands within company policy via CSR. Ireland, it seems, is destined to dependence on capital, without gain, as the size of its consumer base is yet another potential disadvantage in ever emerging as an 'equal' with regard to CSR policy. The same can be said for small open economies generally. The limitation of the consumer base has a corresponding limitation to the capacity for CSR policy. Investment takes on a different trajectory in comparison to larger economies like the US or the UK.

Small open economies are at a systemic disadvantage in the journey towards a more robust CSR framework. Initiatives at global and EU levels are firmly grounded in the 'voluntary' nature of CSR. However, recent advances by the EU suggest that a commitment to voluntary CSR can be accompanied by stringent regulatory controls. The promise of these controls cannot be realised for many small open economies. This section, in focusing specifically on the BitC approach to CSR demonstrates the difference in success that two countries – Ireland and the UK – engaging with this model have had. The UK, in a much stronger position than Ireland with regard to dependence, has been able to supplement CSR with a number of initiatives. Whereas the motive for these initiatives is unclear, they have demonstrated a commitment on some level to CSR. It does seem, though, that the spectre of capital flight shapes the conversation around CSR and CSR potential, adding to the idea that dependence is ubiquitous, and it is the level of dependence that demonstrates the need of a region. Ireland, on the other hand, has not gone beyond the voluntary characterisation of CSR, and its experience of CSR is dictated by the initiatives coming from the EU or further afield, with the business and human rights principles appearing increasingly popular. At this point, then, initiatives for CSR do exist at global/international, EU and national levels. All initiatives are grounded in the voluntary nature of CSR. This therefore has an impact on how different states and regions experience CSR. For small, open and, by extension, dependent regions like Ireland, voluntary CSR initiatives are not sufficient to ignite a robust CSR landscape, which, if tailored effectively, could not only alleviate the symptoms of dependence but also carve the potential for development further down the line. A more hardline, mandatory approach to CSR on a national, EU or international level could promote an equality of opportunity for nation states. The question then becomes whether CSR can be effectively expressed through a mandatory policy requirement.

5.5 A Mandatory EU CSR policy – a solution for small open economies within the EU?

If small open states are so constrained by capital that they cannot attempt a legislative approach to CSR, then what is the solution? Are these states to remain hostage to capital and the restraints of the corporatist state – or is there a solution which could perhaps initiate CSR at a national level? For countries in the EU, at least, there is a plausible, albeit unlikely, solution. CSR could be initiated at a supranational level. This would entail a reworking of the fundamental basis of CSR in Europe – the question of 'voluntary' CSR. In proposing an EU-wide mandatory CSR policy, small open economies like Ireland that are within the EU may benefit. They may be able to foster a vibrant CSR policy within their own borders, which may alleviate the symptoms of dependence. Perhaps if the EU model were to be a success, an international CSR policy could be developed which would assist small open economies not in the EU. Although CSR has recently been mandated in India (s. 135, Companies Act 2013), the manner in which it has been drafted into legislation is more akin to an additional tax on the company rather than an innovative or robust attempt to foster a vibrant CSR culture. This is what a European CSR policy needs to avoid because it will not inspire development in the countries that need CSR the most and because it instead resonates with the modernisation paradigms discussed throughout Chapter 1 (Bernstein, 1971).

For small open economies like the example of Ireland used throughout this book, the inability to develop CSR legislation lies not so much in an unwillingness to engage in CSR practice but more due to the systematic limitations that prevail in the state's economic landscape. Small open economies cannot implement domestic CSR legislation. Why? Because they are dependent on foreign capital generated by MNCs. History suggests that in Ireland, innovation is punished with the threat of capital relocation. Legislation at a supranational level, eventually a global level, could solve the problem.

As noted in Section 5.3 above, European advances in the field of CSR, although admirable in many respects, have become entrenched in the idea of a 'voluntary' approach. Whereas self-regulation and the voluntary approach to CSR have many commendable qualities in the way that it encourages brand marketing – for example, an alternative viewpoint that needs to be considered. When assessing all nations as being on 'equal footing', so to speak, the voluntary approach to CSR seems the best possible option as it would operate in a competitive manner in a way which encompasses the ethos of free market capitalism. However, all nations are not equal. Furthermore, as Chapter 2 (and to an extent Chapter 3) considered, the free market approach to the economy fails to acknowledge the impact of historical nuances on development – or lack thereof – within nations. As a result of this and the implications of dependency on nation states, a voluntary approach to CSR is unacceptable for some regions.

Taking Ireland as an example, to focus on 'voluntary' CSR negates the potential of effective social development, due to fears of capital flight, as stated throughout this book. Ireland, and by extension other small open economies based in the EU, is condemned to be an acceptor of standards (e.g. Suiter, 2003) and, as a result, appears unable to innovate. With a more robust supra-level CSR policy, small open economies could have both a CSR policy and potentially a means of alleviating the symptoms of dependence. This policy, however, would arguably have to be enforced by a supra- or inter-national source. Although contravening the very essence of CSR matters, mandatory legislation is essential – on a supra- or inter-national scale – in order to inspire CSR within the dependent nation.

In order for states classified as dependent to have any hope of effective CSR policies within their borders – and in doing so perhaps attain some development potential as a result of MNC operation within the state – legislation is necessary. Domestic legislation is implausible. The fear of capital relocation is always going to outweigh the potential benefits of any mandatory domestic CSR legislation. However, for small open economies operating in the EU at least, CSR legislation at a supranational level (i.e. the European Union) could be the way forward. Why? With the EU firmly on its way to attaining the 'dynamic' and 'competitive' trading bloc

(Report of the Presidency Conclusions of the Lisbon European Council), arguably MNCs will still strive to operate in the 'largest trading bloc in the world'. The likelihood of this ceasing, in the event of EU-wide legislation, seems unlikely. For Ireland in particular, the benefits would be greater than most. Being the only English-speaking member of the Eurozone (the Eurozone being the part of Europe that uses the Euro), it could potentially attain a large number of MNCs. A mandatory requirement for CSR could, then, in effect, serve to develop areas in Ireland – such as the indigenous industrial sector – in a way which may help foster long-term development and even, therefore, alleviate some of the inadequacies arising out of Irish dependence.

For other nations, those not in the EU, it may be the case that international codes and requirements are necessary in order to initiate CSR. Considering the advances that have been made by the International Labour Organisation with regard to child labour laws (www.ilo.org/global/topics/child-labour/lang--en/index.htm), there is potential for the mandatory evolution of CSR in an international context, so as to incorporate developing nations around the world. This would be more complex than the proposal for the EU and even less likely to be instigated in the short term at least. The current 'guideline' approach to CSR, as advocated by the OECD and the more recent UN Guidelines on Business and Human Rights, has a long path to follow before it can even come close to a mandatory CSR policy. If and until processes of globalisation are completed, this idea cannot be developed efficiently. It would assume that all countries will be prepared to come together and accept this mandatory legislation for the benefit of the global economy as opposed to national economies. Whereas there are other benefits associated with EU membership (such as free movement of people, goods and capital), there are no other persuasions on the global market – aside from trade (of course within specific regions there are some initiatives such as TTIP and others). Given the historical responses of states in signing (or not) UN treaties, it is hard to imagine an economic climate where national economies as diverse as the United States, China, Venezuela and Lesotho unite to mandate that corporations contribute to social and environmental issues. If such a model were indeed adopted, it is hard to see how it would be implemented and enforced.

Although an EU-wide mandatory CSR policy represents a potential solution, the possibility of the solution being adapted is slim. It appears as though – despite the potential for the development of mandatory CSR maxims at an EU level – the demands of capitalism will be sufficient to warrant deeming any potential legislative advancement as not cost effective. Yet another reason for my scepticism on an EU-wide CSR policy is that the EU could also be considered dependent. The EU, like most globalised states and regions in the world, is dependent on globalised and financial capital. As stated in Chapter 2, the metropole of today is globalised capital, with the peripheral regions being nation states – and even, to a certain extent, federal areas such as the US and possibly the EU. However, as was also considered, there are different levels of dependence in accordance with historical nuances and even the size of the population. Above, the role of a potential consumer base was explored in the design of CSR policies within a particular region. Small open economies were yet again at a disadvantage here, especially when compared with huge states like China. The EU does not have this problem. The potential size of an EU economy would possibly make them more effective at bargaining with globalised capital for CSR. However, it may be the case that a mandatory CSR policy is simply one step too far and perhaps could compromise their competitive potential.

5.6 Conclusion

CSR has evolved considerably. Corresponding with the evolution of CSR has been the rise in power of the MNC to the extent that they are increasingly being viewed as key actors in a global governance agenda. Nation-state governments have been downgraded to gatekeepers of the MNC and to directing CSR policies as external stakeholders of the MNC. CSR is a concept embedded within the corporate governance framework and specifically the historical Anglo-American governance system. Although now extending far beyond its initial purpose as a concession to stakeholders within the shareholder-primacy corporate-governance model advocated in the UK and US in particular, its history remains relevant. Specifically, the emergence of CSR as a corporate mode of self-regulation prompts discussion of the characterisation of CSR through a corporate lens – something that was teased out in Chapters 1 and 4 in particular. With this comes the language of corporate governance and the identification of nation states within this corporate governance landscape. So, states become stakeholders – external stakeholders, advocates for an electorate who are also identified as stakeholders. By incorporating the dependency debate into discussions around CSR, what emerges is a meshing of political science, international relations and corporate governance. In identifying nation-state governments as stakeholders, the language of CSR is intertwined through the political science and international relations space that this book occupies.

CSR could be used to alleviate some of the conditions of dependence. However, this would mean a concerted effort to engage with CSR on a wider, more mandatory scale. Some influences on CSR do emerge at various levels, with the international guidelines at UN and OECD levels, EU initiatives together with national approaches. However, these influences are very much grounded in the 'voluntary' approach to CSR in a desire to maintain competitiveness. Systemic limitations further inhibit the potential for CSR to be expressed beyond voluntary self-regulation in small open economies such as Ireland. To solve this, mandatory regulation, legislation or policy is needed, ideally at a global level. This does pose many serious issues, and so, in the interim, EU-wide mandatory legislation could be a temporary solution. With the EU's huge population base, it is in a position to develop a high mandatory standard for CSR that could in theory develop the small open economies that exist within it. But dependence on capital is not restricted to nation states. Although the population base sways to the EU's favour, the shift from the current policy approaches to CSR may present too great a move for the EC. The likelihood of such a solution is improbable, due to the demands of capitalism. Any supranational legislative proposal on CSR would have to challenge the very ethos of CSR policy in the European Union – that of voluntariness. The question becomes whether or not competitiveness or CSR is more important to the development of European Union as a leading trading bloc. For the time being, it seems as though the desire to be a competitive bloc supersedes designs on CSR.

Conclusions

This book has charted the relationship between government and MNC through the CSR framework. Chapter 1 looked at the evolution of CSR, and focused primarily on developments in the UK and the US system. Reasons for this were twofold. First, it is within the Anglo-American corporate governance sphere that the CSR rhetoric emerged and developed. Second, the analysis of developments in the UK and the US provide a useful indication of leading trends in the evolution of CSR but still demonstrate how countries, loosely based within the same system, can diverge somewhat in their approach to CSR policy, practice and enforcement. The second chapter was concerned with dependency theory. In its inception, it was viewed as a means of explaining unequal relationships between the colonised and colonisers. This unequal relationship, according to the dependency theorists, led to underdevelopment, or development that was conditioned by the activities and needs of the colonisers (dependent development). This theory fell into disuse, but Chapter 2 explored its relevance when used as a lens to understand relationships between capital generated by MNCs and governments within the global system. In sum, it can be used as a way to explain the relationship between capital and state, a way to consider the disadvantages of the relationship and indeed to recognise the potential for exploitation within the relationship.

Building on this, Chapter 3 focused more on the key actor in a modified approach to dependency. Looking at the class that oversees the MNC, namely the TCC, this chapter explored the challenges for governments of nation states and particularly small open economies. With the rise in power of MNCs, there is an assumption that they have a greater responsibility to society (beyond shareholders). By typically taking on this responsibility through their CSR policy, the issue then becomes the effectiveness and the usefulness of this CSR policy. Does it benefit the nation state? Can it help alleviate the symptoms of dependency on capital? This depends on whether the MNC is held to account for failures in their responsibilities (either through general business practice or through the inadequacy of their CSR policy). As the MNC has risen in power, the nation-state government has seen its power decline. Can governments hold MNCs to account for failing to meet their corporate responsibilities? This question was explored in Chapter 4, which looks at the role of government within the CSR framework. Considering its role as an external stakeholder or perhaps even gatekeeper, the discussion then turned to how effective the government can be in directing or shaping the CSR policy of corporations, especially when considering the limitations of the power of governments within the context of a ubiquitous dependence as discussed in Chapters 2 and 3. However, national governments are not the only ones who can hold corporations to account. Chapter 5 considered the role of international codes and European developments in CSR. Noting that these all did have limitations, the chapter also explored how the legacy of a dependent state may have an impact on how they engaged with CSR. A possible solution to this was explored in the shape of EU legislation on the subject, but while it noted the promise of such a measure, it recognised that systemic limitations may prevent this from occurring and how striving for competition ultimately stymies any potential for innovation.

The conclusions drawn from this study highlight a number of key findings.

1. Our understanding of financial crises is dictated by neoliberal understandings of the market. By addressing financial crisis as a more critical theoretical evaluation of the literature, it may be argued that financial crises are a predictable trend of our market system and simply a symptom of capitalism.
2. CSR has evolved from philanthropic gifts to a more embedded approach to business and society today. The effectiveness of this more embedded approach may be dependent on the state in which the CSR policy is carried out. For example, the UK seems to have a vibrant CSR environment with a number of enforcement mechanisms and tools within the corporate governance structures to direct and enhance CSR. Other states like Ireland may not experience this partnership approach to CSR given systemic limitations. CSR can be an effective mechanism for contributing to social development within a state or region in which the corporation operates. The effectiveness of CSR is dependent on a number of factors, including the relationship between state and MNC and the level of dependence experienced by the state from MNC investment.
3. Dependency exists today. This manifests as a dependence on capital generated by MNCs, which is then invested into a particular region. Development of that state may occur, but this development is conditioned by the continued existence of that particular investment (i.e. jobs, services, infrastructure, etc.). Development is more valuable when it is true development and not dependent development. Dependent development may create the illusion of prosperity, but this is a false promise. The nature of our capitalist system means that crises are the norm. For states where

development has been dependent or conditioned by investment from MNCs, the effect of crises may be more detrimental.

4. States viewed through the lens of dependence warrants a reappraisal of apparent successes. A modified dependency provides an alternative assessment of the global system, especially with regard to the processes of globalisation and the rise of the TCC. Dependency today is a dependence on capital generated by the MNC, as controlled by the TCC. There exist 'degrees' of dependence with small open economies with a history of being colonised increasing the likelihood of states to become more 'dependent' on that capital. However, all states are dependent, and this idea can be expanded to incorporate supranational entities such as the EU. Although this dependence may not yet be as profound as that what exists in small open economies, its presence will become more ingrained as the EU strives to retain capital and remain competitive in the global market.
5. The TCC exists solely for the accumulation of capital, and as such, the individual requirements of nation states are not a conditioning factor. They matter only insomuch as they might impact on the accumulation of capital. The TCC's loyalty lies solely with capital accumulation and, as such, has no loyalty to any country, culture or people.
6. The TCC has significant power and almost ubiquitous reach. As the power of the MNC (as controlled by the TCC) has increased, the power of governments has waned considerably. The TCC has a role to play within this new governance structure in assuming responsibilities beyond profit maximisation. However, given their loyalty to capital accumulation, this will be difficult to direct and enforce. With the diminished power of government, the role of nation-state governments has been downgraded somewhat to that of an external stakeholder. The external stakeholder may have a key role in shaping company policy, but much depends on exogenous factors such as the consumer base, size of the country, natural resources and, indeed, how 'dependent' the country may be on the investments of MNCs.
7. This suggests that CSR is conditioned by the design of the TCC, with that design being solely for the accumulation of capital. MNCs may be said to have responsibilities to society (beyond shareholders), but who will hold the MNCs to account should they fail to meet their responsibilities? Small, open and dependent states are likely to be very dependent and, as such, hostages to capital because the states that most need the MNC to assume and honour responsibilities are the least likely to be able to hold them to account should they fail to do so. Although some guidance may exist at an international (OECD Guidelines, Ruggie Principles, etc.) and federal level, these still fall within

the voluntary rhetoric that continues to inform discussions on CSR. For CSR to be effective and for it to alleviate some of the conditions of dependence, legislation is needed. This legislation cannot come from a domestic level, because again, dependent states will be both unable and unwilling to develop, implement and enforce such legislation. Legislation needs to come initially from an EU level, ensuring continuity across member states. Given the size of the trading bloc, it is less likely that MNCs will withdraw completely from the region. However, this is unlikely to happen. The EU is still to an extent dependent on capital generated by MNCs. Given the diverse range of and expressions around CSR within the EU, it would be extremely difficult to impose a harmonised legislative approach to CSR within the region. Small open economies are resigned to the cyclical nature of the global financial system and are increasingly conditioned to accept and welcome any investment by MNCs regardless of the detrimental impact that this might have on the long-term economic health of the region. Development continues to underdevelop, and it will continue to do so. Investment overrides innovation. Profits before people. Global capitalism has mutated beyond state control, and future generations will be resigned to the whim of the TCC, a collective that is not loyal to people, countries or cultures. A bleak future awaits.

Bibliography

A renewed EU Strategy 2011–2014 for CSR. Available at http://eur-lex.europa.eu/LexUriServ/LexUriServ.do?uri=COM:2011:0681:FIN:en:PDF (Accessed 12 October 2014).

Aaronson, S.A. and Reeves, J. (2002) *The European Response to Public Demands for Global Corporate Responsibility*. USA: National Policy Association. Available at www.centreonphilanthropy.com/files/kb_articles/1251121958European%20Response%20to%20CSR.pdf (Accessed 12 October 2016).

Adelopo, I., Yekini, K. and Raimi, L. (2015) 'Bridging Governance Gap with Political CSR', in Jamali D., Karam, C. and Blowfield, M. (eds) *Development–Oriented Corporate Social Responsibility*. Sheffield: Greenleaf Publishing.

AIB: Corporate Social Responsibility. Available at https://group.aib.ie/content/dam/aib/group/Docs/corporate-social-responsibility.pdf (Accessed 13 October 2016).

Albareda, L., Lozano, J.M and Ysa, T. (2007) 'Public policies on corporate social responsibility: The role of governments in Europe', *Journal of Business Ethics* 74(4): pp. 391–407.

Alkhafaji, A.F. (1989) *A Stakeholder Approach to Corporate Governance: Managing in a Dynamic Environment*. New York: Quorum Books.

All Party Parliamentary Group for Corporate Responsibility. Available at www.apcrg.org.uk/home (Accessed 14 July 2015).

Amin, S. (2014) *Transnational Capitalism*. Paris: Springer International Publishing.

Andreasson, S. (2011) 'Understanding corporate governance reform in South Africa: Anglo-American divergence, the King reports, and hybridization', *Business and Society Review* 50(4): pp. 647–673.

Angotti, T. (1981) 'The political implications of dependency theory', *Latin American Perspectives* 8(3/4): pp. 124–137.

Appleby, P. (2005) 'Corporate Regulation in Ireland', in O'Brien, J. (ed) *Governing the Corporation: Regulation and Corporate Governance in an Age of Scandal and Global Markets*. Dublin: Wiley, J. & Sons, pp. 255-273.

Arghiri, E. (1972) *Unequal Exchange: A Study of the Imperialism of Trade*. New York: Monthly Review Press.

Ashraf, T. (2012) 'Directors' duties with a particular focus on the Companies Act 2006', *International Journal of Law and Management* 54(2): pp. 125–140.

Baber, G. (2014) 'Legislative and regulatory response to the global financial crisis from within the United Kingdom', *Journal of Financial Crime* 21(2): pp. 124–148.

Baber, G. (2012) 'A new approach to financial regulation: a step in the correct direction?', *The Company Lawyer* 33(1): pp. 3–12.

Bach, S. (2012) 'Shrinking the state or the Big Society? Public service employment relations in an era of austerity', *Industrial Relations Journal* 43(5): pp. 399–415.

Backer, L. (2007–2008) 'Multinational Corporations as Objects and Sources of Transnational Regulation', *ILSA Journal of International and Comparative Law* 14(2): pp. 499–615.

Bainbridge, S.M. (1992) 'Interpreting nonshareholder constituency statutes', *Pepperdine Law Review* 19: pp. 991–1025.

Baker, A. (2006) 'The Political Economy of the UK Competition State', in Stubbs, R. and Underhill, G.R.D. (eds), *Political Economy and the Changing Global Order*. Ontario: Oxford University Press, pp. 408–418.

Baran, P. (1957) *The Political Economy of Growth*. New York: Monthly Review Press.

Baran, P.A. and Hobsbawn, E.J. (1973) 'The stages of economic growth: a review', in Wilber, C.K. (ed). *The Political Economy of Development and Underdevelopment*. New York: Random House, pp. 82–94.

Baran, P. and Sweezy, P. (1966) *Monopoly Capital: An Essay on the American Economic and Social Order*. New York: London: Monthly Review Press.

Barnet, R.J. and Müller, R.E. (1974) *Global Reach*. New York: Simon and Schuster.

Baums, T. and Frick, B. (1997) *Co-determination in Germany: The Impact on the Market Value of the Firm*. Osnabruck: Inst. für Handels-und Wirtschaftsrecht.

BBC Thursday 3 April 2008 Available at http://news.bbc.co.uk/1/hi/in_depth/business/2007/globalisation/default.stm (Accessed 12 October 2016).

Benston, G.J. and Hartgraves, A.L. (2002) 'Enron: what happened and what we can learn from it', *Journal of Accounting and Public Policy* 21(2): pp. 105–127.

Berberoglu, B. (1992) *The Legacy of Empire: Economic Decline and Class Polarization in the United States*. New York: Praeger Publishers.

Berger, G., Steurer, R., Konrad, A. and Martinuzzi, A. (2007) *Raising Awareness for CSR in EU Member States: Overview of government initiatives and selected cases, final report to the EU High Level Group on CSR* Available from Project Website www.sustainability.eu/csr-policies (Accessed 25 September 2015).

Berle, A.A. (1931) 'For whom corporate managers are trustees: a note', *Harvard Law Review* 45: pp. 1365 - 1372.

Bernstein, H. (1971) 'Modernization theory and the sociological study of development', *Journal of Development Studies* 7(2): pp. 141–160.

Berrill, K. (1960) *The problem of economic "take off"*. Paper presented to the round table of the IEA on Economic Development with special reference to East Asia.

Biersteker, T.J. (1987) 'Indigenization and the Nigerian bourgeoisie: Dependent development in an African context', in Paul Lubeck (ed.) *The African Bourgeoisie: Capitalist Development in Nigeria, Kenya, and the Ivory Coast*, Boulder, CO: Lynne Rienner Publishers, pp. 249–80.

Bilateral Group on Trade and Corruption. Available at www.anticorruption.ie/ (Accessed 13 September 2015).

Bilgin, P. and Morton, A.D. (2002) 'Historicising representations of "failed states": beyond the Cold War annexation of the social sciences?', *Third World Quarterly* 23(1): pp. 55–80.

Bisconti, A. (2008) 'Double bottom line: can constituency statutes protect socially responsible corporations stuck in Revlon land'. *Loyola of Los Angeles Law Review*. 42: pp. 765–1147.

Blowfield, M. (2005) 'Corporate Social Responsibility: reinventing the meaning of development?', *International Affairs (Royal Institute of International Affairs 1944-)* 81(3): pp. 515–524.

Bodenheimer, S. (1970) 'The ideology of developmentalism: American political science's paradigm surrogate for Latin American studies', *Berkley Journal of Sociology* 15: pp. 95–137.

Bohle, D. (2006) 'Neoliberal hegemony, transnational capital and the terms of the EU's eastward expansion', *Capital and Class* 30(1): pp. 57–86.

Bondy, K. Moon, J. and Matten, D. (2012) 'An institution of corporate social responsibility (CSR) in multi-national corporations (MNCs): Form and implications', *Journal of Business Ethics* 111(2): pp. 281–299.

Booth, D. (1975) 'Andre Gunder Frank: An Introduction and an Appreciation', in Barnett, T., Oxaal, I. and Booth, D. (eds) *Beyond the Sociology of Development: Economy and Society in Latin America and Africa*. London: Routledge and Kegan Paul, pp. 50–86

Bourne, E.J. (2009) *Global Shift: How a New Worldview is Transforming Humanity*, New Oakland: Harbinger Publications.

Bowen, H.R. (1953) *Social Responsibilities of the Businessman*. New York: Harper & Row.

Bowles, M. (2010) *The Big Society and the Responsive State*. London: Community Development Foundation.

Bradley, H. (1996) *Fractured Identities: Changing Patterns of Inequality*. Cambridge: Polity.

Brohman, J. (1995) 'Universalism, Eurocentrism, and ideological bias in development studies: From modernisation to neoliberalism', *Third World Quarterly* 16(1): pp. 121–140.

Browett, J. (1980) 'Revisited: Into the Cul De Sac of the Dependency paradigm with A.G. Frank', in Peet, R (ed) *An Introduction to Marxist Theories of Underdevelopment*. Canberra: Australian National University Canberra.

Bullock, Lord (1977) *Report of the Committee of Inquiry on Industrial Democracy*. London: HMSO.

BBC Business, (2008) *IMF approves $2.1bn Iceland loan*. Available at http://news.bbc.co.uk/1/hi/in_depth/7738874.stm (Accessed on 27 July 2013).

Business in the Community Available at www.bitc.org.uk (Accessed on 14 July 2015)

Business in the Community (Ireland) Available at www.bitc.ie (Accessed 10 September 2015)

Cairncross, A.K. (1961) 'Essays in bibliography and criticism XLV: The stages of economic growth', *Economic History Review*, 13(3): pp. 450–458.

Cairncross, F. (1988) 'Poorest of the Rich', *The Economist*.

Cammack, P. (2002) 'Attacking the poor', *New Left Review*, 13: pp. 125–134.

Cardoso, F. (1977) 'The consumption of dependency theory in the United States', *Latin America Research Review*, 12(3): pp. 7–24.

Cardoso, F. (1972) 'Dependency and development', *New Left Review* 74: pp. 83–95.

Carlos, A.M. (1994) 'Bonding and the agency problem: evidence from the Royal African Company, 1672–1691', *Explorations in Economic History* 31(3): pp. 313–335.

Carlos, A.M. and Nicholas, S. (1990) 'Agency problems in early chartered companies: the case of the Hudson's Bay Company', *The Journal of Economic History* 50(4): pp. 853–875.

Carroll, A.B. (2015) 'Corporate social responsibility: the centerpiece of competing and complementary frameworks', *Organizational Dynamics* 44: pp. 87–96.

Carroll, A.B. (1999) 'Corporate social responsibility evolution of a definitional construct', *Business and Society* 38(3): pp. 268–295.

Carroll, A.B. (1991) 'The pyramid of corporate social responsibility: toward the moral management of organizational stakeholders', *Business Horizons* 34: pp. 39–48.

Carroll, A.B. (1979) 'A three dimensional conceptual model of corporate social performance', *Academy of Management Review* 4: pp. 497–505.

Carson, R. (1962) *The Silent Spring*. Boston: Houghton Press.

Carson, S.G., Hagen, Ø. and Sethi, S.P. (2015) 'From implicit to explicit CSR in a Scandinavian context: the cases of HÅG and Hydro', *Journal of Business Ethics* 127(1): pp. 17–31.

Cernat, L. (2004) 'The emerging European governance model: Anglo–Saxon, Continental, or still the century of diversity?' *Journal of European Public Policy* 11(1): pp. 147–166.

Charlemagne (2009) 'Iceland hunts the Euro', *The Economist* (22 Jan 2009). Available www.economist.com/node/12972641 (Accessed 12 October 2016).

Chimni, B.S. (2007) 'The past, present and future of international law', *Melbourne Journal of International Law* 8(2): pp. 499.

Chew, S.C. and Denmark, R.A. (eds.) (1996) *The Underdevelopment of Development: Essays in Honour of Andre Gunder Frank*. Thousand Oaks, CA: Sage Publications.

Chilcote, R.H. (1978) 'A question of dependency', *Latin American Research Review* 13(2): pp. 55–68.

Clark, G.L. (2002) 'London in the European financial services industry: locational advantage and product complementarities', *Journal of Economic Geography* 2(4): pp. 433–453.

Clark, G.L. and Wójcik, D. (2007) *The Geography of Finance: Corporate Governance in the Global Marketplace*. Oxford: Oxford University Press.

Clarke, T. (2014) 'The impact of financialisation on international corporate governance: the role of agency theory and maximising shareholder value', *Law and Financial Markets Review* 8(1): pp. 39–51.

Clarke, T. and Bostock, R. (1997) *Governance in Germany: The Foundations of Corporate Structure?* Oxford: Oxford University Press.

Clarkson, M.E. (1994) 'A risk based model of stakeholder theory', *Proceedings of the second Toronto conference on stakeholder theory*. Toronto: Centre for Corporate Social Performance & Ethics, University of Toronto.

Clarkson, M.E. (1995) 'A stakeholder framework for analysing and evaluating corporate social performance', *Academy of Management Review* 20(1): pp. 92–117.

Clement, W. and Williams, G. (1989) *The New Canadian Political Economy*. Montreal and Kingston: McGill–Queen's Press.

Cochran, P.L. and Wood, R.A. (1984) 'Corporate social responsibility and financial performance', *Academy of Management Journal* 27(1): pp. 42–56.

Coffee J.C. (2006) *Gatekeepers: The Professions and Corporate Governance: The Professions and Corporate Governance*. Oxford: Oxford University Press.

Coffee, J.C. (2002) 'Understanding Enron: "It's About the Gatekeepers, Stupid"', *The Business Lawyer* 57: pp. 1403–1420.

Coffee, J.C. (2000) 'Convergence and its critics: what are the preconditions to the separation of ownership and control', *Columbia Law and Economics Working Paper No. 179.*

Coffee, J.C. (1999) 'The future as history: the prospects for global convergence in Corporate Governance and its implications', *Northwestern University Law Review* 93(3): p. 641.

Coffee, J.C. and Sale, H. (2009) 'Redesigning the SEC: does the treasury have a better idea?', *Virginia Law Review* 95(4): pp. 707–783.

Collings, D.G., Gunnigle, P. and Morley, M. (2005) 'Exploring the dynamics of industrial relations in US multinationals: evidence from the Republic of Ireland.', *Industrial Relations Journal* 36(3): pp. 241–256.

Commission of the European Communities (CEC), *Promoting a European Framework for Corporate Social Responsibility.* C (2001) 366 final. Brussels. Available at www. europarl.europa.eu/meetdocs/committees/deve/20020122/com(2001)366_en.pdf (Accessed 21 September 2015)

Communication from the Commission of July 2001 European Governance: A White Pape, COM(2001) 428 Final Available at http://eur-lex.europa.eu/legal-content/EN/TXT/?uri=URISERV%3Al10109 (Accessed 12 October 2016).

Communication: *Corporate Social Responsibility: A Business Contribution to Sustainable Development.* COM (2002) 347 – final. Brussels. Available at http://eur-lex.europa.eu/LexUriServ/LexUriServ.do?uri=COM:2002:0347:FIN:en:PDF (Accessed 20 September 2015).

Communication: *Implementing the Partnership for Growth and Jobs: Making Europe a Pole of Excellence on Corporate Social Responsibility.* COM (2006) 136 – final. Brussels, March 22. Available at http://eur-lex.europa.eu/legal-content/EN/TXT/?uri=celex:52006DC0136 (Accessed 20 September 2015).

Compendium: CSR – National Public Policies in the European Union 2014. Available at http://ec.europa.eu/social/main.jsp?catId=331 (Accessed 27 September 2015).

Condorcet, Marquis De (1975) *Outlines of an Historical View of the Progress of the Human Mind: Being a Posthumous Work of the Late M. Condorcet.* (trans from French) London: Printed for J. Johnson.

Conlon, T. (1975) 'Industrial democracy and EEC company law: a review of the draft fifth directive', *International & Comparative Law Quarterly* 24 (02): pp. 348–359.

Conroy, B. (2009) 'Revolutionising Irish Company Law – The proposed new Companies Consolidation and Reform Act', in O'Neil, A. and Keane, R. (Eds.), *Corporate Governance: an Irish Perspective.* Dublin: Roundhall.

Cooke, P. (2005) 'Regional transformation and regional disequilibrium, new knowledge economies and their discontents', in Fuchs, G. and Shapira, P. (eds), *Rethinking regional innovation and change: path dependency or regional breakthrough.* Boston: Springer, Science and Business Media, pp. 43–63.

Copp, S.F. (2009) 'Corporate social responsibility and the Companies Act 2006', *Economic Affairs* 29(4): pp. 16–21.

Corporate Social Responsibility: Accountable Transparent and Responsible Business Behaviour and Sustainable Growth (2013b) Available at www.europarl.europa.eu/sides/getDoc.do?pubRef=-//EP//TEXT+REPORT+A7-2013-0017+0+DOC+XML+V0//EN (Accessed 10 August 2015).

Corporate Social Responsibility in France, Germany, Hungary and the UK. Available at www.eurofound.europa.eu/emcc/content/source/eu03002a.htm (Accessed 10 August 2015).

Corporate Social Responsibility: Promoting Society's Interests and a Route to Sustainable and Inclusive Recovery (2013a) Available at www.europarl.europa.eu/sides/getDoc.do?type=REPORT&reference=A7-2013-0023&language=EN (Accessed 10 August 2015).

Cowles, M.G. (1998) 'The Changing Architecture of Big Business', in Greenwood, J. and Aspinwall, M. (eds) *Collective Action in the European Union.* London: Routledge, pp. 108–126.

Cragg, W. (2002) 'Business ethics and stakeholder theory', *Business Ethics Quarterly* 12(02): pp. 113–142.

Crane, A. and Ruebottom, T. (2011) 'Stakeholder theory and social identity: rethinking stakeholder identification', *Journal of Business Ethics* 102(1): pp. 77–87.

Cueva, A. Villamil, J. and Fortín, C. (1976) 'A summary of "problems and perspectives of dependency theory"', *Latin American Perspectives* 3(4): pp. 12–16.

Davis, K. (1973) 'The case for and against business assumption of social responsibilities', *Academy of Management Journal* 16(2): pp. 312–322.

Davis, K. (1967) 'Understanding the social responsibility puzzle', *Business Horizons* 10(4): pp. 45–50.

Davis, K. (1960) 'Can business afford to ignore social responsibilities?' *California Management Review* 2(3): pp. 70–76.

De La Cuesta González, M. and Valor Martinez, C. (2004) 'Fostering corporate social responsibility through public initiative: from the EU to the Spanish case', *Journal of Business Ethics*, 55(3): pp. 275–293. Retrieved 10 March 2009, from ABI/INFORM Global database (Document ID: 793401791).

Debating Globalisation, BBC (2001) Available at http://news.bbc.co.uk/1/hi/business/1137190.stm (Accessed 21 July 2015).

DEFRA: Environmental Key Performance Indicators: Reporting Guidelines for UK Business. Available at www.gov.uk/government/uploads/system/uploads/attachment_data/file/69281/pb11321-envkpi-guidelines-060121.pdf (Accessed 13 September 2015).

DEFRA, (2011) 2011 Guidelines to Defra/DECC's GHG Conversion Factors for Company Reporting. Available at www.gov.uk/government/uploads/system/uploads/attachment_data/file/69314/pb13625-emission-factor-methodology-paper-110905.pdf (Accessed 13 October 2016).

Dell: Corporate Social Responsibility. Available at www.dell.com/learn/ie/en/iecorp1/cr (Accessed 28 September 2015).

Department of Business Innovation and Skills. Available at www.gov.uk/government/organisations/department-for-business-innovation-skills (Accessed 13 September 2015).

Department of Enterprise Trade and Investment (ROI) DETI Available at www.entemp.ie (Accessed 13 September 2015).

Department of the Environment, Food and Rural affairs. Available at www.gov.uk/government/organisations/department-for-environment-food-rural-affairs (Accessed 13 September 2015).

Department of Jobs, Enterprise and Investment (ROI) (DJEI) Available at www.djei.ie/en/ (Accessed 13 September 2015).

Department of Work and Pensions. Available at www.gov.uk/government/organisations/department-for-work-pensions (Accessed 13 September 2015).

Detomasi, D.A. (2008) 'The political roots of corporate social responsibility', *Journal of Business Ethics* 82(4): pp. 807–819.

Dey, I. (2008) Is Iceland headed for meltdown? The *Telegraph, 5 February 2008*. Available at www.telegraph.co.uk/finance/economics (Accessed 11 November 2014).

Dicken, P. (2015) *Global Shift: Reshaping the Global Economic Map in the 21st Century*. Seventh Ed. London: Sage Publications Ltd.

Dicken, P. (2007) *Global Shift: Mapping the Changing Contours of the World Economy*. London: Sage Publications Ltd.

Dicken, P. (1998) *Global Shift: Transforming the World Economy*. London: Paul Chapman Publications.

Dodd, E.M. (1932) 'For whom are corporate managers trustees?', *Harvard Law Review* 45: pp. 1145–1163.

Donaldson, L. and Davis, J.H. (1991) 'Stewardship theory or agency theory: CEO governance and shareholder returns', *Australian Journal of Management* 16(1): pp. 49–64.

Donaldson. T and Preston, L.E. (1995) 'The stakeholder theory of the corporation: Concepts, evidence and implications', *Academy of Management Review* 20(1): pp. 65–91.

Dornbusch, R., Fischer, S. and Samuelson, P.A. (1977) 'Comparative advantage, trade, and payments in a Ricardian model with a continuum of goods', *The American Economic Review* 67(5): pp. 823–839.

Dos Santos, T. (1970) 'The structure of dependence', *American Economic Review*, Papers and Proceedings 60: pp. 231–236.

Dos Santos, T. (1973) 'The crisis of development theory and the problem of dependence in Latin America', in H. Bernstein (ed.), *Underdevelopment and development*. Harmondsworth: Penguin.

Du, S. and Vieira Jr., E.T. (2012) 'Striving for legitimacy through corporate social responsibility: insights from oil companies', *Journal of Business Ethics* 110(4): pp. 413–427.

Duanmu, J. (2014) 'State owned MNCs and host country expropriation risk: The role of home state soft power and economic gun boat diplomacy', *Journal of International Business Studies* 45(8): pp. 1044–1060.

Dunning, J.H. (ed.) (1997) *Governments Globalisation and International Business*. Oxford: Oxford University Press.

Editorial: Globalization: Lessons Learned. *Business Week*, 6 November 2000. Available at www.bloomberg.com/news/articles/2000-11-05/globalization-lessons-learned (Accessed 30 April 2015).

Edwards, S. and Santaella, J. (1993) 'Devaluation Controversies in the Developing Countries: Lessons from the Bretton Woods Era', in Bordo, M.D. and Eichengreen B. (eds) *A retrospective on the Bretton Woods system: Lessons for international monetary reform*. US: National Bureau of Economic Research.

Eells, R. (1956) *Corporation Giving in a Free Society*. New York: Harper.
Eichengreen, B. (2004) 'Global imbalances and the lessons of Bretton Woods', *International Economy* 100(4): pp. 39–50.
Eisenhardt, K.M. (1989) 'Agency theory: an assessment and review', *Academy of Management Review* 14(1): pp. 57–74.
Ekholm, K. (2013) 'The globalisation of the financial markets following the global financial crisis', *Sveriges Riksbank Economic Review* 1: pp. 6–30.
Elkington, J. (1997) '*"Cannibals with Forks." The Triple Bottom Line of 21st Century*', Oxford: Capstone.
Emmenegger, P. (ed.) (2012) *The Age of Dualization: The Changing Face of Inequality in Deindustrializing Societies*. Oxford: Oxford University Press.
Environmental Protection Agency (EPA) Available at www.epa.gov (Accessed 15 August 2015).
Epstein, E.M. (1998) 'Business ethics and corporate social policy – reflections on an intellectual journey, 1964–1996 and beyond', *Business and Society* 37(1): pp. 7–39.
Equal Employment Opportunity Commission (EEOC) Available at www.eeoc.gov (Accessed 10 September 2015).
Erturk, I., Froud, J., Johal, S. and Williams, K. (2004) 'Corporate governance and disappointment', *Review of International Political Economy* 11(4): pp. 677–713.
European Multistakeholder Forum on CSR. (2004) Final Report. Final Results and Recommendations. Brussels. Available at www.indianet.nl/EU-MSF_CSR.pdf (Accessed 13 October 2016).
European Commission, (2013) *Peer Review of EU Member State's activities on CSR in 2013–2014*. Available at http://ec.europa.eu/social/keyDocuments.jsp?advSearchKey=CSRprreport&mode=advancedSubmit&langId=en&policyArea=&type=0&country=0&year=0 (Accessed 13 October 2016).
Favell, A. and Reimer, D. (2013) 'Winners and losers? Citizens and sceptics? European integration and the spread of cosmopolitanism', *EUCROSS Policy Brief* 1: pp. 1–11.
Featherstone, K. (2012) 'The spatialities of Europeanization: power, governance and territory in Europe', *West European Politics* 35(2): pp. 427–428.
Feng, H., Froud, J., Johal, S., Haslan, C. and Williams, K. (2001) 'A new business model? The capital market and the new economy', *Economy and Society* 30(4): pp. 467–503.
Filatotchev, I. and Stahl, G.K. (2015) 'Towards transnational CSR: Corporate Social Responsibility approaches and governance solutions for multinational Corporations', *Organizational Dynamics* 22: pp. 121–129.
Final Statement of the Irish and Netherlands NCPs on the notification dates 21 August 2008 concerning the Corrib Gas project, pursuant to the OECD Guidelines for Multinational Enterprise.
Finger, J.M. Hall, H.K. and Nelson, D.R. (1982) 'The political economy of administered protection', *The American Economic Review* 72(3): pp. 452–466.
Fisch, J.E. (2009) 'Top cop or regulatory flop? The SEC at 75', *Virginia Law Review* 95(4): pp. 785–823.
Foreign Policy Magazine Globalisation Index TM. (2006) Available at www.atkearney.com (Accessed 10 September 2014).

Fontrodona, J. and Sison, A.J.G. (2006). 'The nature of the firm, agency theory and shareholder theory: A critique from philosophical anthropology', *Journal of Business Ethics* 66(1): pp. 33–42.

Francoise, Christopher N. (2007) 'A critical assessment of the United States' Implementation of the OECD Guidelines for Multinational Enterprises', *Boston College International and Comparative Law Review* 30(1): pp. 223–531.

Frank, A.G. (1966) 'The development of underdevelopment', *Monthly Review* 18(4): pp. 27–37.

Frank, A.G. (1967a) *Capitalism and Underdevelopment in Latin America.* New York: Monthly Review Press.

Frank, A.G. (1967b) 'Sociology of development and underdevelopment of sociology', *Catalyst* 3: pp. 20–73.

Frank, A.G. (1968) 'Who is the Immediate Enemy?' in Cockcroft, J., Frank, A.G. and Johnson D. (eds) *Dependence and Underdevelopment: Latin America's Political Economy.* New York: Doubleday Anchor.

Frank A.G. (1970) *Latin America: Underdevelopment or Revolution.* New York and London: Monthly Review Press

Frank. A.G. (1977a) 'The development of underdevelopment', *Monthly Review* 18: pp. 27–37.

Frank, A.G. (1977b) 'Dependence is dead, long live dependence and the class struggles: an answer to critics', *World Development* 5(4): pp. 355–370.

Frank, A.G. (1991) 'The underdevelopment of development', *Scandinavian Journal of Development Alternatives* 10(3): pp. 133–150.

Frankental, P. (2001) 'Corporate Social Responsibility – a PR invention?' *Corporate Communications: An International Journal* 6(1): pp. 18–23.

Frederick, W.C. (1994) 'From CSR1 to CSR2: the maturing of business-and-society thought', *Business and Society* 33(2): pp. 150–164.

Frederick, W.C. (1960) 'The growing concern over business responsibility', *California Management Review* 2(4): pp. 54–61.

Freeman, R.E. (2001) 'A stakeholder theory of the modern corporation', in Snoebeyenbos, M., Almeder, R.F. and Humber, J.M. (eds) *Business Ethics* (3rd Edition) New York: Prometheus Books, pp. 101–114.

Freeman, R.E. (1984) *Stakeholder Management. A Strategic Approach.* New York: Pitman.

Friedman, M. (1962) *Capitalism and Freedom.* Chicago: University of Chicago Press.

Friedman, M. (1970) The Social Responsibility of Business is to Increase its Profits, *New York Times Magazine.* Available at www.umich.edu/~thecore/doc/Friedman.pdf (Accessed 11 September 2014).

Furtado, C. (1964) *Development and Underdevelopment.* Berkley: University of California Press.

Gamble, A. (1988) *The Free Economy and the Strong State: The Politics of Thatcherism.* Durham, NC: Duke University Press.

Garriga, E. and Mel, D. (2004) 'Corporate Social Responsibility theories: mapping the territory', *Journal of Business Ethics* 53 (1–2): pp. 51–71.

Gerschenkron, A. (1962) *Economic Backwardness in Historical Perspective.* Cambridge, MA: Bellknap Press.

Ghoshal, S. and Bartlett, C. (1986) 'Tap your subsidiaries for global reach', *Harvard Business Review* 64(6): pp. 87–94.

Giddens, A. (2013) *The Third Way: The Renewal of Social Democracy*. London: John Wiley & Sons.

Giddens, A. (2002) *Runaway World: How Globalisation is Reshaping Our Lives*. London: Profile Books.

Giddens A. (ed.), (2001) *The Global Third Way Debate*. London: John Wiley and Sons.

Giddens, A. (1999) *The Third Way and its Critics*. London: John Wiley and Sons.

Giddens, A. (1998) *The Third Way: The Renewal of Social Democracy*. Cambridge: Polity Press.

Gilson, R.J. (2001) 'Globalizing corporate governance: convergence of form or function', *The American Journal of Comparative Law* 49: pp. 329–357.

Globalisation 2007 Index. Available at http://globalization.kof.ethz.ch/ (Accessed 27 September 2015).

Godfrey, P.C., Hatch, N.W. and Hansen, J.M. (2010) 'Toward a general theory of CSRs: the roles of benefice, profitability, insurance and industry heterogeneity', *Business and Society* 49(2): pp. 316–344.

Goergen, M. Martynova, M. and Renneboog, L. (2005) 'Corporate governance convergence: evidence from takeover regulation reforms in Europe', *Oxford Review of Economic Policy* 21(2): pp. 243–268.

Goldfrank, W. (1977) 'Who rules the world? Class formation at the international level', *Quarterly Journal of Ideology* 1(2): pp. 32–37.

Golub, S.S. and Hsieh, C.T. (2000) 'Classical Ricardian theory of comparative advantage revisited', *Review of International Economics* 8(2): pp. 221–234.

Good for Business, Good for the Community: Ireland's national Plan on Corporate Social Responsibility 2014–2016 (2014). Available at www.djei.ie/en/Publications/Publication-files/National-Plan-CSR.pdf (Accessed 21 September 2015).

Gordon, K. (2001), "The OECD Guidelines and Other Corporate Responsibility Instruments: A Comparison", OECD Working Papers on International Investment, 2001/05, OECD Publishing. http://dx.doi.org/10.1787/302255465771

Griffin, K. (1973) 'Underdevelopment in Theory', in Wilber, C. K (ed.) *The political Economy of Development and Underdevelopment*. New York: Random House.

Guinier, Lani. (2004) 'From racial liberalism to racial literacy: Brown v. Board of Education and the interest-divergence dilemma', *The Journal of American History* 91(1): pp. 92–118.

Habib, M.M. and Stracca, L. (2012) 'Getting beyond carry trade: what makes a safe haven currency?' *Journal of International Economics* 87(1): pp. 50–64.

Hackett, C. (2016) 'The challenge of MNCs and development: oil extraction, CSR, Nigeria and corruption', *Journal of Human Rights in the Commonwealth* 2(2).

Hackett, C. (2014) 'The rebirth of dependence – offering an alternative understanding of financial crisis', *International Journal of Law and Management* 56(2): pp. 121–135.

Hackett, C. (2012) 'Accountability for responsibility: an assessment of the transnational capitalist class' role in driving a global CSR agenda', *Australian Journal of Corporate Law* 27(1): pp. 168–187.

Hackett, C. (2011) 'The grass is always greener: reflecting on global disparity in corporate social responsibility', *Commercial Law Practitioner* 18 (July): pp. 151–157.

Hansmann, H. and Kraakman, R. (2000) 'The end of history for corporate law', *Geo. LJ* 89(2): pp. 439–2593.

Harvey, D. (2003) *The New Imperialism*. Oxford: Oxford University Press.

Haxhi, I. and Aguilera, RR. (2012) 'Are Codes Fostering Convergence in Corporate Governance? An Institutional Perspective', in Rasheed, A. and Yoshikawa, T. (eds) *Convergence of Corporate Governance: Promise And Prospects*, Basingstoke: Palgrave Macmillan, pp. 234–249.

Heemskerk, E.M. (2013) 'The rise of the European corporate elite: evidence from the network of interlocking directorates in 2005 and 2010', *Economy and Society* 42(1): pp. 74–101.

Hegel, G.W.F. (1953) 'The Philosophy of History', in Friederich, C.J. (ed.) *The Philosophy of Hegel*. New York: Random House.

Held, D. (2000) 'Regulating globalization? The reinvention of politics', *International Sociology* 15(2): pp. 394–408.

Helleiner, E. (1994) *States and the Re-emergence of Global Finance: From Bretton Woods to the 1990s*. Ithaca, NY: Cornell University Press.

Hess, D., Rogovsky, N. and Dunfee, T.W. (2002) 'The next wave of corporate community involvement: corporate social initiatives', *California Management Review* 44(2): pp. 110–125.

Hilferding, R. (1970) *Le capital financier*. Paris: Éditions du Minuit.

Hillman, A.J. and Keim, G.D. (2001) 'Shareholder value, stakeholder management, and social issues: what's the bottom line?', *Strategic Management Journal* 22(2): pp. 125–139.

Holmes, P. (1986) *Governing the Economy*. London: Polity Press.

Holtbrugge, D., Berg, N. and Puck, J.F. (2007) 'To bribe or to convince? Political stakeholders and political activities in German multinational corporations', *International Business Review* 16(1): pp. 47–67.

Holton, R.J. (1998) *Globalisation and the Nation State*. Basingstoke: Macmillan Press Ltd.

Hunt, J. (2003) 'The European Union: Promoting a Framework for Corporate Social Responsibility?' in Macmillan, F. (ed.) *International Corporate Law*. Oxford: Hart, pp. 123–140.

Hunt, J.P. (2009) 'Credit rating agencies and the worldwide credit crisis: the limits of reputation, the insufficiency of reform, and a proposal for improvement', *Columbia Business Law Review* 2009(1): pp. 109–1014.

Hunt, S.D. and Morgan, R.M. (1995) 'The comparative advantage theory of competition', *The Journal of Marketing* 59(2): pp. 1–15.

Hymer, S. (1979) *The Multinational Corporation: A Radical Approach*. Cambridge: Cambridge University Press

Idemudia, U. (2008) 'Conceptualising the CSR and development debate', *Journal of Corporate Citizenship* 29: pp. 91–110.

ILO Child Labour. Available at www.ilo.org/global/topics/child-labour/lang--en/index.htm (Accessed 27 July 2015).

Iovine, J. (2009) Russia approves 64billion ISK loan to Iceland. (*Ice News Daily News* 16 July 2009) Available at www.icenews.is/index.php/2009/07/16/russia-approves-64-billion-isk-loan-to-iceland/ (Accessed 15 June 2014).

Ishkanian, A. and Szreter, S. (eds.) (2012) *The Big Society Debate: A New Agenda for Social Policy?* Cheltenham: Edward Elgar Publishing.

Jackman, R.W. (1982) 'Dependence on foreign investment and economic growth in the Third World', *World Politics* 34(2): pp. 175–196.

Jacobsen, J.K. (1994) *Chasing Progress in the Irish Republic – Ideology, Democracy and Dependent Development.* Cambridge: Cambridge University Press.

Jenkins, H. (2006) 'Small business champions for corporate social responsibility', *Journal of Business Ethics* 67(3): pp. 241–256.

Jensen, M.C. (2002) 'Value maximization, stakeholder theory, and the corporate objective function', *Business Ethics Quarterly* 12(2): pp. 235–256.

Jensen, M.C. (2001) 'Value maximization, stakeholder theory, and the corporate objective function', *Journal of Applied Corporate Finance* 14(3): pp. 8–21.

Jones, A. *Making Sense of CSR.* Available at www.iaf.gov (Accessed 15 May 2015).

Johnston, D.C. (1999) 'Gap between rich and poor found substantially wider', *New York Times* (5 September 1999). Available at www.nytimes.com/1999/09/05/us/gap-between-rich-and-poor-found-substantially-wider.html (Accessed 28 September 2015).

Kanter, R. (1999) 'From spare change to real change: the social sector as beta site for business innovation', *Harvard Business Review* 77(3): pp. 122–132.

Kay, G. (1975) *Development and Underdevelopment: A Marxist Analysis.* Basingstoke: Macmillan Press Ltd.

Keay, A. (2007a) 'Tackling the Issue of the corporate objective: An analysis of the United Kingdom's "enlightened shareholder value approach"', *Sydney Law Review* 29(4): pp. 577–725.

Keay, A. (2007b) 'Section 172(1) of the Companies Act 2006: an interpretation and assessment. Legislative Comment', *Company Lawyer* 28(4): pp. 106–110.

Keay, J. (1991) *The Honourable Company: A History of the English East India Company.* London: HarperCollins.

Kemper, A and Martin, R.L. (2010) 'After the fall: the global financial crisis as a test of corporate social responsibility theories', *European Management Review* 7(4): pp. 229–239.

Kline, J.M. (1985) *International Codes and Multinational Business: Setting Guidelines for International Business.* Westport: Quorum Books.

Killian, S. (2009) 'Collateral damage? The impact of Ireland's tax strategy on developing countries', *IrishLeftReview.org.* Available at www.irishleftreview.org/2009/07/22/collateral-damage-impact-irelands-tax-strategy-developing-countries-part/ (Accessed 18 August 2014).

Kinderman, D.P. (2013) 'Corporate Social Responsibility in the EU, 1993–2013: institutional ambiguity, economic crises, business legitimacy and bureaucratic politics', *JCMS: Journal of Common Market Studies* 51: pp. 701–720. doi: 10.1111/jcms. 12021.

Kinderman, D.P. (2011) 'Why do some countries get CSR sooner, and in greater quantity, than others? The political economy of corporate responsibility and the rise of market liberalism across the OECD: 1977–2007', *SSRN.*

King, A. (1975) 'Overload: problems of governing in the 1970s', *Political Studies* 23 (2–3): pp. 162–174.

Kirkbride, J. and Letza, S. (2003) 'Corporate governance and gatekeeper liability: the lessons from public authorities', *Corporate governance: An international review* 11(3): pp. 262–271.

Kita, M.H. (2010–2011) 'It's not you, it's me: An analysis of the United States' failure to uphold its commitment to OECD Guidelines for Multinational Enterprise in spite of no other reliable alternatives', *Pennsylvania State International Law Review* 29: pp. 359–809.

Kobrin, S.J. (2015) 'Is a global nonmarket strategy possible? Economic integration in a multipolar world order', *Journal of World Business* 50(2): pp. 262–272.

Kobrin, S.J. (1997) 'The Architecture of Globalisation: State Sovereignty in a Networked Global Economy', in Dunning, J.H. (ed.) *Governments Globalisation and International Business*. Oxford: Oxford University Press, pp. 146–173.

KOF index of globalization. Available at http://globalization.kof.ethz.ch (Accessed 20 July 2015).

KOF Globalisation Index (2008) Download available at http://globalization.kof.ethz.ch (Accessed 13 October 2016).

Kohler, G. and Tausch, A. (2002) *Global Keynesianism: Unequal Exchange and Global Exploitation*. Huntington NY: Nova Publishers.

Korzeniewicz, R.P. and Moran T.P. (1997) 'World economic trends in the distribution of income, 1965–1992', *American Journal of Sociology* 102(4): pp. 1000–1039.

Kraft, K., Stank, J. and Dewenter, R. (2011) 'Co-determination and innovation', *Cambridge Journal of Economics* 35(1): pp. 145–172.

Krugman, P.R. (1991) 'Increasing returns and economic geography', *Journal of Political Economy* 99(3): pp. 483–499.

Lawler, E.E. and Conger, J.A. (2015) 'The sustainable effectiveness model: moving corporations beyond the philanthropy paradigm', *Organizational Dynamics* 44(2): pp. 97–103.

Leamer, E.E. (1984) *Sources of International Comparative Advantage: Theory and Evidence*. Cambridge, MA: MIT press.

Lean, G. (1999) Urban Regeneration? We've Heard it all Before. *The Independent*. London, 27 January.

Lee, K., Fooks, G., Gilmore, A., Collin, J. and Holden, C. (2012). 'The limits of corporate social responsibility: techniques of neutralization, stakeholder management and political CSR', *Journal of Business Ethics* 112(2): pp. 283–299.

Leipziger, D. (2010) *The Corporate Responsibility Code Book*. Sheffield: Greenleaf Publishing.

Letnar Cernic, J. (2008) 'Corporate responsibility for human rights: a critical analysis of the OECD Guidelines for Multinational Enterprises', *Hanse Law Review* 3(1): 71.

Leuchtenburg, W.E. (1963) *Franklin Roosevelt and the New Deal: 1932–1940*. New York: Harper Perennial.

Luetkenhorst, W. (2004) 'Corporate social responsibility and the development agenda', *Intereconomics* 39(3): pp. 157–166.

Levis, J. (2006) 'Adoption of corporate social responsibility codes by multinational companies', *Journal of Asian Economics* 17(1): pp. 50–55.

Levy-Yeyati, E. and Sturzenegger, F. (2001) 'To float or to trail: evidence on the impact of exchange rate regimes', *UTDT Working Paper No.1/01*.

Lewis, S. (2003) 'Reputation and corporate responsibility', *Journal of Communication Management* 7(4): pp. 356–366.

Leys, C. (1996) *The Rise and Fall of Development Theory*. London: James Currey Ltd.

Leys, C. (1977) 'Underdevelopment and dependency – critical notes', *Journal of Contemporary Asia* 7(1): pp. 92–107.

Lipsey, R.G. (1997) 'Globalisation and National Government Policies: An Economist's View', in Dunning, J.H. (ed.) *Governments Globalisation and International Business*. Oxford: Oxford University Press, pp. 73–114.

Lord Carr of Hadley. *Industrial Democracy: Bullock Report*. HL Deb 23 February 1977 380: cc. 79–355. Available at http://hansard.millbanksystems.com/lords/1977/feb/23/industrial-democracy-bullock-report (Accessed 11 March 2014).

Lowndes, V. and Pratchett, L. (2012) 'Local governance under the coalition government: Austerity, localism and the "Big Society"', *Local Government Studies* 38(1): pp. 21–40.

Lozano, J.M., Albareda, L. and Ysa, T. (2008) *Governments and Corporate Social Responsibility*. Basingstoke: Palgrave Macmillan.

Lutts, R.H. (1985) 'Chemical fallout: Rachel Carson's Silent Spring, radioactive fallout, and the environmental movement', *Environmental Review* 9(3): pp. 211–225.

MacKenzie, K. (2015) 'Facing the Future at the IMF' (*In the Balance*, BBC World Service). Available at www.bbc.co.uk/news/business-33652399 (Accessed 27 July 2015).

Mahoney, J. (2000) 'Path dependence in historical sociology', *Theory and Society* 29(4): pp. 507–548.

Mann, M. (1997) 'Has globalisation ended the rise and rise of the nation state?', *Review of International Political Economy* 4(3): pp. 472–496.

Manne, H.G. and Wallich, H.C. (1972) *The Modern Corporation and Social Responsibility* Washington, DC: American Enterprise Institute for Public Policy Research.

Marchak, P.M. (1993) *The Integrated Circus: The New Right and the Restructuring of Global Markets*. Montreal Kingston: McGill–Queen's Press.

Marini, R.M. (1972) 'Brazilian sub-imperialism', *Monthly Review* 9: pp. 14–24.

Marson, J. (2009) 'IMF tentatively approves loan to help Ukraine', *The Wall Street Journal*, 13 July 2009. Available at http://online.wsj.com/article/SB124725645790724641.html (Accessed 27 July 2014).

Marx, K. (1999) *Das Kapital*. London: Gateway Editions.

Marx, K. and Engels, F. (1978) 'The German Ideology', in Tuckers, R. (ed.), *The Marx Engels Reader* (2nd Edition). New York: W.W. Norton.

Marx, K. (1891) 'Wage Labour and Capital in Engels', F. (tr.) *Neue Rheinische Zeitung*. Available at www.marxists.org/archive/marx/works/1847/wage-labour/index.htm (Accessed 9 June 2016).

Marx, K. (1868 (1969)) *Value, Price and Profit*. New York: International Co. Inc.

Marx, K. (1863) *Theories of Surplus Value* (Volume IV of Capital). Available at www.marxists.org/archive/marx/works/1863/theories-surplus-value/ (Accessed 30 May 2015).

Matten, D. and Moon, J. (2008)'"Implicit" and "explicit" CSR: a conceptual framework for a comparative understanding of corporate social responsibility', *Academy of Management Review* 33(2): pp. 404–424.

McBarnet, D. (2007) 'Corporate Social Responsibility Beyond Law, Through Law, For Law, the New Corporate Accountability', in McBarnet, D., Voiculescu, A. and Campbell, T. (eds) *The New Corporate Accountability – Corporate Responsibility and the Law*. Cambridge: Cambridge University Press, pp. 9–59.

MacEwan, A. and Tabb, W.T. (eds) (1989) *Instability and Change in the World Economy*. New York: Monthly Review Press.

McGuire, J.W. (1963) *Business and society*. New York: McGraw-Hill.

McKee, K. (2015) 'An Introduction to the Special Issue—The Big Society, Localism and Housing Policy: Recasting State–Citizen Relations in an Age of Austerity', *Housing, Theory and Society* 32(1): pp. 1–8.

McKenna, C. (1983) 'The Gower Report – A British SEC', *International Financial Law Review* 2: p. 28.

McWilliams, A. and Siegel, D. (2001) 'Corporate social responsibility: a theory of the firm perspective', *Academy of Management Review* 26(1): pp. 117–127.

Merino, B.D., Mayper, A.G. and Tolleson, T.D. (2010) 'Neoliberalism, deregulation and Sarbanes-Oxley: the legitimation of a failed corporate governance model', *Accounting, Auditing & Accountability Journal* 23(6): pp. 774–792.

Merton, R.K. (1995) 'The Thomas theorem and the Matthew effect', *Social forces* 74(2): pp. 379–422.

Merton, R.K. (1988) 'The Matthew effect in science, II: Cumulative advantage and the symbolism of intellectual property', *Isis* 79(299): pp. 606–623.

Merton, R.K. (1968) 'The Matthew effect in science', *Science* 159(3810): pp. 56–63.

Mickels, A. (2009) 'Beyond corporate social responsibility: reconciling the ideals for a for – benefit corporation with director fiduciary duties in the US and Europe', *Hastings International and Comparative Law Review* 32: pp. 271–831.

Midttun, A., Gautesen, K. and Gjølberg, M. (2006) 'The political economy of CSR in Western Europe', *Corporate Governance: The international journal of business in society* 6(4): pp. 369–385.

Milanovic, B. (2003) 'The faces of globalisation: against globalisation as we know it', *World Development* 31(4): pp. 667–683.

Mitchell, L.E. (1992) 'A theoretical and practical framework for enforcing corporate constituency statues', *Texas Law Review* 70(579): pp. 630–639.

Mitchell, R.K., Agle, B.R. and Wood, D.J. (1997) 'Toward a theory of stakeholder identification and salience: defining the principle of who and what really counts', *Academy of Management Review* 22(4): pp. 853–886.

Moon, J. (2005a) 'United Kingdom: an explicit model of Business-Society Relations', in Habisch, A. (ed.) *Corporate social responsibility across Europe*. Berlin Heidelberg: Springer, pp. 51–65.

Moon, J. (2005b) *CSR and Government: Dichotomous and Embedded Views* (Presentation).

Moon, J. (2004) 'Government as a driver of corporate social responsibility: the UK in comparative perspective' *ICCSR Research Paper Series (20/2004)*. Available at http://195.130.87.21:8080/dspace/handle/123456789/1102 (Accessed 6 September 2016).

Moon. J. and Richardson, J.J. (1985) *Unemployment in UK: Politics and Policies*. New York: Grower Publishing Company.

Moore, G. (1995) 'Community Involvement in the UK – Investment or Atonement?' *Business Ethics: A European Review* 4(3): pp. 171–178.

Mosley, L. (2003) *Global Capital and National Governments*. Cambridge: Cambridge University Press.

Mosley, L. and Uno, S. (2007) 'Racing to the bottom or climbing to the top? Economic globalization and collective labor rights', *Comparative Political Studies* 40(8): pp. 923–948.

Müller, R. (1973) 'The Multinational Corporation and the underdevelopment of the third world', in Wilber, C.K. (ed), *The Political Economy of Development and Underdevelopment*. New York: Random House, pp. 124–151.

Myrdal, G. (1968) *Asian Drama: An Enquiry into the Poverty of Nations*. New York: The Twentieth Century Fund.

Narine, M. (2012) 'From Kansas to the Congo: why naming and shaming corporations through the Dodd–Frank Act's Corporate Governance Disclosure won't solve a human rights crisis', *Regent University Law Review* 25: pp. 351–471.

National Contact Points for the OECD Guidelines for Multinational Enterprises. Available at www.oecd.org/document/3/0,3746,en_2649_34889_1933116_1_1_1_1,00.html (Accessed 12 October 2014).

National Pension Reserve Fund. Available at www.nprf.ie/ResponsibleInvesting/responsibleInvesting.htm (Accessed 1 September 2015).

Neilsen, J. (2006) 'Corporate Citizenship, Labour Rights and the Democratic Deficit' in Huniche. M. and Pedesen E.R. (eds) *Corporate Citizenship in Developing Countries*. Copenhagen Business School Press, pp. 233–239.

Newell, P. (2008) 'CSR and the limits of capital', *Development and Change* 39(6): pp. 1063–1078.

Norbäck, P.J. and Persson, L. (2014) 'Born to be Global and the Globalisation Process', *The World Economy* 37(5): pp. 672–689.

O'Brien, P.J. (1975) 'A critique of Latin American theories of dependence', in Oxaal, I. Barnett, T. and Booth, D. (eds) *Beyond the Sociology of Development*. London: Routledge and Kegan Paul, pp. 7–27.

Obstfeld, M. (2012) 'Financial flows, financial crises, and global imbalances', *Journal of International Money and Finance* 31(3): pp. 469–480

Occupational Safety and Health Administration (OSHA) Available at www.osha.gov (Accessed 12 March 2015).

OECD (2015), OECD Economic Outlook, Volume 2015 Issue 1, OECD Publishing, Paris.DOI: http://dx.doi.org/10.1787/eco_outlook-v2015-1-en

OECD Globalisation Report 2006. www.oecd.org/newsroom/36511265.pdf (Accessed 14 October 2016).

OECD Observer Policy Brief, The OECD Guidelines for Multinational Enterprises. Available at www.oecd.org/investment/mne/1903291.pdf (Accessed 2 May 2015).

Ohmae, K. (1999). *The Borderless World: Power and Strategy in the Interlinked Economy, Management Lessons in the New Logic of the Global Marketplace*. New York: Harper Business.

Ohmae, K. (1995a) *The End of the Nation State: The Rise of Regional Economics*. New York: Free Press.

Ohmae, K. (ed.) (1995b) *The Evolving Global Economy: Making Sense of the New World Order*. Cambridge, MA: Harvard Business School Press.

Omarova, S.T. (2010–2011) 'Wall Street as community of fate: toward financial industry self-regulation', *University of Pennsylvania Law Review* 159(2): pp. 411–492.

Orts, E. (1992) 'Beyond shareholders: interpreting corporate constituency statutes', *George Washington Law Review* 61: pp. 14–1955.

Oshionebo, E. (2013) 'The OECD Guidelines for Multinational Enterprises as Mechanisms for Sustainable Development of Natural Resources: real solutions or window dressing', *Lewis & Clark L. Rev.* 17(2): pp. 545.

Oxley, M.G. (2007) 'The Sarbanes-Oxley Act of 2002 – restoring investor confidence', *Current Issues in Auditing* 1(1): C1–C2.

Padfield, S.J. (2009–2010) 'Finding state actions when corporations govern', *Temple Law Review* 82: pp. 703–736.

Parker, R.W. and Alemanno, A. (2014) *Towards Effective Regulatory Cooperation Under TTIP: A Comparative Overview of the EU and US Legislative and Regulatory Systems 15 May 2014*. Brussels: European Commission., May 2014. Available at SSRN: http://ssrn.com/abstract=2438242 (Accessed 23 January 2015).

Parkes, C., Scully, J. and Anson, S. (2010) 'CSR and the "undeserving": a role for the state, civil society and business?', *International Journal of Sociology and Social Policy* 30(11/12): pp. 697–708.

Parmar, B.L., Freeman, R.E., Harrison, J.S., Wicks, A.C., Purnell, P. and de Colle, S. (2010) 'Stakeholder theory: the state of the art', *Academy of Management Annals* 4(1): pp. 403–445.

Peston, R. (2008) *Markets call time on Iceland*. BBC. Available at www.bbc.co.uk/blogs/thereporters/robertpeston/2008/10/creditors_call_time_on_iceland.html (Accessed 13 April 2015).

Peters, B.G. (1993) 'Managing the Hollow State', in Eliassan, K. and Kooiman, J. (eds) *Managing Public Organisations: Lessons for Contemporary European Experience*, 2nd Edition. London: Sage.

Pettet, B. (1997) 'The stirring of corporate social conscience: from "cakes and ale" to community programmes', *Lectures on Current Legal Problems* 50(1): pp. 279–314.

Pilling, G. (1972) 'The law of value in Ricardo and Marx', *Economy and Society* 1(3): pp. 281–307.

Post, J.E., Preston, L.E. and Sachs, S. (2002) 'Managing the extended enterprise: the new stakeholder view', *California Management Review* 45(1): pp. 6–28.

Prebisch, R. (1950) *The Economic Development of Latin America and its Principle Problems*. Lake Success, New York: UN Department of Economic Affairs.

Rapp, G.C. (2012) 'Mutiny by the bounties? The attempt to reform Wall Street by the new whistleblower provisions of the Dodd–Frank Act', *Brigham Young University Law Review* 2012 (1): pp. 73–152.

Ravallion, M. (2003) 'The debate on globalisation, poverty and inequality: why measurement matters', *International Affairs* 79(4): pp. 739–753.

Reidenbach, R.E. and Robin, D.P. (1991) 'A conceptual model of corporate moral development', *Journal of Business Ethics* 10(4): pp. 273–284.

Report by the Comptroller and Auditor General (2009) The Nationalisation of Northern Rock, National Audit Office www.nao.org.uk/wp-content/uploads/2009/03/0809298.pdf

Report of the Committee on the Financial Aspects of Corporate Governance (1992). (The Cadbury Report). Available at www.ecgi.org/codes/documents/cadbury.pdf (Accessed 10 August 2015).

Report of the Presidency Conclusions of the Lisbon European Council 23 & 24 March 2000. Available at www.europarl.europa.eu/summits/lis1_en.htm#b (Accessed 26 February 2014).

Rhodes, R. (1994) 'The hollowing out of the state: the changing nature of the public service in Britain', *The Political Quarterly* 65(2): pp. 138–151.

Richards, S. (2000). 'Still panicking after all these years', *NewStatesman* 31 July 2000. Available at www.newstatesman.com/node/193652 (Accessed 13 October 2016).

Rowbottom, R. and Schroeder, M.A.S. (2014) 'The rise and fall of the UK operating and financial review', *Accounting, Auditing & Accountability Journal* 27(4): pp. 655–685.

Robins, N. (2006) *The Corporation that Changed the World: How the East India Company Shaped the Modern Multinational*. London: Pluto Press.

Robinson, W.I. (2012) 'Global capitalism theory and the emergence of transnational elites', *Critical Sociology* 38(3): pp. 349–363.

Robinson, W.I. (2007) 'Beyond the theory of imperialism: global capitalism and the transnational state', *Societies Without Borders* 2(1): pp. 5–26.

Robinson, R.B. and Pearce, J.A. (1983) 'The impact of formalised strategic planning on financial performance in small organisations', *Strategic Management Journal* 4(3): pp. 197–207.

Robinson, W. and Harris, J. (2000) 'Towards a global ruling class? Globalisation and the transnational capitalist class', *Science and Society* 64(1): pp. 11–5411.

Rodney, W. (1981) *How Europe Underdeveloped Africa* (Revised Edition). Washington D.C.: Howard University Press.

Rostow, W.W. (1960) *The Stages of Economic Growth: A Non-Communist Manifesto*. Cambridge: Cambridge University Press.

Roxborough, I. (1979) *Theories of Underdevelopment*. London: Macmillan Press.

Roxborough, I. (1976) 'Dependency theory in the sociology of development: some theoretical problems', *West African Journal of Sociology and Political Science* 1(2): pp. 116–133.

Sadler, D. and Lloyd, S. (2009) 'Neo-liberalising corporate social responsibility: a political economy of corporate citizenship', *Geoforum* 40(4): pp. 613–622.

Sassen, S. (1998) *Globalisation and its Discontents*. New York: The New Press.

Savage, G.T., Nix, T.W., Whitehead, C.J. and Blair, J.D. (1991) 'Strategies for assessing and managing organizational stakeholders', *The Executive* 5(2): pp. 61–75.

Scherer, A.G. and Palazzo, G. (2011) 'The new political role of business in a globalized world: a review of a new perspective on CSR and its implications for the firm, governance, and democracy', *Journal of Management Studies* 48(4): pp. 899–931.

Schmidt, R.H. and Spindler, G. (2002) 'Path dependence, corporate governance and complementarity', *International Finance* 5(3): pp. 311–333.

Scholte, J.A. (2008) 'Defining globalisation', *World Economy* 31(11): pp. 1471–1502.

Schuler, G. (2010) 'Effective Governance through Decentralized Soft Implementation: The OECD Guidelines for Multinational Enterprises', in Von Bogdandy, A., Wolfrum, R., Von Berstorff, Dann, P. and Goldmann, M. (eds) *The Exercise of Public Authority by International Institutions*. Berlin, and Heidelberg: Springer, pp. 197–226.

Schuurman, F.J. (2000) 'Paradigms lost, paradigms regained? Development studies in the twenty first century', *Third World Quarterly* 21(1): pp. 7–20.

Schwartz, M.S. and Carroll, A.B. (2003) 'Corporate social responsibility: a three-domain approach', *Business Ethics Quarterly* 13(4): pp. 503–530.

Scott, J. (1997) *Corporate Business and the Capitalist Classes*. Oxford: Oxford University Press.

Scully, G.W. (1988) 'The institutional framework and economic development', *The Journal of Political Economy* 96(3): pp. 652–662.

Sealy, L.S., Alexander, B. and Rider. K. (1998) *The Realm of Company Law: A Collection of Papers in Honour of Professor Leonard Sealy*. London: Kluwar Law International.

Selekman, B. (1959) *A Moral Philosophy for Business*. New York: McGraw-Hill.

Sethi, S.P. (1975) 'Dimensions of corporate social performance: an analytical framework', *California Management Review* 17(3): p. 58.

Sethi, S.P. and Williams, O.F. (2000) *Economic Imperatives and Ethical Values in Global Business: The South African Experience and International Codes today*. London: Kluwer Publishers.

Sheehy, E.J. (1996) 'The growing gap between rich and poor countries: a proposed explanation', *World Development* 24(8): pp. 1379–1384.

Siggins, L. (2009) 'OECD to offer mediation in Corrib gas dispute', *The Irish Times*, 7 March 2009. Available at www.irishtimes.com/newspaper/ireland/2009/0307/1224242448347.html. (Accessed 10 March 2014).

Silberhorn, D. and Warren, R.C. (2007) 'Defining corporate social responsibility: a view from big companies in Germany and the UK', *European Business Review* 19(5): pp. 352–372.

Skelcher, C. (2000) 'Changing images of the state: overloaded, hollowed out, congested', *Public Policy and Administration* 15(3): pp. 3–19.

Sklair, L. (2006) 'Capitalist globalisation: fatal flaws and necessity for alternatives', *Brown Journal of World Affairs* 13: pp. 29–37.

Sklair, L. (2002a) 'Democracy and the transnational capitalist class', *The Annals of the American Academy of Political and Social Science* 581(1): pp. 144–157.

Sklair, L. (2002b) *Globalisation: Capitalism and its Alternatives*. Oxford: Blackwell Publishing.

Sklair, L. (2001) *The Transnational Capital Class*. London: Wiley Blackhall.

Slocock, C. (2015) 'What happened to David Cameron's Big Society?' *Huffington Post*, 2015 (January). Available at www.huffingtonpost.co.uk/caroline-slocock/big-society_b_6505902.html (Accessed 2 September 2015).

Smith, T. (1979) 'The underdevelopment of development literature: the case of dependency theory', *World Politics* 31(02): pp. 247–288.

Sommer Jr, A.A. (1991) 'Whom should the corporation serve – the Berle–Dodd debate revisited sixty years later', *Delaware Journal of Corporate Law*. 16: pp. 33–57.

Sparkes, R. and Cowton, C.J. (2004) 'The maturing of socially responsible investment: a review of the developing link with corporate social responsibility', *Journal of Business Ethics* 52(1): pp. 45–57.

Spruyt, H. (2002) 'The origins, development, and possible decline of the modern state', *Annual Review of Political Science* 5(1): pp. 127–149.

Sternberg, E. (2011) 'How Serious is CSR? A Critical Perspective', in Crouch, C. and Maclean, C. (eds) *The Responsible Corporation in a Global Economy*. Oxford: Oxford University Press, pp. 29–54

Sternberg, E. (2009) 'Corporate Social Responsibility and Corporate Governance', *Economic Affairs* 29(4): pp. 5–10.

Sternberg, E. (2000) *Just Business: Business Ethics in Action* (2nd Edition). Oxford: Oxford University Press.

Steurer, R. (2010) 'The role of governments in corporate social responsibility: characterising public policies on CSR in Europe', *Policy Sciences* 43(1): pp. 49–72.

Stiglitz, J. (2003) 'Toward a New Paradigm of Development' in Dunning, J. (ed.) *Making Globalisation Good*. Oxford: Oxford University Press.

Stiglitz, J. (2002) *Globalisation and its Discontents*. London: Penguin.

Stilpon, N. and Thompson, J.K. 'Corporate Governance Patterns in OECD economies: Is convergence underway?', *Directorate for Financial, Fiscal and Enterprise Affairs, OECD*. Available at www.oecd.org/corporate/ca/corporategovernanceprinciples/1931460.pdf (Accessed 12 June 2015).

Stopford, J.M. and Strange, S. (1991) *Rival States, Rival Firms: Competition for World Market Shares*. Cambridge: Cambridge University Press.

Strange, G. (2014) 'Depoliticisation, the management of money and the renewal of social democracy: New Labour's Keynesianism and the political economy of "discretionary constraint"', *New Political Economy* 19(1): pp. 138–154.

Strange, S. (1997) 'An International Political Economy Perspective', in Dunning, J.H. (ed.) *Governments Globalisation and International Business*. Oxford: Oxford University Press.

Strange, S. (1996) *The Retreat of the State: the Diffusion of Power in the World Economy*. Cambridge: Cambridge University Press.

Suiter, J. (2003) 'Compliance Rules Could Hit "Foreign Investment"', (2003) *The Times*.

Sullivan, H. (2012) 'A Big Society needs an active state', *Policy and Politics* 40(1): pp. 145–148.

Sunkel, O. (1973) 'Transnational capitalism and national disintegration in Latin America', *Social and Economic Studies* 22(1): pp. 132–176.

Swagel, P. (2015) 'Legal, political, and institutional constraints on the financial crisis policy response', *The Journal of Economic Perspectives* 29(2): pp. 107–122.

Taylor, C. (1989) 'The Diversity of Goods', in Clarke, S.G. and Simpson, E. (eds) *Anti-Theory in Ethics and Moral Conservatism*. Albany: SUNY Press.

Taylor-Gooby, P. (2013) 'Why do people stigmatise the poor at a time of rapidly increasing inequality, and what can be done about it?', *The Political Quarterly* 84(1): pp. 31–42.

Taylor-Gooby, P. (2012) 'Root and branch restructuring to achieve major cuts: the social policy programme of the 2010 UK coalition government', *Social Policy & Administration* 46(1): pp. 61–82.

Tausch, A. (2010) 'Globalisation and development: the relevance of classical "dependency" theory for the world today', *International Social Science Journal* 61(202): pp. 467–488.

Teasdale, S., Alcock, P. and Smith, G. (2012) 'Legislating for the big society? The case of the Public Services (Social Value) Bill', *Public Money and Management* 32(3): pp. 201–208.

Teubner, G. (2012) *Constitutional Fragments: Societal Constitutionalism and Globalization*. Oxford: Oxford University Press.

The Cabinet Office. Available at www.gov.uk/government/organisations/cabinet-office (Accessed 9 September 2015).

The Responsible Business Champions Scheme. Available at www.apcrg.org.uk/responsible_business (Accessed 10 August 2015).

The Turner Review. Available at www.fsa.gov.uk/pubs/other/turner_review.pdf (Accessed 31 August 2015).

Thorhallsson, B. and Kattel, R. (2013) 'Neo-liberal small states and economic crisis: lessons for democratic corporatism', *Journal of Baltic Studies* 44(1): pp. 83–103.

Thorsteinsdottier, H. (2010) 'CSR in Iceland', in Visser, W. (ed.) *World Guide to CSR: A Country by Country Analysis of Corporate Sustainability and Responsibility*. London: Greenleaf Publishing.

Titiroglu, D., Bhabra, H.S. and Lei, K. (2004) 'Political uncertainty and asset evaluation from business relocations in Canada', *Journal of Banking and Finance* 28(9): pp. 2237–2258.

Townsley, N.C. and Stohl, C. (2003) 'Contracting corporate social responsibility', *Management Communication Quarterly* 16(4): pp. 599–605.

Traynor, I. (2009) 'Iceland to be fast-tracked into the EU', *The Guardian*, 30 January 2009. Available at www.theguardian.com/world/2009/jan/30/iceland-join-eu (Accessed 29 September 2015).

Valenzuela, J.S. and Valenzuela A. (1978) 'Modernization and dependency: alternative perspectives in the study of Latin American underdevelopment', *Comparative Politics* 10(4): pp. 535–557.

Vallentin, S. (2013) 'Governmentalities of CSR: Danish government policy as a reflection of political difference', *Journal of Business Ethics* 127(1): pp. 33–47.

Van Apeldoorn, B. (2003a) 'The struggle over European order: transnational class agency in the making of embedded neo-liberalism', *State/Space: A Reader*, pp. 147–164.

Van Apeldoorn, B. (2003b) *Transnational Capitalism and the Struggle over European Integration*. Oxford: Routledge.

Van Apeldoorn, B. (2000) 'Transnational class agency and european governance: the case of the European round table of industrialists', *New Political Economy* 5(2): pp. 157–181.

Von Stange, G. (1994) 'Corporate social responsibility through constituency statutes: legend or lie?', *Hofstra Labor and Employment Law Journal* 11(2): pp. 461–499.

Vurro, C. (2006) 'The Evolutionary Path of the Concept of CSR', in Perrini, F., Pogutz, S. and Tencati, A. (eds) *Developing CSR*. Cheltenam: Edward Elgar Publishing.

Wade, R.H. (2004) 'On the causes of increasing world poverty and inequality, or, why the Matthew Effect prevails', *New Political Economy* 9(2): pp. 163–188.

Wallerstein, I. (2001) *Unthinking Social Science: The Limits of Nineteenth Century Paradigms*. Philadelphia: Temple University Press.

Wallerstein, I. (1974) 'The Rise and Future Demise of the World Capitalist System: Concepts for Comparative Analysis', *Comparative Studies in Society and History* 16(4): pp. 387–415.

Walton, C.C. (1967) *Corporate Social Responsibilities*. Belmont, CA: Wadsworth.

Ward, H. and Smith, C. (2006) *CSR at a Crossroads: Futures for CSR in the UK to 2015*. London: International Institute for Environment and Development (iied).

Warren, B. (1980) *Imperialism: Pioneer of Capitalism*. London: Verso.

Westwood, A. (2011) 'Localism, social capital and the "Big Society"', *Local Economy* 26(8): pp. 690–701.

Wheeler, S., (2001) *Corporations and the Third Way*. London, Hart Publishing.

Wheeler, S. (2007) 'Ethics in the workplace', *Law and Critique* 18: pp. 1–28.

Williams, C.A. and Conley, J.M. (2006) 'Triumph or tragedy – the curious path of corporate disclosure reform in the UK', *William & Mary Environmental Law and Policy Review*. 31(2): pp. 317–927.

Williams, C.A. and Corely, J.M. (2005) 'An emerging third way? The erosion of the Anglo-American Shareholder Value Construct', *Cornell International Law Journal* 38(2): pp. 493–1049.

Williamson, L. (2002) 'Globalisation: Good or Bad', *The Guardian*, 31 October 2002. Available at www.theguardian.com/world/2002/oct/31/globalisation.lewiswilliamson (Accessed 21 July 2015).

Wilmarth Jr, A.E. (2010) 'The Dodd–Frank Act: a flawed and inadequate response to the too-big-to-fail problem', *Oregon Law Review*. 89: pp. 951–1057.

Windsor, D. (2001) 'The future of corporate social responsibility', *The International Journal of Organizational Analysis* 9(3): pp. 225–256.

Withnall, A. (2015) 'Refugee Crisis: David Cameron says Europe must get better at sending migrants home', *The Independent*, 23 September 2015. Available at www.independent.co.uk/news/world/europe/refugee-crisis-david-cameron-says

-europe-must-get-better-at-sending-migrants-home-10513581.html (Accessed 23 September 2015).

Wójcik, D. and MacDonald-Korth, D. (2015) 'The British and the German financial sectors in the wake of the crisis: size, structure and spatial concentration', *Journal of Economic Geography* lbu056.

Wolf, M., (2015) 'A refugee Crisis that Europe cannot escape', *Financial Times*, 22 September 2015. Available at www.ft.com/content/3967804c-604b-11e5-a28b-50226830d644 (Accessed 23 September 2015).

Wood, D.J. (1991) 'Corporate social performance revisited', *Academy Of Management Review* 16(4): pp. 691–718.

Woody, K.E. (2012) 'Conflict minerals legislation: the SEC's new role as diplomatic and humanitarian watchdog', *Fordham Law Review.* 81(3): pp. 1315–1351.

Woolas, P. (2007) MP 17/01/07 *Localism – Lyons, CSR and Beyond.* Available at www.communities.gov.uk (Accessed 31 August 2014).

Wright, O. (2014) 'Exclusive: David Cameron's Big Society in tatters as charity watchdog launches investigation into claims of Government funding misuse', *Independent*, July 2014. www.independent.co.uk/news/uk/politics/big-society-is-a-sham-that-s-hurting-the-small-charities-sector-says-report-9571816.html (Accessed 2 September 2015).

Wynn-Evans, C. (2007) 'The Companies Act 2006 and the interests of employees', *Industrial Law Journal* 36(2): pp. 188–193.

Zartman, I.W. (1976) 'Europe and Africa: decolonisation or dependency', *Foreign Affairs* 54(2): pp. 325–343.

Index